UNTHINKABLE SACRIFICE

John Battaglia said hello and it grated on Mary Jean to hear her ex-husband's voice.

"Hi, John," she said lightly. "I got a message that the girls wanted to ask me something."

"Yeah," he said, and Mary Jean could hear the echo-like sound that always accompanied his punching of the speaker phone button.

"Ask her!" John's voice pounded. *"Ask her,"* he repeated in a louder, harsher voice.

"Mommy?" Faith stammered. She was noticeably crying and her voice sputtered in short sobs. "Why do you want Daddy to have to go to jail?"

Mary Jean could feel her body temperature climb. "Oh come on, John, don't do this to them."

Then Mary Jean heard the screams that will forever haunt her. Faith cried out, "No, Daddy, don't! Oh please no, Daddy. Don't do it. No, no, no!"

Over her daughter's piercing cries, Mary Jean heard the blast of a gun. "Run, babies, run!" she screamed. "As fast as you can, run for the door!"

Other Pinnacle Books by Irene Pence

A CLUE FROM THE GRAVE

TRIANGLE

BURIED MEMORIES

NO, DADDY, DON'T!

IRENE PENCE

PINNACLE BOOKS
Kensington Publishing Corp.
http://www.kensingtonbooks.com

PINNACLE BOOKS are published by

Kensington Publishing Corp.
850 Third Avenue
New York, NY 10022

All Kensington Titles, Imprints, and Distributed Lines are available at special quantity discounts for bulk purchases for sales promotions, premiums, fund-raising, and educational or institutional use. Special book excerpts or customized printings can also be created to fit specific needs. For details, write or phone the office of the Kensington special sales manager: Kensington Publishing Corp., 850 Third Avenue, New York, NY 10022, attn: Special Sales Department, Phone: 1-800-221-2647.

Pinnacle and the P logo Reg. U.S. Pat. & TM Off.

First Printing: July 2003
10 9 8 7

Printed in the United States of America

For Faith and Liberty

ACKNOWLEDGMENTS

It is impossible to tell a true story that took place over seventeen years without the help of a great many people. At the same time, people prefer anonymity when they relate a story as sensitive as this one. For those who helped but did not want their names published, I give my sincerest thanks. I could not have written this book without you.

Thank you to District Attorney Bill Hill, who encouraged me to tell this story. State Congressman Toby Goodman wrote the new Texas law on unsupervised visits by abusive spouses and walked me through the process. Defense attorney Paul Johnson worked harder than any defense attorney I have ever witnessed. Judge Harold Entz was the only jurist who stood up to John Battaglia before the murders. Thank you to Assistant District Attorney Megan Miller for her firsthand information, and to Michelle's attorney in her protective order battles, Leota Alexander. Prosecutor Keith Robinson helpfully answered my questions.

Kudos to the staff of *The Dallas Morning News*. Steve McGonigle, a tenacious investigative reporter, generously shared his information; David Woo, photo editor, was patient with my many requests; and photographer Richard Michael Pruitt took excellent photos. Thanks also to fellow journalists

Lance Brennan with *The Turtle Creek News* and Denise McVea with the *Dallas Observer.*

Dedicated police officers Dane Thornton and Zane Murray helped explain the frenzied night of the murders. Gigi Ray, death investigator for the Dallas County Medical Examiner, is a woman of great integrity. She guided me to tell the story accurately.

I appreciated the hospitality of Judge Janice Warder's court, including court reporter Judy Belton, and bailiffs Gary Detrick, Cindy Pollard, and Joe Collard.

Thanks to Karen Haas, who knows the magic of New York City. Others who deserve my appreciation are Anthony Steele, Linda Murphy, Lucinda Monett, Mary Catherine Smith, Lisa and Mike Kittrell, Cassidy Murphy, Mike Glassco, Tami Thomsen, Mike Lester, Margaret and Howard Neff, Cindy Joungwaard, John Grimes, Ed Buford, and Gloria Somerville Wagner.

Dan Hurwitz, a fellow writer, is a most conscientious editor and a very good friend.

I was fortunate to have the gracious advice and encouragement of Kensington's Editor-in-Chief, Michaela Hamilton, and her editorial assistant, Miles Lott.

"Domestic violence is always about power and control."
Professor Michelle Laborde Ghetti

ONE

"Stop! Please help me!" screamed a hysterical woman as she waved down a passing squad car.

Dallas police officer Dane P. Thornton immediately hit the brakes and flipped on his red-and-blues. Pulling a U-turn, he screeched to a halt directly behind the woman's sleek black Mercedes.

He opened his door, and she reached out to him, begging and crying. "My babies! My babies!" she sobbed.

Thornton wondered what a woman like this was doing in this older, tattered part of town. Even though her smartly tailored beige linen pants were creased and wrinkled, and her matching silk blouse was tearstained and smudged with makeup, she was clearly from someplace much more refined and affluent. She didn't fit this bohemia of Deep Ellum, an eclectic mix on the edge of downtown clogged with trendy restaurants and after-hour bars. Within the blocks, hip young singles and black-garbed "Goths" filled neon-splashed sidewalks.

"Slow down, lady," Thornton instructed. "Just tell me what's happened."

"You don't know?" she screamed, her long brown hair wild around her tear-streaked face. "I'm Mary Jean Pearle! I called 911!" She turned and pointed

to the red brick, four-story Adam Hats Lofts that
stood ten feet away. "I've got two little girls up there.
I heard a gun go off. Five times maybe. I was on the
phone with them. My babies were shouting, 'No, no,
no,' and the gun kept firing again and again. That's
when I called police. My little kids . . . ," she trailed
off, breaking into more frenzied sobs. She became
incoherent and almost impossible to understand as
each syllable came out in a shriek. She gulped for air
and tried to talk to the officer. "Aren't you responding to my call?"

The cop had thirty-two years of experience, but he
felt a shiver rush down his spine. Shots? Children? It
never got any worse than that. As a traffic officer, he
had his radio tuned to accident calls, so he quickly
switched his signal to Channel One, which covered
the Central Business District where they were now.
Thornton repeated the woman's story to his dispatcher, but no one there had heard anything about
the shooting. Regardless, he decided to act. Giving
the dispatcher his location, he barked, "Get someone over here right now. I'm going inside, and I'll
need backup."

He grabbed a twelve-gauge shotgun out of his car,
then turned to Mary Jean. "Ma'am, this is my beat. I
was just returning to District with a traffic report. No,
I didn't get any 911 call, but I'll check it out."

Tears streamed down Mary Jean Pearle's cheeks.
Her voice barely contained her hysteria. "This
doesn't make sense," she cried. "I called 911 a half
hour ago from University Park. I can't believe I beat
the Dallas police down here! Oh my God, please
hurry! You've got to get to them! Hurry!"

"Lady, I know this is rough, but calm down. Now
tell me, who lives here?"

"My ex-husband, John Battaglia. He's in 316. No, no, 418. He just moved. Only a couple days ago." Each word she uttered was loud, shrill, and filled with panic.

"Do you have a key?"

"God, no! I have *nothing* to do with him."

The officer ran to the loft's main entrance, where overhead hung a white wood awning supported by heavy chains. Forty lights tucked inside the canopy illuminated the area to daylight brightness despite the setting sun. Officer Thornton neared the door and the overhead lights glistened on his shaved, tan head. He reached the building's front door and grabbed the handle. It was locked. A man stood nearby, smoking a cigarette and watching the officer jerk on the door.

"Do you live here?" Thornton asked.

"Yeah, do you want in?" The man took a card from his pants pocket and swiped it across a magnetic eye.

The lock beeped and Thornton took hold of the handle, but the sound of another car screeching to the curb made him turn around. Two other policemen, Officers Zane Murray and Ray Rojas, dashed from their vehicle and ran toward him. Thornton grabbed a nearby flowerpot to prop open the door, and went over to the other officers.

"I just got a call that someone heard shots coming from inside one of these lofts," Officer Murray told Thornton.

"I called," Mary Jean said, then repeated the story she had told the traffic officer.

Officer Murray snapped on his radio mike. "Get an ambulance over here!" he told the dispatcher, shouting over the traffic noise on Central Expressway, the elevated thoroughfare that divided downtown Dallas from Deep Ellum. "We have reason to believe that kids have been injured."

The three policemen ran inside, leaving Mary Jean alone on the sidewalk. She crossed her arms over her shaking body and paced back and forth. Everything was playing out in slow motion. *This is what you hear about happening to other people,* she thought as her stomach continued churning.

The massive downtown buildings towered over her, and their interior lights began to flicker alive as the sky darkened.

Mary Jean grabbed her cell phone and punched in a number for Melissa Lowder, the friend she had been visiting when she last talked with her daughters. Melissa picked up on the first ring.

"Melissa, the police are finally here," she said in a shaky voice. "They've gone inside."

"I can get someone to take care of my kids," Melissa said. "Do you want me to come down?"

"Oh yes, please, please. I really need you."

Mary Jean clicked off her phone and looked around the empty street. The last orange streaks of the sunset had left the sky, darkening her world all the more.

The officers ran into the lobby. Thornton passed an abstract, four-story, yellow-and-orange sculpture in the core of the lobby, and headed for the elevator while the other two officers ran to the stairs. They believed that Battaglia was inside, and they were prepared.

The elevator crawled to the fourth floor, and

Thornton's tension climbed with it. It jolted to a stop and the doors slid open. At the same time, the other two officers reached the fourth floor, panting.

The three hurried along the hall, their rubber soles thudding on the concrete floor. When they arrived at Battaglia's door, they knocked and stepped to the side. The man could be inside with a gun trained on them. When there was no response, they tried to open the heavy commercial door. They weren't surprised to find it locked.

They knew what they had to do next and were well aware of the risk they were taking. Because they suspected that someone was injured, they could legally enter the loft without a warrant, but once they kicked the door open, they'd be at risk from whoever was on the other side.

They didn't hesitate. Murray, who stood six feet tall and weighed 220 pounds, told the other two officers to stand back.

Rojas and Murray drew their service revolvers. Thornton's pistol was holstered, but he had already switched off the safety of his shotgun.

Murray eyed the place on the door right by the lock, its weakest point. The burly, barrel-chested officer took a couple of steps backward, and with adrenaline pumping, powerfully kicked the door with his black leather boot. The entire wall shook, but the door remained closed. Murray sucked in another breath and rushed at it a second time. As his boot made contact, the wooden doorjamb cracked and splintered around the lock.

The instant the door slammed open, the officers tore inside, hollering, "Police!" with their guns pointed in three different directions. The lights were off in the apartment, but the afterglow from the setting sun glimmered through three huge, multi-paned windows, casting broken shadows across the room.

Their eyes swept the cavernous loft that was still hazy with gunsmoke.

Then they froze.

Even for experienced officers, the sight of a little barefoot girl lying on her stomach only twelve feet from the door was shocking. Her arms were stretched out toward them. She had obviously been trying to reach the door. She had to have known what was happening in the last few moments of her life.

The child's hair haloed around her head just as she had fallen, and blood puddled on the cold, brown painted concrete in a two-foot-diameter circle. A piece of a copper bullet jacket glinted in the pool of blood. Her light blue shorts were intact but her pink-and-blue floral T-shirt was riddled with bullet holes. One shot had entered and exited her arm. Another had ripped her side, and an additional shot had hit her back. The officers were sickened to see the hair on the back of her head parted by a shot that had been obviously fired at close range, execution style. That bullet had exited through a gaping hole by her nose.

What kind of man could have done this?

Thornton knew that there was no chance that she could be alive, not with such heavy blood loss. From working traffic wrecks, he was used to seeing dead people. He'd come to accept that when someone had already expired, there was nothing you could do for them and you just had to get on with the investigation. But this was different. This was no accident. He'd be seeing that little body again when he shut his eyes tonight and tried to sleep.

He picked up his walkie-talkie and demanded, "Get homicide over here right now!" At this point, his reactions were automatic: shotgun in one hand, radio in the other.

Mary Jean Pearle had said there were two girls. They'd found one. Where was the other?

The officers turned to their right. They saw a closed door, and gripped their guns more tightly. Then Thornton grabbed the door handle, threw it open, and switched on a light. It was a large walk-in closet. Before they did anything else, it had to be secured. They moved methodically, quickly, as they had been taught. Thornton entered the closet, stepped to his right, and kept his back flat to the wall. Murray squatted down and covered him, while Officer Rojas took the left-hand side.

Using their guns, they poked through closely packed, hanging clothes and stacked boxes. They found five long guns leaning against the back wall behind the clothes in addition to a couple of pistols that sat on white, plastic-coated wire shelves.

The next door led to the bathroom, where they found two more rifles. They quickly secured that area and moved to the first bedroom.

The room was small and partially walled off from the rest of the loft. Two stacked metal bunk beds, probably for the children, were pushed against one wall. The beds were neatly made up. A soft pastel coverlet with dainty flowers and ribbons covered the bottom bunk. It contrasted sharply with the top bunk's spread of bold red and blue, splashed with big white stars. There was little else in the room, except two packing boxes stuffed with toys and children's books.

Stepping further into the loft, they came upon the

master bedroom to their left. A double bed covered with a shiny purple spread sat across from a gun rack that held three rifles in plain view. So far, they had seen at least a dozen long guns. On a nearby night-stand sat a Glock, a semiautomatic handgun similar to police issue. It had probably been used for that last shot to the little girl's head, because the tip of the muzzle still held a few strands of hair and bits of flesh. They were careful not to touch anything. Headquarters was probably looking for a judge to sign a search warrant right now.

They reluctantly left the loaded Glock where it sat. If Battaglia were hiding in the hall, all he had to do was rush in, pick up the gun, and the officers would be sitting ducks. When they had stormed through the entrance, they had left the loft door open. Right now they didn't want to waste time to retrace their steps to close it.

The huge number of guns made them apprehensive. If they did encounter Battaglia, what kind of a hell would they face? The two younger officers wore bulletproof vests, but Thornton never did. He found the vests hot and confining; he'd just as soon take his chances.

It was obvious that Battaglia had only recently moved in. Packing boxes were stacked six feet high in the back of the loft. They provided a perfect hiding place for someone watching the officers, waiting for them to get closer, waiting for them to be easy targets. The place was disorganized but not disheveled. The bedroom furniture was arranged in place, and Oriental rugs gave further definition to room areas. The loft's living room was so large it echoed. The ceilings rose about fourteen feet and were supported by three-foot-thick concrete columns, ribbed in Romanesque style.

The officers' eyes continuously scanned the packing boxes for movement. They still didn't know if Battaglia were hiding there or in some other dimly lit corner of the loft.

Tightly clutching their guns, they systematically cleared each area. The officers examined a large black sound system that sat behind two huge speakers. CDs and tapes cluttered the floor, and several spent bullet casings littered the area. Gun drawn, Officer Thornton stood in front of the sound system while Officer Murray checked behind it.

Stacks of books leaned against every wall and crowded each room while bare bookshelves stood ready to house them. The books defined Battaglia. One pile held *Hangover Soup*, appropriate for a man they later learned had addictions. That lay on top of *The Bell Curve*, a controversial book with racial overtones suggesting that blacks performed lower on IQ tests. There was *Neo-Conservatism* balanced above *A History of Western Morals*, and, under that, a copy of *The Art of War* by Sun Tzu. What kind of problems had sent Battaglia in search of answers in books like these?

With guns still drawn, the police covered the areas in front of, behind, and inside the boxes. When they had satisfied themselves that those areas were secure, they turned toward the kitchen. Seconds later, they stopped.

A speakerphone and a pistol sat on the countertop. On the floor directly beneath them, an older girl lay on her side. Her left arm was tucked under her chin as if she had fallen asleep, and a tiny gold earring glistened in her lobe. A bow held her ponytail in place, and a blue Band-Aid circled her middle finger. Her red shorts were clean, but her white Highland Park hockey T-shirt was splashed with blood. A stylized cartoon hockey player, stenciled in yellow-and-blue plaid on the back of her shirt, wore a determined look with his hockey stick raised high. Two bullet holes marred her back, and she too had suffered that final execution-style shot to the back of her head. The blackened, powder-burned flesh around the wound indicated that the gun had been shoved into her scalp. That bullet had exited through an open starburst gash in her forehead. There was way too much blood on the floor to hope that any life still clung to that little body.

Officer Thornton needed a flashlight to look under beds and around darker areas. He left Murray and Rojas at the scene. When he entered the hall outside the loft, he noticed a closed door that wasn't an entrance to any apartment.

He jerked open the door and pointed his revolver into the dark interior. It was a janitor's closet. Even filled with brooms, mops, and other cleaning equipment, it was definitely large enough to hide a man. He made a mental note to check that closet on each floor. Then he hurried to the elevator and rode down to the lobby on his way to get a flashlight from his squad car.

As he stepped outside on the sidewalk, he almost collided with Mary Jean Pearle. She had been talking on her cell phone. Her face was deathly white and her brown eyes puffy from crying.

"Are they there?" she asked.

"Yes, ma'am, they are," he replied gravely.

"Are they . . . ?" she asked, unable to utter the unspeakable word.

"Yes, Ma'am. I'm afraid so."

Mary Jean screamed, and collapsed in Officer Dane Thornton's arms. He grabbed her to keep her from falling. As she sagged against him, he said, "Ma'am, I think you better stay here. You just don't need to be up there."

She visibly gathered her strength so she could stand alone. Sobbing, shoulders slumped, she turned to a pretty, young brunette. Tears also ran down the cheeks of the other woman, who reached out to hug Mary Jean.

"This is my friend, Melissa Lowder," Mary Jean told the policeman. "She just got here."

"Do you know the little girls?" Thornton asked Melissa. "I mean, could you identify them?"

Melissa nodded solemnly, then clutched her wadded Kleenex and mopped her eyes.

"I hate to ask you, but we need to have their identification verified. Why don't you take Ms. Pearle to the squad car. My officer will stay with her."

Melissa nodded and ushered Mary Jean to the waiting car.

As her heart pounded, Melissa Lowder accompanied the officer through the lobby and into the elevator.

Once the door slid shut, Thornton asked, "What do you know about this Battaglia guy?"

"He's a CPA. Had his own business until recently, but he still keeps his office. A few months ago, a small oil exploration company hired him as their chief financial officer. That business is downtown." Then she cautioned, "He's been a Marine, and he's still very fit and strong."

As the elevator stopped at the fourth floor, Melissa was filled with foreboding. The doors slid open and the two began their way down the long hall. In the distance she could see the opened loft door. Everything looked hazy and smoky inside, but even from this distance she could detect the outline of a small child stretched on the floor. A gasp of horror caught in her throat. She was doing this for her friend, and that thought was the only thing keeping her going.

She entered the loft, careful not to step on spent bullet casings, and then hesitantly headed toward the first body. Tears filled her eyes. It took every bit of resolve for Melissa to look down.

"This is Liberty," she stammered. "She was only six years old."

Police escorted Melissa into the kitchen; tears were still rolling down her cheeks. "Faith," she said somberly. "She was nine."

She turned to leave the most devastating scene she had ever witnessed in her life, but one of the officers stopped her.

"One more thing, ma'am. We found this picture on the countertop. Can you identify him?"

Melissa glared at the smiling face. "Yes, that's John Battaglia," she said bitterly, tapping the photo with her forefinger. "That's who you need to find."

Two

Dark clouds hovered over the family of John Battaglia Jr. even before he was born on August 2, 1955. After his birth, tragedy continued to shadow him.

His Grandfather Battaglia, an Italian immigrant, lived in Brooklyn, New York, where he raised his family. Rumors abounded that Grandpa crossed the ocean with more than just his family and dreams of finding success in the New World. Through his contacts from the land of the Mafiosi, the family patriarch was said to have had a connection with organized crime. John Jr. would later brag that his grandfather had been a Mafia chief in Chicago. In any event, John Battaglia Sr. was just a boy when his father robbed a bank at gunpoint, was arrested, and was sent to prison.

Because of the disgrace he brought upon his family, Grandmother Battaglia divorced her husband. She took her children and fled to Florida, hoping that nobody there would learn the family's ugly little secret.

In the next generation, John Battaglia Sr. married a pretty, sensitive blonde named Julia Christine. Soon after their marriage, he joined the military and served as a specialist in logistics with the Army Medical Corps.

Their first child, John David Battaglia Jr., was born at a military base in Alabama. John Jr. took after his mother. At two, he was a beautiful child with green eyes and blond ringlets.

The Battaglia clan grew rapidly, and two brothers and two sisters soon followed. The house was filled with the aroma of Italian dishes, but also with intimidating threats, harsh discipline, and drunken brawls.

The large Catholic family stayed closely connected to the church. As the oldest, John was nudged into serving as an altar boy. That gave some structure to John's fragmented life as he began to spend three to four hours a week assisting priests to prepare the sacraments. But he fought wearing the black floor-length cassock covered with a lace-trimmed white surplice.

Because of John Sr.'s military career, the family moved like gypsies. They were always pulling up stakes and having to make new friends. Their nomadic life took them from Alabama to Texas, then to Washington, D.C., Germany, Oregon, and New Jersey. As a career military man, John Battaglia Sr. disciplined his children like a drill sergeant. Their father's rule was "Do as I say and don't ask questions." Questions earned them swift punishment—their father's belt on their backsides.

However, John Battaglia Sr. disagreed with anyone who said he was a harsh taskmaster, insisting that he only "paddled some rumps." But the punishment he dished out went further than that. He broke one son's guitar over his back.

In 1970, John Battaglia Sr. left the military after fifteen years of service. He continued to stay in the

Army Reserve for many years, ultimately retiring as a lieutenant colonel. With his medical background, he landed a job in Oregon as a hospital administrator and emergency services manager.

It was in Oregon that John Jr. began his first year of high school, where he also played football. The following year, his father was transferred to New York City, much to John Jr.'s disappointment. He was yanked out of high school and forced to give up his football team and all the new friends he had made. But his father had a chance to set up the first addict-run drug clinic and the first publicly financed abortion clinic in the country.

They lived in Dumont, New Jersey, a town of 20,000 in the upper northeast corner of the state, where John Jr. attended Dumont High School. Dumont was just across the Hudson River from New York.

It was difficult for John to get close to his father, whom he saw as intolerant. Instead, he saved his attention for his mother, Julia, whom he loved very much. When his father became agitated and demanding, his mother would say, "Don't get your dad upset. Just go to your room."

Always the peacemaker in the family, Julia was a woman with fragile emotional health. She suffered from severe depression for weeks at a time, and once had been treated at Englewood Hospital for eighteen days. She drank heavily to alleviate her depression, but that merely intensified her problem.

Her hospitalization at Englewood had provided only temporary relief, because her despondency came back. On the evening of December 5, 1972, her husband broke the news that he was going to commit her to Bergen Pines, a psychiatric hospital in New Jersey. She flew into a frenzy at the prospect of being sent to what she viewed as a prison. Finally, a doctor came to the house to administer a sedative. John Jr. was only seventeen at the time he witnessed the confrontation.

The next morning, John Jr. was the last person to speak to his mother before she climbed into her year-old Buick and drove one hundred miles north along the Hudson River, crossing into New York State. She found a scenic overlook not far from the West Point Academy, and pulled off the road.

The river splashed over granite boulders, and had, over time, carved deep slices into the rock cliffs that supported the Palisades Parkway. Dense vegetation of every description—tall pines, huge leafy oaks, and wildflowers—covered the hilly terrain and trailed down to the water's edge. Surrounded by all this beauty, she stepped out of her car and walked almost fifty feet. As she stared down at the pounding river, she pulled out a 9-millimeter German Mauser. Placing it to her right temple, she squeezed the trigger. She dropped to the pine needle-covered ground, falling on top of the gun. The Palisades Parkway Police found her lifeless body at 2:15 P.M.

A note in her pocket described the depression that had caused the young mother to take her own life, leaving five children behind.

Gossip suggested that John Sr. was terribly abusive to Julia and that he contributed to her mental problems. In any event, their mother's suicide shattered the family so severely that some family members still don't speak. John, more than his brothers and sisters, was particularly depressed and subject to explosive mood swings. At times he blamed himself. Could he have said something during those last few moments when he had spoken with her? Could he have been more sympathetic? Could he have changed her mind? To relieve his nagging guilt, he threw himself into his studies and graduated from high school in just three years.

A year later, John's father remarried. His new wife, a woman named Kathy, was a statuesque blonde. She brought an additional son into the family, whom John Sr. immediately adopted.

In a family of six children supported by a sole breadwinner, no one expected to be sent to an exclusive Ivy League school or given money for an expensive dorm or apartment. So, while still living with his family in Dumont, John Jr. began attending one of the four extensions of Fairleigh Dickinson University, a large private New Jersey university. His first major was pre-med, but after plodding through his courses for a year, he realized that math was his forte, and switched to accounting.

With all the volatile family arguments, living at home had its disadvantages. As the oldest, John received his father's harshest discipline, causing his brother Marc to call him an "emotional cripple."

At another time, during an explosive rage, John pulled a pistol on Marc.

In 1976, although John Jr. was busy in college studying accounting, his friends found it easy to talk him into leaving school for a year to travel with the rock band Emerson, Lake & Palmer. He took off like he had been handed a ticket to freedom and excitement. He enjoyed the band's fireworks and loud rock music, and relished being the group's business manager as they toured the country.

In 1977, he completed his year's tour with the band, but he still wasn't ready to head back to college. Although his college major had been accounting, he frequently toyed with the idea of becoming an artist.

The decadence of the seventies, coupled with the rock scene's mentality, had made it easy for him to hurl himself into drugs. He found that cocaine stabilized his mood swings, and he began selling the drug to finance his habit. Inevitably, he got caught. He was arrested, charged with delivery of a controlled substance, and given a suspended sentence.

To escape his problems, Battaglia joined the U.S. Marine Corps and worked in logistics, mirroring what his father had done in the army. After eleven weeks of basic training in San Diego, he began a four-year tour of duty that took him all over the country and also to Hong Kong.

Standing six feet tall and weighing two hundred pounds, he looked proud and handsome in his dark wool dress uniform. It was cinched at the waist with a white belt and topped off with a matching white hat.

Born under the zodiac sign of Leo, the demanding, aggressive lion, Battaglia found that the most rugged branch of the military suited him. Proud of his sign, he had a large head of a lion tattooed on his upper left arm.

By the end of his hitch in 1982, he had risen to the rank of sergeant. He decided it was time to go back to school and get on with the business of becoming a CPA. He took his honorable discharge and left his military career behind.

At the time, his father was working in Dallas, managing emergency physician services at the Baylor University Medical Center. John had always wanted a closer association with his father. Having spent a lifetime trying to win his father's approval, he moved to Dallas, where he found a job as an accountant.

At first, John lived with his father and stepmother. Kathy worked in the office of the Kim Dawson Agency, the premier Dallas modeling agency. She knew her handsome, dark-haired stepson could be a sought-after model, and she encouraged him to have portfolio photos taken.

He followed her suggestion and was soon hired for photographic shoots, mainly advertising upscale clothing. The camera captured his sad green eyes and wistful gaze.

Now he was juggling modeling along with his accounting position, in addition to taking night classes to reach that long-postponed CPA goal.

It was a frenetic but happy time for John Jr. For the first time in his life, he had formed a positive alliance with his father, and was on a solid career path.

THREE

In 1971, Michelle Ward graduated eighth of 400 in her Baton Rouge, Louisiana high school class. In the summer just prior to entering Louisiana State University, she began dating Dale LaBorde, and they fell in love. Her academics slipped slightly during her freshman year when she eloped with Dale.

Still, Michelle Ward LaBorde graduated with honors from college with a B.A. in Education, and began teaching fifth grade. Five years into her marriage, she gave birth to a son, Billy, on November 4, 1977. After the baby arrived, the young couple found that school, work, and parenthood took their toll. Dale wanted to continue partying with friends, while Michelle taught school during the day and stayed home with the baby at night. With such diverse interests, the marriage disintegrated and they divorced in 1980.

Afterward, Michelle took custody of her three-year-old son, and applied to Louisiana State University Law Center. She was immediately accepted. In law school, she rose to the top 1 percent of her class, automatically qualifying her for the honorary Law Review. In May 1983, she graduated first in a class of 184, and began working for Akin, Gump, Strauss, Hauer & Feld in Dallas. The highly respected law firm had more than one hundred lawyers. It also had offices in New York and Washington, D.C. The "Strauss" in the firm's name was Robert Strauss, a one-time chairman of the Democratic National Committee who would later become the ambassador to the Soviet Union.

By mid-1984, John Battaglia Jr. needed a few more classes before he could take the CPA tests. The attractive man was the antithesis of an introverted, bespectacled accountant. Instead, he was gregarious around people and could be very charming.

One of his best friends—and roommate—Mark Weisbart, was a bankruptcy attorney at Akin, Gump, Strauss, Hauer & Feld. Weisbart was sure that the pretty blond bankruptcy and estate lawyer with whom he worked, Michelle LaBorde, would enjoy meeting John. She was tall, poised, and possessed a model's good posture that exuded self-confidence.

Michelle LaBorde was two years older than thirty-year-old John Battaglia, but anyone would have guessed she was much younger, due to her unlined face and pretty brown eyes. Michelle wasn't just smart; she was brilliant, and it would take someone with a fine intellect to interest her.

Mark Weisbart suggested that Michelle and her fellow lawyer, Kitty O'Connell, join him and John Battaglia for a drink at a local restaurant. Michelle and John were instantly drawn to each other. As soon as she began talking with him, she appreciated his intelligence. He knew a great deal about art, music, and the theater. In fact, she found that he could talk extensively and with authority about many subjects.

They immediately began dating, but before their

first date, Michelle wanted to clear the air and let him know that she had a seven-year-old son.

John Battaglia's face brightened when he heard about Billy. He told her that he loved children. During his four years in the Marines, he had volunteered to help with Special Olympics because he wanted to work with children. He couldn't wait to meet her son.

Michelle soon realized that of all the things she liked about John Battaglia, she was most impressed with his interest in Billy. When Battaglia brought toy soldiers to Michelle's two-bedroom, one-bath rental house, Billy was delighted to see him walk through the front door. As John and Billy made the soldiers march up and down the furniture, he told the young boy about his experiences in the Marines. Soon, Michelle began to wonder if Battaglia was more interested in Billy than in her. Michelle had a rule that she wouldn't leave the house until after 8:00 P.M., when Billy was put to bed. So Battaglia came early before their dates to play with him, and at other times would take just the boy out for pizza.

Billy became very attached to John. The seven-year-old's father lived in Baton Rouge, and Billy wasn't seeing him on a regular basis. John took over that role, and the two became very close.

When Michelle and John attended law firm parties, her colleagues would exclaim how lovingly he looked at her. There was no doubt in anyone's mind that the new man in her life adored her.

On New Year's Eve, three months after they began dating, Billy was scheduled to visit his father in Baton Rouge, freeing Michelle for three full days. At the same time, one of her law school friends offered to loan Michelle her New York City apartment on

Third Avenue while the friend was visiting relatives in Shreveport.

Michelle and John flew to New York for three romantic days. They bundled up for the crisp, cold weather and strolled down Fifth Avenue, delighted by the spectacular Christmas decorations in all the upscale store windows. They stopped at Rockefeller Center to watch the locals ice skate and were awed by the spectacular jewel-toned lights decorating the tree beside the rink.

The crowded, fast-paced city captivated their imaginations. Yellow taxis streaked by them as they walked the streets deeply inhaling the wafting aroma of freshly baked pretzels.

They made love for the first time, which made the trip all the more special.

Only one incident marred their vacation. Michelle had run across the street to a grocery store, and when she returned, Battaglia was sitting on the bed with a goofy expression on his face.

Michelle looked into eyes that stared blankly at her. She was positive he had taken some kind of drug. But he wouldn't admit to anything and his behavior appeared normal. Still, Michelle couldn't get his silly look off her mind.

As the weeks passed, Michelle saw no other indication of drugs, and John seldom drank, so their whirlwind courtship returned to its original happy, and now intimate, state.

In February of 1985, they decided to drive to New Orleans to celebrate Mardi Gras. It was only a forty-five minute drive from Baton Rouge, and Michelle wanted to introduce John to her family.

At five o'clock, he picked her up at her glass-and-granite office building on Pacific Street. Once in his car, she took off her heels and slipped into a pair of loafers she had pulled from her suitcase. He had already been home and changed into jeans and a casual shirt.

They headed east on Interstate 80, through a chain of small Texas towns. They crossed the Louisiana border near Shreveport and drove southeast for several more hours.

At pitch-black midnight, they were nearing Baton Rouge when a car full of teenagers roared past them. No sooner had it passed, then it pulled in front of them and slowed down, causing Battaglia to slam on his brakes. That enraged him, but when the kids flashed a bright floodlight directly into his eyes, he went crazy. It was impossible for him to see the road.

"Those goddamn kids!" he bellowed. "Are they trying to get us both killed?"

In the glow of the light, Michelle could see Battaglia's face visibly change. His eyes narrowed and his mouth twisted into a threatening grimace.

He reached down, his right hand fingering the carpeted floor, searching for something.

"What do you want?" Michelle asked

"The duffel bag," he said as he groped in vain under the seat. "I've got a gun in the bag. Get it for me!"

The thought of a gun frightened her. "That's the last thing you need," Michelle said, her concern growing. She kept glancing at his face. It was a face she hadn't seen before. For the first time since she had met him, he looked panic-stricken. His eyes stared wildly and he began yelling at her. "Give me the goddamn duffel!"

As they fought over the bag, Battaglia began weaving across lanes.

"Stop it," Michelle screamed. "Now *you're* going to get us killed!" *What's wrong with him?* she asked herself.

As he sped up the car, his driving became more erratic. Michelle was so frightened that she grabbed the duffel and threw it into the backseat. A few moments later, they passed the car full of boys and Battaglia screamed obscenities at them.

When the teenagers' car was only pinpoint headlights in their rearview mirror, the atmosphere in the car was still heated.

"Why in the world are you bringing a gun?" Michelle asked, her temperature still climbing.

"New Orleans is a dangerous place," he told her.

"It'll be a lot more dangerous if you're carrying a gun!"

She thought she knew him, but this man sitting beside her was a total stranger.

It was almost one in the morning in Baton Rouge when they pulled into the driveway of Michelle's sister's house where they would be spending the weekend. One look at Michelle, and her sister could tell that she was upset and asked her what was wrong. Michelle explained about the incident in the car.

The rest of the weekend flew by in a blur for Michelle. She couldn't erase the craziness of the highway episode, although no further bizarre incidents occurred during the rest of the trip. John Battaglia behaved normally in spite of the loud and colorful Mardi Gras crowds and the parades that covered them with confetti and plastic jewelry.

However, by the time Michelle returned to Dallas, she had made up her mind. She wouldn't tolerate anyone who had such drastic mood swings and was so scary and unpredictable. No longer would she be seeing John Battaglia.

Then she found out she was pregnant.

FOUR

Despite the circumstances, Michelle was excited to be pregnant. She didn't want to raise her son as an only child. Then as the reality of her situation settled on her, she began to wonder what in the world she had gotten herself into. She didn't want to be married to John Battaglia, but she didn't want to have a child out of wedlock. Overall, she was surprised to be pregnant since she had been on birth control pills and was diligently taking them.

When she finally built up the courage to tell John that she was pregnant, he immediately wanted to marry her. But she wasn't sure that she wanted to jump into such a commitment. She kept pondering her options, although she never considered having an abortion. Then reconsidering marriage, she wondered if she could have the baby on her own and not marry John, but she was afraid to discuss single parenthood with him.

In late March, she sat down and wrote a letter to her mother, telling her about her plan. Her mother's explosive response came back by return mail.

Michelle,
   How dare you think of having that baby all by yourself?

Her mother went on to question whether she had the right to deprive her child of a father and make it illegitimate.

Michelle had hoped for a little support; she had no idea that her mother would blow a gasket.

In mid-April, Michelle slid up the zipper of her skirt and noticed a gap where the last half inch didn't meet. Although she hadn't gained much weight, she knew that time was running out and she had to make a decision.

On April 28, 1985, she took her mother's words to heart and married John Battaglia in an unromantic civil ceremony at the courthouse. Amid cluttered desks and ringing phones, they were married by a justice of the peace. John slid a plain gold ring on her finger and gave her a peck on the cheek after the brief ceremony; then they stepped aside for the next couple to get married in assembly-line fashion.

Only one month after they were married, to Michelle's shock, John disappeared. He was gone for two days. On the morning of the third day, Michelle was frantic, not knowing if he were dead or alive. When he finally called mid-morning, she was relieved to hear his voice.

"Michelle, I'm really sorry," Battaglia stammered. "I know I should have called you before now. See, here's what's happened. I'm over at Janet's. She's kinda my ex-girlfriend. I'm really sorry about this."

"Janet?" Michelle asked, ice forming on her words.

"Well, right before I met you I was engaged to her. I'm sorry, I should have told you all this before now.

I'm really sorry. I'm at her place now, but I'll be right home."

Michelle hung up the phone and dropped to her sofa. Tears filled her eyes. She had known nothing about any Janet. What had she gotten herself into? Married and pregnant. What were her options?

Minutes later, a repentant John Battaglia quietly padded through the front door of Michelle's small house and began apologizing all over again.

Michelle listened. Today they had planned to drive to Austin, Texas, where John would be awarded his CPA license. Not one person in his family had called about his passing the tests, nor had anyone offered to go with him to the awards ceremony. His parents still lived near Dallas on Lake Ray Hubbard. He looked so pathetic that Michelle felt sorry for him and thought that someone should accompany him to Austin. She would go on one condition. As soon as they returned, they were going to have a very important meeting with this Janet. She wanted to know exactly how her new husband felt.

Mark Weisbart, John Battaglia's friend who had introduced him to Michelle, let them use his apartment for their meeting with Janet. Weisbart even whisked Billy to McDonald's while the confrontation took place.

John stood up in front of both women. He shook from fear, nervously licking his lips and running his fingers through his hair. Without eye contact, he told Janet that he wasn't in love with her anymore and that he loved Michelle.

Only later would Michelle learn that while she was pondering whether or not to marry John, he was conspiring with Janet to leave Michelle after the baby was born, and to take his child and raise it with Janet.

FIVE

Once he became a CPA, John Battaglia's accounting firm gave him a handsome raise in addition to larger, more prestigious clients. Now he looked forward to the day he would become a partner.

By July of 1985, Michelle was five months pregnant and the family would soon be needing a larger home. They began searching in neighborhoods close to their offices, and found a three-bedroom house on Bellewood Drive in the Lake Highlands area. There was also an excellent school for Billy only a half block from the new house.

Michelle was in the master bedroom, filling boxes with belongings. She called to her husband, who was watching television, "John, will you please come help pack this stuff?"

"Nah," he replied. "Most of that's yours. I don't see why I should pack it."

Michelle frowned, wondering why he'd have that attitude. It was true that almost everything belonged to her. She had accumulated a house full of lovely traditional furniture; some from her first marriage, and other pieces that she had inherited from her grandmother.

After packing another box, she walked into the living room and again asked for help as she passed by John.

He jumped up and grabbed her from behind, jerking his arm around her neck, his elbow bent in front of her.

Michelle's eyes widened in disbelief. He was hurting her, but more than that, he was frightening her.

His mouth was only inches from her ear when he hissed, "I'll help when I'm good and ready, if at all. Do you understand?"

He released his grip and Michelle angrily shoved him away, then ran crying to the bathroom. She stayed in there, holding a damp washcloth to her face and shaking with fear. He was so strong; she was totally under his control. If he had continued squeezing her neck, she couldn't have stopped him. Thinking back to their ride to Baton Rouge and the gun he had carried, she realized that this marriage had been a terrible mistake.

When she came out, he was packing boxes as if nothing had happened.

The next week, the Battaglias moved to a Beaver Cleaver kind of neighborhood. Three- and four-bedroom homes graced neatly trimmed lawns that were laced with beds of begonias and caladium. Huge live oak trees made leafy green canopies over the streets.

Their new house, built of beige bricks, had a long porch spanning the front that was supported by decorative white wrought-iron columns.

The house was less than a mile from White Rock Lake, a city reservoir built in 1912. The lake rested in a natural cauldron and the entire area was a series of green, heavily treed hills that gently sloped toward the lake's shores.

With more room for both her seven-year-old son and the new baby they were expecting, Michelle relaxed, knowing that now they were settled in their new home, her existence would be more peaceful.

The cool October nights held a hint of fall as summer finally lost its grip on Dallas. Michelle stood in the kitchen, cooking spaghetti. As she inhaled the spicy aroma permeating the room, the phone rang. She tucked the receiver between her shoulder and her ear and kept stirring. "Hello," she said, and her mother's voice greeted her.

John Battaglia was wrestling with her son in the living room. As she listened to her mother, she kept smiling to herself, thinking how wonderful her husband was with Billy.

She heard Battaglia say, "Okay, that's enough." Then she heard her son plead, "Just five more minutes." Suddenly there was a loud thump and her son's piercing scream.

She dropped the phone, leaving it to dangle and bang against the kitchen wall as she ran to the living room. She saw her son holding his arm and crying.

"He threw me against the wall," Billy sobbed.

Wide-eyed, Michelle looked at her husband in horror.

"I told him I didn't want to play anymore," John said, showing no remorse. "Besides, it was an accident. I meant to throw him on the sofa."

But only weeks later, Battaglia kicked her son's rear, raising him off the floor. Again, John showed no remorse and went off to their bedroom to watch television. Michelle followed him, screaming at him to *never* do that again. Without looking away from the screen, he said that he wouldn't.

Michelle's frustration soared. At first, Billy had loved John; they were best friends. But now she could see her son begin to cower whenever John entered the room. She vowed to protect her son at all costs, but she was due to give birth in a month, and it seemed like the worst possible time to move out. Other than the two times John had hurt her son, he was wonderful to her and Billy, which only made her decision to leave more difficult. John effectively orchestrated his wife's emotions. There were just enough good times to keep her staying with him.

Also, Michelle didn't know that most batterers would not abuse a pregnant wife. Until the baby was born, they took their rage out on other family members.

A little after 6:00 P.M. on November 10, 1985, their beautiful, eight-pound daughter, Laura Julia, was born at Presbyterian Hospital. John Battaglia chose his mother's name, Julia, for the child's middle name. He was thrilled to have a daughter and spent many hours doting on her. She was his "Laurie Mouse" and he was her "Ba-ba."

Battaglia was always around, playing with his daughter, grinning, waving his arms, making up funny words—anything to entertain her and hear her baby giggles.

However, the happiness of having a child was short-lived. In mere months, Battaglia switched back to his pattern of abusing Michelle. But he never again abused Billy.

Michelle began to detect a cycle. He seemed to explode every three months as circumstances would build. He never went into a depression; he'd just wind up tightly, like a clock. At the beginning of the cycle, he appeared normal, but tension would mount every few days. Then, as time progressed, he'd turn into a ranting, screaming stranger who was abusive and unrepentant for his actions. At those times, Michelle would be scared out of her wits, not knowing what John would do or who he might hurt.

After that, Battaglia would orchestrate the "honeymoon phase" of their relationship: an abuser's modus operandi. He'd surprise her with gifts and sprinkle her with compliments. They would go out, just the two of them, and have dinner, see a movie, or spend a Sunday afternoon at the Dallas Museum of Art.

In the spring of 1986, their life changed. Michelle had hired a young girl from France to care for the children. The woman didn't speak English, nor was she attentive to the children. Michelle's requests to discuss getting rid of her were met by disinterest from Battaglia.

Finally he said, "Will you leave me alone? It's tax season and I don't want to talk about it now!"

"We *have* to talk about it now," Michelle retorted. "Laura is in danger because the woman's not really taking care of her."

John Battaglia's eyes grew large and the veins on his neck bulged out. "I said not now!" he screamed. "Do you understand English? *Not now!*" He punctuated his words by jabbing his finger at Michelle's face and backing her up until she reached the wall of the breakfast area; then he began punching her chest. John's hands were so strong and his demeanor so hateful that she shook from fright.

His punches left ugly purple bruises that immediately began swelling. They were particularly painful because she was still nursing.

Michelle was horrified. John was becoming more violent. She tried to tell herself that he didn't know what he was doing. When her mind flashed back over the last few months, she realized that she had been explaining away Battaglia's sudden, angry outbursts. Months ago she'd rationalized that he was too busy with his increased CPA responsibilities. Other times, she'd blamed herself for saying something that irritated him. Ultimately, she had brushed off episodes of hostility as unimportant because they were only verbal, and her husband frequently apologized and became very remorseful.

She had adopted those excuses to keep the peace, but striking her was going too far.

Grasping her chest, she screamed, "Get out of here this minute! Get out!"

Thus began a scenario that would play out over and over. He left that night, but he was back the next morning, very sorry. Once the honeymoon phase was in place, he explained that when he was under so much stress at work, he "got like that" and didn't know what he was doing or who he was doing it to. If only she'd take him back he'd seek anger counseling to rein in his violent behavior. He'd never hurt her again, he promised.

Each time, the Battaglia charm worked, and each

time, with the compassion of a saint, Michelle let him move back in. But her submissive manner simply increased his power and tightened his control over her. Unbeknownst to her, she was teaching him what he could get away with.

One night Laurie cried out, and Michelle went to the nursery to comfort her. She changed her diaper, then sat down with her in the padded, comfortable rocking chair. As Michelle rocked her, Laurie snuggled her little face into her mother's neck. Everything was so quiet. Michelle started thinking about her life. She had a wonderful son and a beautiful, sweet daughter. She also had an incredible job and was making great money. She looked around the room. Even if they didn't own it, they had a beautiful home. She had her health, and, at times, she had a good husband. She had everything to be happy about. Then reality set in; in her soul, she knew that things were frightening and terribly wrong.

On a Monday morning in June of 1986, Michelle lay in bed, trying to get ten more minutes of rest before starting her busy day.

Battaglia walked into the bedroom, fresh from taking a shower, and announced, "I'm thinking of quitting my job and going to art school."

Michelle opened one eye. "You're kidding, of course." She could not imagine he was serious because she hadn't seen anything artistic about him. He would draw little pumpkins—flat, one-dimensional, juvenile sketches that showed little talent.

"No, I'm not kidding," he said angrily. "I'm just

not fulfilled doing accounting and I always wanted to be an artist," he told her as he shoved his arms into a starched white shirt.

Michelle couldn't believe he was serious. "There's no way you can do that," she told him. "You're in your thirties; you're married with two children to support. I think that's just a ridiculous idea!"

Her words infuriated him and started his motor churning. How dare she tell him he couldn't go to art school? He was losing control at that moment, and to him, control was everything. He raised his bare fist, and she quickly turned her back to him. He hit her again and again as she tried to get away, all the while screaming at him to stop. She was in so much pain that she thought if he didn't stop, he'd seriously injure her. She scooted to the other side of the bed and dropped to the floor. Terrified, she shouted for him to get out of the house, and stayed hidden under the bed until he left.

When everything became quiet, Michelle pulled herself up and managed to stand. She stumbled into her son's room to see if he had heard the commotion. Unbelievably, he lay quietly; apparently oblivious to his mother's beating. It would be many years until he admitted lying in his bed in shock, unable to move as he listened to Michelle scream.

Michelle didn't report the abuse to police or seek medical help because she knew that would only anger John all the more. She was so afraid of him. But she did want someone to know what kind of punishment he had inflicted. When she walked into work, she took her secretary into the ladies' room and raised her blouse to let the woman view the purple bruises on her back. Her secretary was horrified.

When a managing partner of the firm walked by

and saw the two women frowning and talking, he asked, "Is everything okay?"

Michelle, by now the typical abused wife, looked up at the man and smiled. "Sure," she said. "Everything's just fine!"

And when she talked to her family, she forced herself to sound lighthearted. She was too ashamed to tell them about the man she had married.

Three days after he beat her, Battaglia begged, charmed, and bargained his way back into Michelle's life. He promised to seek counseling. Although he had promised that before, he seemed more sincere this time, and actually began seeing a counselor. When he moved back home, he was wonderful again.

John's periods of being kind made Michelle's situation all the more frustrating. She was trying to keep her marriage together for her children, herself, and John, but she knew her husband could change in a heartbeat.

That positive phase lasted for three months. At times during that summer John Battaglia took his violence out on inanimate objects. Still, it was terrifying to see him assault the bathroom wall, knocking a hole in the plasterboard.

Late one night toward the end of August, they both sat propped up in bed reading. John was reading a book on Buddhism, while Michelle was studying a legal brief.

The phone rang. Michelle answered and listened in disbelief to the voice on the other end. She had heard John talk about his grandfather, saying at one time he was a Mafia chief in Chicago, but, like many things, she thought it was something he had invented and that the grandfather lived only in John's mind. Many times he had told her things that weren't exactly lies, but rather what he believed to be true.

However, the voice she heard asking to speak to John was the voice of the Godfather. He had a thick, old-world Italian accent, all raspy like he had a mouthful of marbles. In disbelief she handed the phone to John, then left the room so he could talk in private. After she returned, John never offered to discuss the call.

On September 5, 1986, the children were tucked in bed when Battaglia went to take a shower. Michelle hoped it would freshen his ugly mood, which had permeated the house all day. She heard a crash and the sound of glass shattering on the floor. She rushed from the bedroom into the bathroom and saw that John had put his fist through the glass shower door. Blood was everywhere. She offered to take him to the emergency room, but he was still angry and insisted on going by himself. She let him. He returned with his hand in a cast, having severed a tendon.

In the days that followed, his anger continued. She felt like she was always walking on eggshells as his mood plunged deeper into an abyss. The tension in the house was thick, so she kept quiet, not wanting to anger him further.

Two days later, Michelle was in Laurie's room getting her ready for bed when John walked past the door.

"You're ignoring me," he accused.

"No, I'm not," she said as she picked up their ten-month-old daughter. "Guess I'm just in a quiet mood."

"You're ignoring me because you think you're better than I am. You and your highfalutin' lawyer friends."

All of a sudden John flew across the room and raised his cast-enclosed fist. Michelle was petrified. She screamed and turned her head just in time to save her face; his blow landed behind her ear. The pain was incredible. His punch shoved her backwards so that she fell with the baby in her arms. The child Battaglia professed to love was no deterrent to his rage. The room seemed to turn upside down as Michelle fell, and the bedroom's pink-and-white plaid wallpaper spun around her. She clung to her daughter, trying to protect her, but as they both fell, Michelle heard the thud of her daughter's little head bumping against the wall. Then, Michelle's head smacked on the floor and she lost her grip on the child. Michelle could do little about her daughter's screams as she herself lay on the floor, dizzy and disoriented. Her head pounded and she saw everything around her in double vision. Finally, she collected her thoughts and crawled to Laura and picked her up. As she tried to soothe her screaming daughter, she looked up and saw that Billy had come running to the bedroom door. His frightened face mirrored her thoughts. She was now convinced that if John attacked her again, he would kill her.

The assault erased any care she once had felt for John. It was the final alarm bell that she needed to force her out of this sick relationship. He was leaving today, this minute, and forever.

She grabbed both children and rushed to her next door neighbor's, the Dicksons. For the first time, she told them about John's beatings. They insisted on calling the police to make a report.

Even though Michelle was miserable, she still went to work that day. Once in the office, her secretary insisted on driving her to a Prima Health Care facility for treatment.

A week later, when she felt stronger, she would file for divorce.

Six

John Battaglia kept Michelle under close scrutiny by renting a one-bedroom, lonesome-looking garage apartment only two blocks from where she lived on Bellewood. His apartment sat behind a house that was similar to Michelle's, only now he was the boarder living in guest quarters that had been built over a detached garage. Its dismal appearance only added to his sour mood.

He paced the floor, thinking how furious he was that his wife had threatened to divorce him. But he'd shown her. As soon as he moved out, he'd hired an attorney, James Newth, and filed for divorce. He'd also followed his attorney's suggestion and quit his job as a CPA so Michelle would have to pay *him* child support. Michelle only *thought* she was getting away.

Michelle finally sought counseling, which was her first step in gaining strength. She spent months at The Family Place, a privately supported community organization that dealt mainly with victims of domestic abuse. Her counselor, Susan Bragg, soon learned that Michelle had little control over her life with John Battaglia, and that she would cave in to him just to avoid mistreatment. The counselor urged her to stand strong against any of Battaglia's demands, regardless of how difficult he became.

The court ordered Battaglia into counseling to curb his anger. At times, Michelle met with John's counselor, Randy Severson, at Hope Cottage, an organization dating back to the 1800s. Severson also encouraged her to stand up to John.

In mid-September, a distraught Michelle LaBorde took Billy and Laurie and flew home to Baton Rouge to talk with her parents. Her parents' marriage was one filled with love; she had never seen one second of abuse.

Michelle finally had to tell her parents the truth about her volatile relationship. She was embarrassed that not only had she married such a man, but she hadn't left him earlier. Like most abused wives, she had always believed that somehow she could change him.

Sitting on a down-filled sofa in her parents' living room, she tearfully began describing her life over the past year. Her parents shook their heads in dismay. Then her father, who was also an attorney, decided to act.

While Michelle wiped her puffy eyes, her father began calling lawyers he knew in Dallas. One suggested Josh Taylor, a specialist in family law. Her father hired Taylor, who promised to immediately file a protective order against Battaglia. Taylor assured her father that Michelle would finally be safe.

As soon as Michelle returned to Dallas, her baby-sitter, Odice Cooper, a large black woman who was warm and loving to her children, came running to her. Odice was anxious to show Michelle something in the master bedroom. Michelle hesitantly walked into the room and found hundreds of wire coat hangers clustered in a semicircle on the floor surrounding her bed. A wooden bat lay on the bed alongside an imprint the size of a man. Battaglia had obviously been waiting for her. If he had fallen asleep, anyone stepping on the hangers would have woken him.

Michelle was shaking as they searched the house for Battaglia, but he had apparently left. During the search, Michelle checked the closet shelf where John kept his gun. It was gone, and that terrified her.

Michelle could always feel John's presence. Even if she couldn't see him, she knew he was near, following her, watching her.

On several occasions, he hid in the tall bushes behind her house, waiting for her to drive home. When she pulled into the garage, and before the door closed, he'd scoot inside like a man hyped on amphetamines. Then he'd crawl behind her car and suddenly pop up at her driver's-side window. Michelle's hands would involuntarily fly up from the steering wheel and she'd gasp with fright.

Hearing her counselor's voice in her mind, she fought to appear unruffled. She'd raise her garage door and point to the opening for Battaglia to leave. Sometimes he did. But sometimes he'd rush past her and push his way into her house.

On Monday, September 30, 1986, Michelle and John were with their lawyers in the family courthouse discussing their pending divorce. John had asked for child custody in addition to child support from Michelle.

Over the hum of the air conditioner, Michelle sat at the witness stand outlining Battaglia's assaults, including the latest where he had apparently planned to beat her with a bat.

Suddenly, he became angry and screamed that she was lying. He ran to her like a wild animal, and tried to strike her with his cast-covered hand. The bailiffs grabbed and restrained him.

The following week, Judge Gibbs of the 256th Family District Court surprised no one by issuing a restraining order against John Battaglia for clobbering Michelle's head as she held baby Laura. The order spelled out that John Battaglia was prohibited from directly communicating with Michelle or her son. The only contact he could have was when he picked up their daughter for visitations. He was forbidden to enter her house. Even so, Michelle panicked, for, given the rage Battaglia had vented on her and her son, what might he do to a defenseless little baby when he had her to himself?

If Battaglia violated the order, he could be fined as much as $2,000 or confined in jail for one year, or both. In order to collect evidence of future violations, Michelle began keeping a log detailing Battaglia's harassment. When he phoned screaming curses and threatening her, she would automatically hit the "record" button and capture his calls on tape.

On October 26, 1986, Michelle was sleeping too soundly to hear the footsteps approaching her bedroom door that led to an outside patio. But the sound of a key in her lock and the door being pushed open woke her. Slowly, she fluttered her sleep-filled eyes and glanced over at her digital clock on the nightstand: 12:20 A.M. She looked up to see John Battaglia standing over her. Anxiety flooded through her. Unconsciously, she grabbed a wad of the sheet, twisting it with nervous hands.

John placed a hand on her shoulder to hold her down. Trapped, with no way to escape, she started crying, dreading what he might do. With his other hand, John stroked her hair and cooed, "What's the matter, Michelle? Something wrong? I could make it better. We could make love."

Filled with nightmarish fear, Michelle shook her head. Perspiration moistened her nylon gown until it stuck to her like a second skin.

Her refusal angered him. "I could snuff you out right now," Battaglia said. "Should I beat you until you're covered with bruises, or maybe put this pillow over your head until you're begging me to stop?"

Michelle's teeth were chattering so hard she couldn't talk.

"Just wait," Battaglia threatened. "I'm going to get you. I will come after you in more ways than you can imagine."

Then he left.

Shortly afterward, he phoned. "I've stolen your protective order," he boasted. "Guess what, Michelle, you have no more protection," he said with a sick, sinister laugh. "You're just a whore and a liar. Just wait. I'll show you."

Michelle was so scared that she bundled up Billy

and Laurie and ran to her next-door neighbor's, where she phoned the police.

Fifteen minutes later the police knocked on her neighbor's door and asked Michelle to show them a copy of her protective order. Believing it was still in her briefcase in her car, she led police to her home. Her briefcase contained all of the documents and evidence she had against John. She opened the door to her garage and found that the order was not the only thing Battaglia had taken. Her car was gone. He had apparently grabbed the car keys that she kept on a wooden hook by the kitchen door.

When police called their headquarters to check on the protective order, they found none. Her attorney, Josh Taylor, had apparently not bothered to file it with them. The police refused to do anything without that order.

The police left, and Michelle collapsed on the small gray velvet chair in her darkened living room. She was sobbing, and furious at how law enforcement refused to help.

When her car was found the next day, Michelle went to see Josh Taylor to tell him what had happened and to get another copy of the protective order. She told him how upset she was that he had not filed the order with the police.

Taylor frowned and his face turned scarlet as he glared at her. Then he stood up and forcefully slammed a book down on his desk. "Don't tell *me* how to practice law, young lady!" he yelled.

Michelle had heard from other attorneys that Taylor had a terrible temper. She was literally shaking when she left his office to seek a new lawyer.

* * *

All through November and December, John Battaglia continually broke into Michelle's house at night. She had already changed her locks twice, but, each time, John had called a locksmith and convinced him that it was his house and he had misplaced his key. In no time, Battaglia had a set of keys for the new locks. She called the locksmith to add more dead bolts. She had to find a way to stop him.

Once Michelle had received another copy of her protective order, she picked up the phone and called the Municipal Court of Dallas and spoke with an Officer James Shivers. She told him she couldn't count the times Battaglia had broken into her house or peered at her through the windows. He had scared and shocked her, then threatened her with bodily harm. The officer wrote up a report charging Battaglia with violation of the protective order, and issued a warrant for his arrest.

Until the court completed the paperwork and the police could take action, John Battaglia was totally unaware of his pending arrest. Many times he'd wait until Michelle had left, then slip into her house after Odice had unlocked the doors. He threatened to harm the sitter if she told. Odice knew what harm meant; she had seen enough bruises on her employer. Whenever Michelle called to check on the children, she didn't have to ask if her husband was there; she could hear Odice's stammering voice, sounding like a frightened child's. Michelle constantly worried that Odice would quit.

When John Battaglia learned through a friend at the police department that Michelle had reported him, he was furious. He knew that his actions could result in an arrest—an arrest that could mean jail time. In desperation, he took a different approach to restrain his wife. On November 21, he called Dean Gandy, her boss at Akin, Gump, and fabricated a wild account of Michelle having an affair with the managing partner while she was pregnant with another attorney's child. He threatened to take the information public to tarnish the firm's reputation.

"What the hell are you talking about?" Gandy demanded, fully exasperated.

"If you'd just persuade Michelle not to press those criminal charges, I won't call the newspaper about this. Talk to her and make her drop . . ."

Gandy slammed down the receiver in Battaglia's ear.

After all the months of harassment, the employees at Akin, Gump were painfully aware of Michelle's out-of-control husband. Solely because of him, the firm placed panic alarms on all four floors of their tastefully decorated offices. Next to each alarm, a photo of Battaglia was taped to the wall. Oddly, the photo was from his modeling portfolio. Whoever saw Battaglia first was to press the buzzer to warn other employees. Because of Michelle's restraining order, John was not allowed within 100 feet of her, but that didn't deter him.

* * *

During the Thanksgiving holiday, Michelle took
her two children and flew to Baton Rouge for a long
weekend away from Battaglia's harassment. Helping
with Thanksgiving rituals at her parents' home, she
was making a sweet potato casserole when her next-
door neighbor in Dallas, Dick Dickson, called. Dick
had now become a surrogate father to Michelle.
Knowing her circumstances, he and his wife tried to
look out for her whenever they could. Today he was
calling to report having seen Battaglia unscrewing
the hinges on her back door. Dickson had immediately called Michelle's landlord and sent him over.
The perplexed landlord later told Dickson that
when he entered the house, he'd found Battaglia
standing in the living room like he owned the place.
He noted that Battaglia had unlocked three windows, he assumed for future break-ins. The landlord
contemplated soldering bars on each window, but he
shuddered at the thought. It would make the pretty
rental home look like a fortress, and the way things
were going he imagined that Michelle wouldn't be
living there much longer.

SEVEN

Michelle returned home from Baton Rouge, uneasy about entering her house knowing that John had been there. She had felt so secure in Baton Rouge and wondered if she could move back there once her divorce was final. Would joint custody be a problem? It was increasingly important that she find out.

She opened a kitchen drawer to tuck away some mail, and stared in disbelief. The drawer was empty. She was stunned and furious, but it took her no time to realize that when John had broken into her home, he must have stolen all of her personal files. She felt so violated.

The next day she received another blow: the bank was repossessing her car. Shaking with rage, she went to see her loan officer. He indignantly told her that a man had called, warning them that she had taken the car to Baton Rouge with no intention of continuing payment. It took Michelle an hour to convince him that she had never considered defaulting.

The phone rang a week later and Michelle heard John Battaglia's ugly voice yelling at her. She actually preferred to have a listed number because she then knew where John was. If he couldn't call her, he would make more surprise visits to her home. This time he called to tell her that he had been arrested on the warrant she had filed.

Michelle uttered a silent prayer. *Thank God. Finally, justice.*

Battaglia continued raving. "I had to stay in jail three hours while they fingerprinted me and did the damn paperwork on the bail bond. Had to put up two hundred dollars. See what you've done to me?" His loud voice was filled with rage. "After I put up the money for surety, I made a beeline out of that place!"

She closed her eyes and her body tensed. It made her cringe to know that he was free and able to inflict more abuse. Now he'd be like a mad hornet. The more she tried to stop him, the worse her life would become.

Hardly a week after being sprung from jail, Battaglia boldly called Michelle at a client's office in Houston.

Michelle was shocked to hear his voice. How could he have found her? The law firm certainly wouldn't have told him where she was.

While she pondered the possibilities, he ranted that he would report her to the ethics commission of the bar association if she didn't drop the latest charges against him.

John was taking more than an emotional toll on Michelle; he was ruining her health. She couldn't sleep and her waking hours were terrorized by his threats. Normally she weighed 135 pounds, but with a constant knot in her stomach, she had lost 18 and had begun looking anorexic.

* * *

Battaglia's phone calls were followed by a new series of breaking and entering, sometimes three or four nights in a row. The police would be called, petitions filed, arrest warrants issued, and still Battaglia roamed the streets making life unbearable for Michelle.

Sometimes he'd do irritating things like canceling her membership at Blockbuster Video. Then he caused more serious problems like running up $110 on Michelle's Cetelco long-distance service. Michelle thought she was losing her mind, and then learned she was losing her credit. In one of Battaglia's break-ins, he had stolen her credit cards and was busy using them. As they were still married and living in a community property state, he could legally use her cards. He especially abused her Exxon and Lord & Taylor cards. She refused to pay for his charges, and the companies canceled her credit cards.

Michelle's bills for attorneys and counseling were adding up, and now the unpaid credit cards were pushing her over the edge. She was forced to file for bankruptcy.

Three days before Christmas 1986, John Battaglia tore the plastic from his freshly cleaned, charcoal-gray suit and slipped it over his crisp white shirt and gray-and-red tie. He smiled as he admired his reflection in the mirror. Yesterday he'd had his hair trimmed a little shorter than normal, and now he looked like a solid, conservative citizen.

His appearance before the Dallas County Grand Jury was at ten that morning to hear charges for violating his court order. Prosecutors spelled out several offenses. Breaking and entering, peeping into Michelle's windows, the threatening phone calls, and general harassment were rolled into one big ball of misconduct.

No lawyer could be present at a grand jury hearing, and whatever John Battaglia said to the jury that day would not be reported. He relished his opportunity to present his response to Michelle's accusations. After less than two hours, the sophisticated liar had greased his way through the hearing, and the jury promptly voted to "no bill" him. In other words, they couldn't find enough evidence to indict him, and immediately released him from all of the charges Michelle had brought against him.

Michelle was outraged when she heard the news. What good did it do to itemize Battaglia's every despicable offense if the court refused to act? That night, she was soaking in her tub. As she tried to force herself to relax, to concentrate on the Christmas holidays and her upcoming flight to Baton Rouge, she thought that she had heard a noise. She stepped out of the tub and tiptoed from the bathroom into her adjoining bedroom. There was no mistake this time; someone was knocking on her bedroom door. She threw on her terry-cloth robe and finger-combed her wet hair. As she opened the door a crack, her breath caught in her throat as she stared into the smiling face of John Battaglia.

"What are *you* doing here?" she screamed in panic.

"Just wanted to make sure you heard the grand jury's decision."

"I *can't* imagine what you told those people!" she yelled. She tied the sash on her robe more tightly, while thinking he had to be the best con artist she had ever met.

"Told them the truth," Battaglia said. "How you're always badgering me. Won't let me see Laurie." He inhaled deeply on his cigarette and blew smoke into Michelle's face.

"Leave right now or I'll call the police," she said, coughing, and fanning away the smoke. However, the last time she had called the police, they had told her that they couldn't arrest Battaglia at home for a misdemeanor, but only if they happened to stop him for another infraction somewhere else. Legally, the couple was still married, and the police viewed the house as also belonging to John Battaglia. They didn't feel they could arrest him for being in his own home. This only made Michelle more furious with how the courts treated women in domestic disputes.

"Police never touch me," he said cockily. "Or haven't you noticed, bitch?" Then he strolled down the hall. She shook her head, amazed at how well he had mastered sliding open bolted doors. He was Superman, Spider-Man, or any other inhuman being undeterred by locks, laws, or protective orders. She felt like a very frightened sitting duck.

When Michelle left for work on January 2, 1987, she pulled out of her driveway and groaned to see John parked in his red Jeep at the top of the hill behind her house. He was waiting to follow her, as he had many times before. Whenever she looked in her rearview mirror, he was smiling at her.

He kept up with her through Lake Highlands, down Mockingbird, and then to busy Central Expressway, the freeway leading to downtown. Michelle

was furious with the way he stayed on her bumper.
She drove in the middle lane until she spotted an
opening, and moved to the far-right lane. He pulled
along side and forced Michelle toward the shoulder.
Her moist hands tightened on the steering wheel
while the heat of tension flushed her cheeks. The
exit was still another mile away. She looked over at
him in panic. He smiled. Then he picked up a rock
the size of a grapefruit from his front seat, and threw
it at her. She swerved in time to miss it. Fortunately,
she didn't hit any other cars. He pulled beside her
and laughed.

Still staying with her, he raised his hand. With his
thumb and forefinger, he created a gun. And shot
her.

EIGHT

It was a crisp Tuesday, January 6, 1987, when police knocked on John Battaglia's apartment door and shoved an arrest warrant into his hands. He wasn't surprised, after having thrown the rock at Michelle's car. He'd felt sure she'd file charges as soon as she got back to her office.

He couldn't help but smile inwardly at how irritated Michelle was with the legal system. He'd blithely go through the process of being fingerprinted, posting bail, and getting out. Later, he'd go back for a hearing, pay a fine, and leave.

Battaglia grabbed his jacket and followed the police to their car.

At the Dallas County jail, Battaglia took a "business as usual" attitude as he strolled over to the desk to take care of the paperwork. He'd put up $100 for the $1,000 surety bond. After filling out forms, he'd be out the door. For just such situations, he always carried a $1,000 in cash in his billfold. It had frequently come in handy.

Battaglia turned to the clerk behind the counter and asked, "Could you shove that phone over here, please? I need to call the guy about my bail bond."

"Not so fast," the officer behind him said. He laid another form in front of Battaglia. "You can't use a surety bond on this one. Judge Entz raised your bond to ten thousand dollars. Cash."

Battaglia stared at the policeman in disbelief.

"Nobody ever told me about this. A surety bond was always okay before."

The officer shrugged and picked up the form. "Says here that there's good cause to believe you won't appear when directed by the court. Anyway, it doesn't matter. Judge Entz asked for the ten-thousand-dollar cash bond and that's what he'll get, or you'll get jail time."

Battaglia sighed. "Give me the phone," he said. "I'll call my lawyer."

Battaglia called his attorney, James Newth. After a brief wait, he explained that he couldn't come up with the $10,000 in cash right then. Newth told him he'd file a writ of habeas corpus to try to get him out of jail, but cautioned that it would take a couple of days. Battaglia gave him the information he needed and hung up. Then, he quickly punched in another number for a call he was craving to make.

He reached Michelle Laborde at work. Cupping his hand over the mouthpiece, he moved as far as the phone cord would stretch. When Michelle answered, he asked, "Well, bitch, aren't you proud of yourself? They have some fucking bond deal here where I have to come up with ten thousand dollars in cold, hard cash. This time they're gonna lock me up. Aren't you as happy as shit about that?

"You are going to be sorry. Some dark night when you're out by yourself I can disable your car, and I'll be following you. I'll know where you are—alone with nobody to help you."

Michelle listened to him rant, then hung up the phone and shuddered. Once he got out of jail, would he be all the worse?

Three days in the county jail made John Battaglia furious. His confinement was all Michelle's doing, since his problems were always someone else's fault. And even worse, he still couldn't come up with the $10,000 in cash. It was Friday, and all he could think was that his damn attorney better have something up his sleeve to get him out, for he certainly didn't want to spend the weekend in this godforsaken place.

Judge Harold Entz entered Dallas County Criminal Court No. 4 and took his seat at the bench. A large man with a reputation for being firm, he had served fourteen years as a judge. He nodded to the lawyers. "Is the defendant ready?"

Battaglia let his attorney do all the talking. James Newth pleaded that the court had previously accepted John Battaglia's surety bonds and now the judge had issued only a verbal order to the county clerk to increase the bond to $10,000. And cash at that. The lawyer complained that the court had given no notice of the bond change, so his client had been denied due process of law, and that the bond had been increased without a prior hearing or evidence. He ended by asking that the defendant be discharged from such illegal confinement and restraint.

Michelle had hired a new attorney, John Barr, and he accompanied her to the hearing.

John's father, John Battaglia Sr., had not seen his son for several months. Among his other complaints, he was furious that John had filed for divorce. But today John Jr. was desperate and had invited his father to attend the hearing. He hoped that his father had brought along his checkbook.

When Michelle described how Battaglia had thrown a rock at her car, John Jr. turned around and caught his father's eye. He raised his right arm and flexed his bicep, then grinned.

Judge Entz listened to both sides. The judge had read about John Battaglia's offenses himself rather than relying on a paralegal or a clerk to do his research. He saw that Battaglia's history of getting probation had not deterred him from committing offenses. Judge Entz slid his finger down the column of entries in the document, counting the times Battaglia had violated Michelle's protective order. Experience had taught him that those were only the reported occurrences. After noting the number of offenses, the judge announced that the bond would remain at $10,000 cash.

The police returned Battaglia to his cell.

Monday came, and John Battaglia was still in jail and desperate. He again phoned Michelle.

"Listen, I'll do whatever you want," he said, sounding hoarse and frantic. "I've been here for eight days and I'm going nuts. I'll drop everything I've asked for in the divorce and you can have Laurie for the lion's share of the time. Please, Michelle," he begged. "Listen to me. I'm stuck in here. I need to get a job so I can come up with the money. Please, Michelle, please."

Michelle thought about Battaglia's plea, but she

was tired of giving in to his demands. An hour later, she was surprised when he called back.

"I'm out," he announced.

"You are?" she said, astonished. "How'd you manage that?"

"Dad came through at the last minute. I'm under big time pressure to pay him back, but at least I'm free. Now I need to come over and talk about those charges."

When John Battaglia arrived at Michelle's house that night, he looked terrible. His skin was chalky white, and he resembled a whipped hound dog. He sat quietly on the small gray chair in Michelle's living room, looking tired and remorseful. When he talked to her about dropping the charges, he sounded frantic. *Maybe*, Michelle thought, *his confinement had been long enough to get his attention.*

The next day, Michelle called her attorney, John Barr, to discuss Battaglia's request to drop the charges. Her lawyer told her that if there were a trial and they found Battaglia guilty, he would probably be given a penalty of no more than the time he had already served.

Resting her forehead on her hand, Michelle reflected on the injustice of it all. There was almost no consequence for violating a protective order.

At lunch the next day, she drove to the county courthouse and signed an affidavit of non-prosecution to dismiss the charges. Michelle desperately hoped that John had learned his lesson, and would start listening to reason. Had John not acted so calm, insisting how much counseling had changed him, she would have realized that John had just sweet-talked her through another phase of the abuse cycle.

NINE

After John Battaglia's time in jail, he was contrite, and even seemed calm. He continued in counseling with Randy Severson once a week. Michelle also met with Severson for updates on Battaglia's progress. The counselor told her that John was doing much better "adjusting" to the divorce, and made a special point of saying, "John is *no* danger to you."

The following spring, Dick Dickson was working in his yard. He began weeding the flower garden on the side of his house that faced Michelle's, and noticed two electric wires coming from her attic. Concerned, he went over to tell her about them. They both went up to her attic to investigate, and saw that the wires had been spliced into her telephone line.

Outside, they traced the wires, following them as they stretched across the newly green grass and into several bushes at the rear of the lot. Crawling underneath, Dickson found the wires plugged in to a recorder. There was only one explanation as to how those wires became attached to her phone.

A few days later, Michelle confronted John Battaglia and he admitted connecting the wires to her telephone line. He proudly told how he would set his alarm for 2:00 A.M. and walk down to her house. After scrambling under the bushes, he'd take out the tape, insert a fresh one, then go back to his apartment and listen to all of her conversations. He knew exactly who she was talking to and what she was doing. He wasn't the least repentant. In fact, he was arrogant, boasting that he had learned several of those clandestine tricks in the Marines.

So many happenings that appeared coincidental now had a logical explanation. John could have heard her making plans for her trip to the client's office in Houston. Four months earlier, Laurie had fallen and bumped her head, and Michelle had called the doctor. Battaglia was at her door the next morning screaming that she was an unfit mother and that if she had been watching Laurie more closely, that wouldn't have happened. Michelle couldn't imagine how John had known of Laurie's fall. When she called the doctor back, he insisted that he had never talked to Battaglia.

After speaking with the doctor, she contacted her lawyer, who had sent out a private investigator to check her phones for "bugs." None were found, for he hadn't looked in the attic.

Battaglia's wiretapping was a federal offense, but any week now they would sign their final divorce papers, and Michelle didn't want to file charges that would only interrupt the proceedings and give John another reason to delay giving her a divorce.

Over five months, James Newth, John Battaglia's lawyer, had sent him several requests for payment and had received nothing. In addition to covering the habeas corpus hearing in front of Judge Entz,

Newth had been representing Battaglia in his divorce. On June 18, James Newth wrote Battaglia, stating that without payment he would no longer represent him. Battaglia shot back his reply:

> *I received your letter today regarding your proposed withdrawal from the . . . cases in which you 'represented' me. It is unnecessary for you to file these motions to withdraw . . . since I am firing you.*

Battaglia twisted the knife further and closed with:

> *I am in the process of contacting counsel regarding the proper legal actions to take relating to your negligent representation of me.*

James Newth took his motion to withdraw before Judge Harold Entz, who knew the situation all too well, and quickly released Newth.

During the summer, John Battaglia had many unsupervised visits with Laurie. It was a relief for Michelle to not have to include Billy in these exchanges. She had too much firsthand evidence of how Battaglia had treated the boy.

However, Laurie had atopic dermatitis—she was highly allergic to grasses, trees, and animal hairs, and these allergies were also aggravated by stress. John complained that every night she spent with him, her scratching made it difficult for either one of them to sleep.

When John returned Laurie after a weekend visitation, her little legs, feet, and hands would be scratched and bleeding.

* * *

At last, on July 10, 1987, the final divorce decree was ordered, and the marriage of John Battaglia and Michelle LaBorde was dissolved.

Michelle was awarded managing conservatorship of Laura. Battaglia would be allowed unsupervised weekly visitation in addition to other specified holidays. Although Michelle emphasized John's physical abuse of herself, the judge declared that it didn't matter what John had done to her. The judge wouldn't order supervised visits because John had not harmed Laurie.

The very first time John Battaglia was scheduled to visit Laurie after the divorce, he appeared at the house late and in an angry mood.

"Hey, bitch!" he yelled. "Give me my kid!" He grabbed for Laurie and she started crying.

Michelle held her daughter tightly. "You're in no condition to take her," she said firmly. "Just leave!"

"Look, whore, we all know you're an unfit mother, and I'm not going anywhere without Laurie!"

Michelle started to carry the baby back in the house, but John wouldn't leave. She was terrified to turn Laurie over to him, and angry that he would come for her in this condition.

Blocking Michelle's open door so it wouldn't close, he got in her face and continued screaming. "Okay, bitch, what are you going to do about it now? I'm not leaving, what are you gonna do about it? Huh? Call the police? Huh? Huh, bitch?"

Catching him off guard, Michelle pushed him out of the door, slammed it shut, and locked it. Then she spent the next thirty minutes trying to calm her daughter.

Battaglia angrily returned to his apartment and picked up the phone. He called the police and filed an assault and battery charge against Michelle. The police came out to John's apartment and took his complaint.

The black Dallas skies unleashed a torrent of rain, unusual for August 13, a time when the sun normally beats down on the baked ground and sunburned flowers.

Michelle LaBorde was driving on the busy, eight-lane LBJ Freeway when a car pulled into her lane as if she were invisible. The sedan clipped her fender and threw her into a spin on the slick pavement. She twirled 180 degrees. To her horror, she found herself sliding backward, looking directly into the oncoming traffic. Another car hit her head-on and spun her around again. Her car crashed into the concrete median, where it finally came to rest.

Twenty-month-old Laurie was with her. The child was screaming from fright, but miraculously had suffered no injuries. Michelle fared almost as well, with only a bruised left thigh and upper arm, but her car was totaled.

Because of a mix-up with insurance forms, the claim wouldn't be settled for over a month, and she would be forced to ride the city bus to work each day. Walking to and from the bus stop would be the problem. She'd be out alone, and vulnerable to John's whims. This would prove more hazardous than she could ever dream.

TEN

Needing to leave early to catch the bus to work, Michelle LaBorde hurriedly gulped down a cup of coffee in her kitchen. She grabbed her briefcase and walked out into the warm August morning.

She froze when she spotted John Battaglia's car. He didn't have a scheduled visit with Laurie, so he had no right to be there. His sudden appearances always scared her to death.

She saw him walking toward her house. Although she was shaking, she decided to take her counselor's advice and be firm with him. She turned and stormed up the sidewalk. "I have legal rights and it's about time you started observing them!" she yelled. "I want you to leave immediately!"

She approached the first set of five concrete steps leading to her front door, but Battaglia held his ground on the top step and made no attempt to move. She closed in until she was standing on the stair immediately below him, close enough to feel his hot breath on her face. In a strong voice she said, "Get out of here or I'm calling the police!"

Battaglia's eyes narrowed with rage. There was no stream of obscenities this time. He simply raised his fist and knocked Michelle down the concrete steps. She tumbled onto the unforgiving sidewalk. Her briefcase flew from her hand and legal papers scattered across the lawn. She was dazed at first, not truly comprehending what had happened. When her mind cleared, she sat up and touched her torn hose and skinned knees. She was furious.

Battaglia stomped right by her as she sat on the sidewalk. Then he climbed into his car and roared up the street.

Odice Cooper cautiously opened the front door and peeked out. The whites of her eyes were large and she looked panicky. Michelle saw Odice's frightened face and realized that her baby-sitter had endured more than any employee should have to.

"Call the police!" Michelle shrieked. "This time he's going to be arrested and he can rot in jail!"

Twenty-eight-year-old Bonnie Kingman lived in the same hilly, tree-shaded neighborhood as Michelle LaBorde, but she had no idea what the woman who lived two blocks from her had been going through.

Clad in khaki shorts and a pink T-shirt, Bonnie was enjoying a chat with her next-door neighbor as both women watched their toddlers play in the hot afternoon sun.

A bus rumbled down the street in front of them and slid to a stop. A pretty woman stepped off whom Bonnie recognized, but didn't know by name. As always, the woman was dressed with bandbox precision. Her smart red suit was accented with black and she carried an expensive-looking briefcase. Diamond studs sparkled in her earlobes.

With a subtle hint of recognition, the stylish woman smiled at the two women and said, "Hi."

They said, "Hello," and stared admiringly as she began to cross the street. Bonnie glanced at her watch. "Five-thirty," she said. "Time to start dinner."

Both women began heading home with their children. Just as Bonnie reached her front door, she heard a scream. She turned and saw that the woman in red had crossed the street and was several feet from the entrance to the teachers' parking lot at the White Rock Elementary School, directly across from Bonnie's house.

A flurry of movement caught Bonnie's attention next. A man was beating the woman, who appeared to be fighting for her life. She was raising her hands and using her expensive briefcase to fend off his blows. He wore only tight white tennis shorts and no shirt. Bonnie thought she heard him call the woman a bitch, and she wondered *what had the woman done to make that jogger so mad?*

Then the man, a muscular six feet or taller and probably weighing 200 pounds, pulled back his fist and slammed it into the woman's face. The blow connected with her left eye. Now he was gearing up for another shot. Bonnie could see the muscles bulge in his bare back. The woman's pathetic cries continued. The attack had happened so suddenly. The man was like a striking cobra—giving no advance warning of the venom that was coming. His punches came faster and faster, and his fists drove deeper into the woman's face, now white with fear.

Bonnie called to her neighbor to take her son. She let go of his hand and took off running, leaping across the green yard. In seconds she was in the street, her pink sandals slapping the pavement.

"Stop that!" Bonnie screamed, but the man continued to hit and yell at the terrified, defenseless woman. He hit her other eye; then his next blow slammed her nose until it lay flat against her left cheek. The snap of cartilage popping through skin nauseated Bonnie. Blood oozed from the woman's crooked nose and flooded past her lips, staining her teeth red.

While Bonnie stood inches away, pleading to the man to stop, he blasted the woman with one final strike, this time hitting her jaw and knocking her unconscious. She dropped to the blistering sidewalk like a rag doll.

Bonnie was panting, and numbed by shock. She fought to stay calm as she knelt by the woman. Then she turned to her neighbor, who was watching from just inside her front door.

"Call 911!" Bonnie shouted.

The attacker must have heard her, but he appeared unconcerned at the thought of police coming for him. As the woman lay unconscious, the man slowly picked up a bike that Bonnie hadn't noticed before. She wondered, *had he been hiding somewhere, stalking this woman, waiting for her bus to arrive?* He sat down on the bicycle seat and casually began to pedal away as if he were out for a leisurely ride.

Bonnie had been so traumatized by the brutality of the assault that she had given no thought to her own safety. Her blood chilled when the man stopped and turned back toward her. He glanced down at the broken, bleeding woman, then gave Bonnie a proud, smirky, confident, arrogant smile, as if he were enjoying the woman's pain. Then he pedaled on.

A few seconds later, a young man on a motorbike slowed down when he saw the injured woman. "My God!" he said.

"Help us," Bonnie pleaded. "That's my house right

there," she said, pointing. "Go inside. The kitchen's down the hall toward the back. Find a dish towel or something and fill it with ice."

The man nodded and pulled his motorbike onto the sidewalk. Without asking questions he headed toward Bonnie's house. She was so concerned about the blood-covered woman at her feet that only later would she realize that she had ordered a complete stranger into her home. In moments, the man hurried back with a terry-cloth towel bulging with ice.

Bonnie knelt down and placed ice on the woman's jaw. She grimaced when she saw that one of the woman's earrings had been pulled out, leaving the lobe torn and bloody.

Ever so slightly, the woman began to move. Her jaw was crooked and grotesque, even worse than her nose. She tried to open her eyes, but they had already begun to swell shut. She peered up at Bonnie through narrow slits.

"Did you know that man?" Bonnie asked.

"He's my ex-husband," she answered through clenched teeth, unable to open her mouth.

"Why did he do this?"

"He's after me. He's always been after me. I've been petrified that something like this would happen."

"Why?" Bonnie asked, more puzzled than ever. She was on her knees, trying to hear the battered woman as they waited for the ambulance.

"He hates me," the woman said, her voice barely above a whisper. "He's been beating me. Harassing me. It's been going on for so long. You did see that, right?"

Bonnie nodded, and with bravado and great compassion said, "I saw it and believe me, he's not going to touch you again."

The woman seemed to find peace from that assurance. She forced her swollen eyes to focus. "You saw that," she repeated for confirmation. "Nobody has ever seen him hit me before. Thank the Lord that somebody finally did. Maybe the cops will believe me now. Yesterday he pushed me down the front steps. He's done so many things. Terrible things." Warm blood trickled from her earlobes into her hair. The woman reached to touch her ear. "Oh no," she groaned, "my earring."

Bonnie could only marvel at the woman, who seemed so mentally aware. She had quickly gathered her wits about her only seconds after gaining consciousness.

Within minutes Bonnie heard sirens, and soon the police and an ambulance were beside them. The young man helping them took off. He hadn't witnessed the beating and would be unable to give a statement.

The police tried to pull as much information from the woman as they could, but she could barely speak. She told them that her name was Michelle LaBorde and her attacker had been her ex-husband, John Battaglia.

Bonnie was still shaking as she watched the paramedics gingerly lift Michelle. Michelle gasped and cried out as they placed her broken body on a gurney. After they raised the cart, its wheels clicked into place, and they rolled her to the ambulance and slid her inside.

As the ambulance driver prepared to leave, he flipped on the siren. It seemed impossibly loud at this close range. The noise dissipated as the ambulance turned toward the LBJ Freeway, where it would travel farther north to the emergency room at Presbyterian Hospital.

Bonnie watched the ambulance until it was out of sight, then she went to the squad car and slumped down next to the officer. She disclosed every detail she could remember about the attack. The officer jotted down the details. After Bonnie signed her statement, she stepped out of the car and watched the police disappear down her street. She glanced around at the neatly kept homes, the towering trees, and the beds of flowers, thinking what a nice quiet neighborhood she'd always thought it was. She realized she didn't know what went on inside those houses and what hell some people were living.

Before going back to her house, something made her look down. She saw several spots of Michelle's blood that had baked on the sidewalk. Then, in horror, she watched a few tufts of blonde hair circle in the afternoon breeze.

The green scrub-clad emergency team at Presbyterian hospital hurried Michelle's gurney up a ramp and through the double doors that led to the emergency room. The metal wheels of the gurney squeaked over the shiny vinyl tile floor.

Covered with blood, Michelle was rolled past other waiting patients and immediately taken into an examining room where the doctors began assessing her wounds. Sliding in and out of consciousness, she managed to ask that her baby-sitter be called. Although speaking was painful and difficult, she also told one of the nurses to notify her parents in Baton Rouge.

She didn't want the doctors to wipe off any blood

until her picture had been taken for evidence, but her bleeding was so profuse that the doctors needed to find the source, and were forced to clean off her face.

An orderly wheeled her into surgery. In minutes, a doctor found her vein and inserted a needle to administer a general anesthetic. The doctor then popped her nose into place and packed it with cotton to stabilize the cartilage, and bandaged the bridge where the broken bone had burst through the skin. Examining her jaw, the doctor saw that it wasn't broken, but was severely dislocated. He wired it into place, fearing his patient would suffer temporomandibular joint disorder and a lifetime of pain because of the injury. It would be a month before Michelle could eat solid foods.

Of all her injuries, the doctors were most concerned about her eye. Michelle had told them earlier that when John first struck her, it felt like her eyeball was hitting the back of her skull. There was nothing they could do for it now because the area was so severely swollen.

After surgery, she was checked into the hospital and wheeled to a private room. A sympathetic woman from a battered women's shelter came and took her photograph.

"We're here for you," the woman said, as she patted Michelle's hand. She left a card from the shelter on a table by the bed.

The anesthetic caused Michelle to keep dozing off. A nurse came by periodically to slip ice chips in her mouth.

Then she was awakened by a uniformed officer who had come to take her statement. He had introduced himself, and his name sounded familiar. After trying to answer his questions, she realized that he was the same policeman who had taken John's complaint when he filed an assault charge against her.

The connection dawned on the policeman as he wrote her name. He said, "Oh, you're the gal who beat up your husband."

Michelle groaned and closed her swollen eyes.

ELEVEN

On the evening of the attack, Michelle's parents flew in from Baton Rouge and rushed from the airport to Presbyterian Hospital. When they reached their daughter's room, the sight of her shocked them. They walked in quietly, barely recognizing the once-pretty face that was now shaded black and purple. Her swollen eyes, nose, and jaw rounded out her features, making her look like a balloon. They hovered by her bed most of the night, not wanting to leave her side.

The next day, on Thursday, Mark Weisbart visited Michelle at the hospital and brought her the Texas Penal Code. She was anxious to begin her research. She wanted to find something solid so the police could charge John with a felony assault and arrest him immediately.

After Mark left, she pored over the Code, but everything classified her beating as a misdemeanor. She glanced at her swollen face in her compact mirror and scoffed. The bruises didn't look like a misdemeanor to her. Finally, she found a passage about breaking someone's nose. That constituted a felony assault. She called the police.

On Friday, after two days in the hospital, she checked out and spent the weekend with her parents at their hotel. She couldn't bring herself to return home until John had been arrested. Now she was completely terrified of the man.

When Michelle was finally able to describe the beating to her parents, they listened with tears in their eyes.

"For months we've been anxious for you to get away from John," her mother said. "Then once you're divorced, he attacks you worse than ever."

Michelle nodded. "People always ask, 'Why doesn't the woman leave her abuser?' But I've read the statistics. Three-fourths of murders and serious abuse take place *after* the couple has separated. John must have felt he was losing control since I was no longer legally his, and he was determined to prove that he was still the boss.

"I'm so grateful for one thing," Michelle said. "A fire truck arrived first and blocked the view between my house and where I was on the sidewalk. The kids usually come out on the porch and wait for me to get off the bus. I'm so glad they didn't see the beating."

Michelle was trying desperately to protect her children. She had been thinking about them as she lay semiconscious on the sidewalk. In her mind she had seen a fire truck hovering there like a guardian angel. However, no witness ever reported seeing a fire truck on the scene.

John Battaglia was arrested at his garage apartment on Sunday afternoon. He made his familiar trek down to the courthouse and was fingerprinted, but he had to spend one night in jail as arrangements were made for his bail bond. The next day, he paid his ten percent and left. However, this time he was charged with a felony assault and would stand trial for his crime. Until then, he was a free man.

Unbeknownst to Michelle, he continued to follow her every activity like a hunter stalking prey. When the hospital released her with ice packs on her face, he tailed her parents' rental car from a safe distance as they drove her to their hotel.

Michelle was sad to see her parents leave on Monday, for now she felt truly alone and more defenseless than ever before. While she was gone, her son had stayed with a friend's family. Odice had taken care of Laurie for the past four days and nights with frequent and welcome visits from Michelle's parents, but Michelle needed to give Odice a break.

However, there was no way Michelle could stay alone at night after the beating. Her friends were eager to help. Old law school buddies volunteered to stay a few nights, paralegals and secretaries from her firm took turns staying over, and many times she and her children slept next door at the Dicksons'. If John Battaglia were to touch her again, she was positive he would kill her.

Once Michelle returned home, she found that there was little food in her house. The food brought by generous friends when they came to spend the night had run out. Although she was mainly on a liquid diet, she eventually had to go to the grocery store where she would also buy school supplies for Billy. Still swollen and bruised, she gingerly placed large sunglasses over her eyes, which now resembled two chunks of black coal. She grimaced as the glasses touched the red scar on the bridge of her broken nose.

She walked into the store, hating to embarrass her son, who was with her. Every customer turned to stare at her as if she had "Abused Woman" tattooed on her forehead. She hurriedly pulled canned fruits and vegetables from shelves and quickly tossed them into her basket, trying to get in and out of the store as fast as possible. Laurie was sitting in the child's seat of the cart, but Billy had wandered into another aisle and Michelle went to search for him.

She froze.

There was John Battaglia. And worst of all, he had Billy by the arm. The child stood wide-eyed and scared. John, down on one knee, had made a fist and was holding it in front of Billy's face.

"Did you see what happened to your mama?" he hissed.

Billy was too frightened to respond.

"Well, just remember. That could happen to you!"

Michelle grabbed her son's hand and raced off to find the store's security guard. She explained the situation to the uniformed woman, who accompanied Michelle around the store and out to her car.

At that moment, Michelle decided to buy a gun.

Tuesday morning, Michelle drove to the Oshman's Sporting Goods on Abrams Road and went to the rear of the store where the firearms counter was located. The potbellied clerk had only to glance at Michelle's battered face before suggesting a .38-caliber pistol for its power and accuracy. He patiently explained how to operate it. He also persuaded her to buy a purse that had a side pocket for the gun.

She could place her hand on the gun with her finger on the trigger and no one would know. He also suggested a firing range where she could get some practice.

Michelle wasted no time. That afternoon she went to a firing range that was located in an old warehouse. It was hazy and smelly from the smoke of spent bullets. In no time, she had unloaded two boxes of shells into paper targets that had the outline of a man printed on them. Once she could cover the heart and head with bullet holes, she knew she was ready.

Billy's school began its fall session the following week. Still wearing dark glasses to cover her bruised eyes, Michelle accompanied him on the first day to explain Billy's possible danger to the principal, teacher, and counselors. She gave them a photo of John Battaglia with instructions that under no circumstances was Billy to be released to John. To further protect him, Odice went to the school daily to walk Billy home.

The first week in September, Mary McGee, a paralegal at Akin, Gump, was spending the night with Michelle.

Michelle's evening ritual was to shove a heavy chest of drawers in front of her bedroom door that opened to the rear patio. Double-bolted locks were affixed to all the doors leading outside her house. Her once-lovely home now reminded her of a prison. All of her curtains were closed and pinned shut. She thought how unfair it was; she was living in a prison and John Battaglia was roaming free.

About 11:30 P.M., Michelle and Mary tucked themselves into her four-poster bed. By 2:00 A.M. Michelle was sleeping soundly with the gun under her pillow.

Neither woman heard the footsteps outside on the thick summer lawn. But the first thump against the door woke Michelle. Repeated thuds sent her into a frenzy.

Mary slowly sat up in bed. "What on earth?" she asked, still groggy.

"It's gotta be John," Michelle whispered.

The banging on the door intensified and Battaglia shouted, "Michelle? Michelle? Open the door!"

Mary picked up the phone and called 911 while Michelle broke into hysterical sobs. "How could he? How could he?" she screamed repeatedly. "This can't be happening again!"

Michelle tried to calm herself. She took several deep breaths, wiped her eyes, and stuck her hand under her pillow. The coldness of the gun felt reassuring in her hand.

TWELVE

In the three weeks since Bonnie Kingman had watched the ambulance rush Michelle LaBorde to the emergency room, she had thought of her many times.

Today Bonnie was hurrying to finish a client's proposal for her part-time advertising job before her son awoke from his nap. She heard someone knock on her front door. The last thing she needed was an interruption. She stood up, pushed her chair back from the computer, and went to see who it was.

When she opened her door, she didn't recognize the woman in sunglasses who stood before her.

"Remember me?" the woman asked, her purple-and-yellow-splotched face still swollen from the beating. "I'm Michelle LaBorde."

"Oh my gosh!" was all Bonnie could manage when she saw what Michelle looked like.

"I came by to thank you," Michelle said. "You helped me when I really needed it." She paused a moment, then said, "I truly feel you saved my life."

Bonnie didn't have to be reminded of that awful day and the crumpled body on the sidewalk. She broke into a wide grin, knowing that Michelle was out of the hospital and on the mend. Opening the door, Bonnie invited her in, but Michelle shook her head and remained on the porch.

"I can't stay. I'm leaving town and I just wanted to come by and say thank you. Remember what you said to me right after the attack? That John wasn't ever going to touch me again."

Bonnie looked down at her entry's parquet floor, embarrassed by the bravado of her own words. "I remember. But thinking back, it was such an emotional thing. I realize now that there wasn't anything I could do to stop him."

"No, not in that way," Michelle agreed. "But your written testimony can stop him. You were great to get involved and talk to the police."

Bonnie stepped out on the porch, wondering how Michelle had remembered her words. Michelle had been almost comatose when Bonnie had said that to her. Both women sat on the concrete steps of the porch.

"Look at my eyes," Michelle said as she carefully removed her sunglasses. "They're still pretty red."

Bonnie had to stifle a gasp at the sight of Michelle's swollen, bloodshot eyes. "I just can't imagine all that you've been through," Bonnie told her.

"Turns out he broke my nose—a compound fracture, and dislocated my jaw. So the doctors had quite a time of it putting me back together." She replaced her glasses and tucked a strand of blond hair behind an ear.

"Did you hear what he said to me?" Michelle asked.

"I heard him call you a name. I know he was screaming at you, but I really couldn't hear any conversation."

"Oh, we had a conversation, all right. Albeit brief.

When he first rode up to me on his bike, I was just shaking. He kept smiling at me and I could feel my heart pound. I was so scared.

"I had a protective order against him, and the day before the beating, I had filed charges because he shoved me down the steps. So he knew there was a warrant out for his arrest.

"That really made him mad because of the possibility he'd go to jail. When he came up to me that day, I tried not to make eye contact. But he said, 'Well, if you're going to put me in jail, there might as well be a darn good reason.' After that I saw stars.

"I've finally come to the realization that I'm no longer safe here. John won't stop till he kills me. Just last week he came pounding on my bedroom door, but by then I had bought a gun. I was really scared, but when I yelled that I had a gun, he left." Michelle shook her head. "That man will stop at nothing. But that night after he left, I got up and looked in the mirror. I saw a very frightened face staring back at me, but I also knew it wasn't the face of a murderer. I just couldn't kill my daughter's father. He'd be dead and I'd be in jail and she'd be an orphan. That's when I decided I had to move. But I still carry that gun. Someday, I might be forced to use it."

"You've been through so much," Bonnie said. "Where will you go?"

"My family's in Louisiana. Baton Rouge. My dad's an attorney and he's giving me advice. He'll protect me. I'm also an attorney," Michelle added.

"You make me feel like a frumpy housewife," Bonnie confessed. "You're dressed sharp even now, and here I am." She looked down and realized she was wearing the same khaki shorts and pink T-shirt she'd had on three weeks ago.

"I remember the outfit," Michelle said and smiled.

"You're one neat lady. I'm going to miss you."

"I wish there was some way I could thank you."

"You already have," Bonnie assured her. "You've thanked me by coming back and showing me that you're going to be okay."

Michelle walked back to her rented car. She gave Bonnie one last wave, then drove away.

The following month, Bonnie spotted a large white moving van parked in front of Michelle's house. She felt sad, realizing that she'd probably never see her brave neighbor again.

THIRTEEN

Awash in sixty inches of rainfall each year, Baton Rouge is a lush subtropical city of a quarter million people. Magnolia trees blossom with white flowers as big as dinner plates. Baton Rouge, the state's capital, hugs the shores of the Mississippi River, where commerce crawls from St. Louis to the mouth of the Gulf of Mexico.

"Baton Rouge" is French for "red stick," and it was a red stick, or maypole, that the soldiers saw in 1699, laden with fish and bear heads and dripping with blood that gave the city its name.

Michelle LaBorde happily reclaimed her birthplace when she moved back to Baton Rouge on September 14, 1987, and even welcomed its humid, eighty-five-degree days.

Michelle had left Dallas under cover of darkness, taking the 9:17 P.M. flight. She and her children took only the clothes they could wear and what they could pack in suitcases.

The following week, Michelle and her mother returned to Dallas to pack up the rest of the house, again at night.

* * *

Now in Baton Rouge, Michelle was happy to be back in the arms of her large, outspoken, southern Louisiana family, who raised their voices when they were excited, happy, sad, mad, or just wanted to be heard. Her parents and a brother and sister lived in Baton Rouge, and another sister in Lafayette. The antithesis of Battaglia's distant, noncommunicative family, Michelle's family gathered at least once a month to share dinner and catch up on each other's lives.

Michelle moved back with no job, no car, no place to live, and no school for her children, but she thanked God for the way her life began to heal itself. She may have missed the glamour of working for the large Dallas legal conglomerate, but she relished the calm of the small law firm, Anderson, Holliday and Jones, that immediately hired her. Then the insurance company paid her claim, allowing her to replace the car she had wrecked in the Dallas rainstorm. To her surprise, a nun at the best Catholic school in Baton Rouge made an exception and let Billy enroll in midyear. Then two weeks later, she found a lovely home to rent. Around the same time, the court had granted her bankruptcy discharge, so she now had a fresh financial start.

Knowing that John Battaglia would not suddenly appear on her doorstep made life more tolerable. Her children loved the hugs of their doting maternal grandparents. Life had finally become peaceful, or so she thought.

Once she had found a new home, she hired a moving company to take everything from her Dallas house. She provided the movers with the divorce de-

cree declaring that everything in the house belonged to her, and warned that although John
Battaglia would probably show up, under no circumstances were they to let him in.

Within hours of the moving van's arrival, John appeared at the front door of the Bellewood house.

The first mover found him in the front entry and
asked for his ID.

Battaglia ignored the man and tried to walk into
the living room. Gesturing, he said, "Everything here
belongs to me. I don't want you people to touch a
thing."

A fellow worker joined the mover, and both men
stood their ground, telling John he couldn't enter.
One man unfolded the court documents that had
been stuffed in with their moving instructions. He
showed them to John. "Guess you'll have to leave,
buddy," the mover said.

John smiled. "I can't believe she's doing this to me.
You guys know how divorce works. You buy these
things for the woman and she takes them all with her."

The men smiled and nodded like they knew what
he meant.

"Tell you what, fellas, just for old times' sake, let
me take one last look at the home I shared with my
wife and kids. Just for sentimental reasons. It'll mean
a lot to me."

He was capable of looking sympathetic, and apparently did at that moment. "Oh okay, we understand,"
they told him, and stepped aside so he could enter.

He waited until the men were loading a large
chest of drawers into the van, then sneaked into the
master bedroom. He knew that one of Michelle's
most prized possessions was the antique four-poster
bed that she had inherited from her grandmother.

Rushing to the bed, he knelt down on the area rug under the footboard and took out his car keys. Working quickly, he carved "CUNT" into the wood in two-inch high letters, then hurried out before the men returned.

Michelle LaBorde had been strong throughout her recovery from the attack, through her move, and through all the adjustments of getting settled in Baton Rouge. However, once she heard what Battaglia had done to her grandmother's bed, she fell apart.

The following month, John Battaglia was still angry about Michelle's sudden departure. Feeling revengeful, he decided to take her to court. He recruited his father to write Judge Carolyn Wright to tell her of the family's concern about the welfare and well-being of Laura Julia.

In his letter, the senior Battaglia lamented that when he was in Dallas, Michelle had thwarted his efforts to see his granddaughter. Now that Laura was no longer in Dallas, he felt forced to turn to the Wards, Michelle's parents, to learn of Laurie's whereabouts. He moaned to the judge that when he had phoned the other grandparents, he received a frosty reception, describing Mrs. Ward as "barely coherent."

The Wards were equally shocked that he had called. Didn't the man know that his son had beaten their daughter to a pulp only two months before?

Michelle received a distinguished honor in November 1987 when she was inducted into the Louisiana

State University Law School's Hall of Fame for her performance in law school and her legal service to the community. She was presented with an impressive plaque that still hangs on her office wall today.

In the kitchen of her new home, Michelle sat at her desk, sorting mail. She stopped when she came to an envelope with the return address of the 256th Family District Court in Dallas.

Michelle ripped it open and read a subpoena demanding that she return to Dallas for a custody hearing. It contained John Battaglia's accusation that she took his child out of state, thus limiting his access to her—and he even wanted increased visitation rights.

She typed a note to Judge Carolyn Wright, reminding her of the original custody ruling and outlining John Battaglia's history of abuse. If court records were any consideration, a blind man could see that John didn't need increased time with his daughter.

However, the judge replied there was nothing she could do, for regardless of what Battaglia had done in the past, Michelle had taken their daughter to another state. The fact that Michelle left Texas to save her life and keep her children from harm was not an adequate excuse.

Michelle flew back to Dallas for a tension-filled visit.

During the proceedings, Judge Wright asked Michelle's new lawyer, Leota Alexander, to meet with her in chambers to review the documents. During their discussion, the judge exclaimed to Leota, "That

John Battaglia is the best-looking man I've ever seen in my life!"

Michelle's attorney was startled that the judge would make such a complimentary statement about someone with John Battaglia's shameful assault record.

In court, the judge decided that Battaglia would be allowed to see his daughter as per his original custody agreement, but because Michelle had moved, the amount of time per visit had to be increased in order to get the child back to Texas. Therefore, Michelle would be forced to turn over two-year-old Laurie to John for three days a month, every month—in Dallas. That horrified Michelle.

John Battaglia turned around and gave Michelle a smug "You deserve this" glance.

Michelle's lawyer brought the court's attention to records that showed Battaglia still had a felony assault tagged to his rap sheet. This was the man who had knocked Michelle down as she held Laurie, injuring both of them. What would he do to Laurie if he had her for three days all to himself? Michelle knew in her heart that he was dangerous and capable of anything. She'd tried to tell so many people, but to no avail. Would she see Laurie again? Would he abduct her, or for God's sake, would he do something even worse? Was the legal world insane?

FOURTEEN

The Court's decision was much to John Battaglia's liking. But there was no denying that he still had two dark legal clouds hanging over his head, which meant visitation was out of the question until those issues were resolved.

Those protective order violations of pushing and beating Michelle both occurred in August 1987. With postponements and rescheduling, the hearing was pushed forward to July 1, 1988, almost a year after the attacks. In the court documents, the hearing had been postponed twenty-six times. That meant that Michelle had been notified twenty-six times to appear in a Dallas court. Sometimes she found herself flying to Texas twice a month.

Michelle had endured a year of subpoenas ordering her to attend hearings, only to see each hearing canceled and rescheduled. The entire process left her exhausted and upset. Battaglia had managed to weasel his way out of all of his other offenses, and now his lawyer contacted Michelle, urging her to drop the beating charge from a third degree felony, aggravated assault to a Class A misdemeanor. If she would do that, Battaglia agreed to waive a jury trial and plead guilty to the lesser offense. The lawyer said that Battaglia's punishment would be set at 364 days of confinement in the Dallas County jail.

That was hard for Michelle to believe, so she asked for a copy of the judgment. When it arrived, she studied it thoroughly. True, the judgment mentioned 364 days of confinement, but reading further, Michelle saw that the court, "In the best interests of society and of the defendant," would withhold execution of the sentence and grant probation instead of jail time. Also, an additional provision of the agreement would dismiss Battaglia of the charge of shoving Michelle down the steps at her home.

How many times had Michelle been faced with these dilemmas? She didn't want to cave in to her ex-husband yet again, but it would mean no more flying back to Dallas for court appearances, no more testifying in front of the man she had grown to hate. Battaglia would have to attend monthly probation meetings at forty dollars a session. That meant that the county would be keeping track of his attendance. He'd be restrained from further contact, either in person or by phone or mail with Michelle without the approval of the court. Michelle shook her head. She had heard that one before. But now she lived in Louisiana, so the next item in the judgment caught her eye. "John Battaglia cannot leave Dallas without the written consent of the Court." That phrase would make it much more difficult for John Battaglia to visit his daughter.

Michelle agreed to Battaglia's plea bargain, but his next harassing phone call made her realize that she would never be rid of the man. He called to carp about not having seen Laurie for almost a year.

Michelle then realized that he would always be there, that figure slinking in the shadows, ready to pounce when he didn't get his way.

Only months after Michelle had moved back to Baton Rouge, she was devastated to learn that her father, whom she adored and had modeled her career after, had been diagnosed with cancer and given only six months to live.

Many pictures of little blond Laurie crowded John Battaglia's accounting office, and numerous others lined his North Dallas apartment. Some were of John holding Laurie as a brand-new baby. Others were of Laurie grinning while she took her first steps. Those taken in the last year were rare, for he had not seen Laurie in that amount of time and he was dependent on Michelle to send him photos. He found that irritating. Everyone at his accounting office was well aware of his daughter, for he talked about her constantly and told everyone how much he loved her.

Now that his sentence for the assault had been reduced to mere probation, he began pressuring the Dallas County family courts to help him arrange visits with his daughter. The court ordered an evaluation to decide if it was safe for Battaglia to have visitation rights. A well-known Dallas psychologist, Linda M. Ingraham, Ph.D., was assigned to interview and test both warring parties.

Battaglia and LaBorde were evaluated separately by Dr. Ingraham at her Oak Lawn office. Battaglia, dressed in a freshly pressed double-breasted suit, sat down on the counselor's cushioned sofa. He was at his schmoozing best. Dr. Ingraham characterized John as "outgoing and talkative during the interviews." He described his attack on Michelle as merely an "incident where he blackened her eyes," because he had been "frustrated." The doctor saw John as a nonaggressive, nonassertive person whose "overt hostility measured well below average." The doctor described his attacks as "generally directed at the person provoking them rather than expressed as random outbursts."

Michelle flew back to Dallas for her interview. Dr. Ingraham reported that she had a sincere concern for her daughter's safety, but determined that Michelle had "passive-aggressive tendencies" in addition to being "impulsive." She also found that Michelle tended to minimize her role in the problem relationship for she "provoked others to rage and then complained about the resulting mistreatment." In other words, the doctor blamed Michelle for being assaulted.

The psychologist had given John and Michelle the Minnesota Multiphasic Personality Inventory (MPPI). She may not have known that John had already taken the test on four different occasions. The test scans for personality disorders, and includes 567 questions that are answered in two hours. The built-in validity of the test rests on the same question being asked in four different ways to help guarantee consistency of answers. Anyone as bright as John Battaglia could figure out how to manipulate the test by the fifth time he took it. How else could he have gotten his "overt hostility" to register well below average?

Based on her personal interview and John's test results, the psychologist decided that he was basically an "insecure person who needed assertiveness training." She found that "the danger to Laura appears minimal because John's outbursts are not likely to be directed at her." Then, arriving at a solution that could have prevented future problems, the psychologist suggested that the initial visits be supervised, as John's outbursts "can be unpredictable."

Finally, she concluded, "There does not seem to be a compelling reason why John should be denied access to his daughter."

Michelle knew that John was capable of being two different people. He could be fun and caring, and at other times hateful and violent. There was no question which person showed up for the interview with Dr. Ingraham.

Michelle's father died only five months after his cancer had been detected. It was a double blow for Michelle. Not only had she lost her father, but she lost his legal advice and emotional support, as well.

For once, the slow turn of the judicial wheels worked in Michelle's favor. After Dr. Ingraham's psychological test tilted in John's favor, it wasn't until August 11, 1989, that the family court finally completed the visitation agreement.

The courts forced Michelle to relinquish her daughter for three days every month, plus additional holiday visits. On top of that, she had to fly Laurie to Dallas each month, and then John would fly her back. All this for the man who had beaten her so savagely.

How she wished she were in a position to write abuse laws. The courts just didn't understand what a woman had to go through. She would love to tell them.

Fifteen

When President Reagan deregulated banking in the 1980s, John Battaglia was working as an accountant for the Federal Deposit Insurance Corporation (FDIC). Reagan's decision opened the gates for anyone to jump on the trolley and start a bank. All new banks received the protection of the FDIC. Having been granted charters indiscriminately, many banks and savings and loans lost their conservative moorings and, without due diligence, granted loans to inexperienced clients who were undertaking high-risk ventures. Bank executives lavishly decorated their offices and added corporate jets and other luxuries worthy of oil sheiks.

The financial debacle that followed clobbered the federal government with $300 billion in debt, and left no way to pick up the pieces. Finally, in 1989, Congress created the Resolution Trust Corporation (RTC) to plow through the fiasco and, it was hoped, to salvage some of the banks' assets. In addition, Congress earmarked a large chunk of accounting contracts for minority companies.

Dallas, and Texas in general, had more than its fair share of failed thrifts. Banks were sold and resold, and names of financial houses that had been solidly etched in granite now fluttered on painted canvas banners draped over the fronts of their buildings.

In 1990, John Battaglia enthusiastically vaulted from his FDIC job to the new organization charged with the task of retrieving assets of failed financial institutions. He had no way of knowing how much this decision would alter his life.

Battaglia took on the job with patriotic zeal; he wanted to impress people with his determination. He voiced concern that the RTC had no structure. After all, it had been hurriedly created out of smoke and mirrors. The Dallas office alone oversaw a hefty $10 billion in assets.

Furthermore, RTC employees were given no quotas, so they were under no pressure to complete their assignments. If they closed all of their ailing financial houses with dispatch and liquidated assets promptly, their job would be finished, the RTC dissolved, and they'd be tossed out on the street. Therefore, efficiency was of little concern. Battaglia claimed to be infuriated by this lackadaisical attitude, and decided to apply his Marine discipline to his job, which proved to be an unpopular move. He began taking notes so he could alert his supervisors to the poor internal business practices.

SIXTEEN

In October 1990, Mary Jean Pearle was twenty-eight and had dated many young, eligible men. Still, she had not found that one person with whom she wanted to spend the rest of her life. Many of her friends had already married, but although the idea of getting married appealed to her, she felt no panic to rush to the altar.

The tall brunette was blessed with a head of thick chestnut brown hair, which she casually brushed off her face and let fall down her back. Her large expressive brown eyes were accented by conservative makeup, and a warm red polish covered her long, tapered nails. She had outgrown all of the teenage fads, and her taste leaned toward fashionable tailored pants and cashmere sweater sets.

Looking for a husband to support her was not a goal. Her parents were wealthy and generous and, in addition, she supported herself by working in the family antique business. Not yet an antique expert herself, she could at times differentiate between fine antiques and well-made imitations.

The crowded, noisy atmosphere of The Mucky Duck in the Oak Lawn area was one of many favorite hangouts for Mary Jean Pearle's crowd. The English pub ambiance was inviting, and drinking beer and meeting new people was a good way to spend a Saturday night.

This cool fall evening, as she laughed with friends, Mary Jean noticed a handsome man watching her from two tables away. When she made eye contact with him, he came over and introduced himself. John Battaglia was seven years older than Mary Jean and very suave. The age difference made him seem worldly and sophisticated. Just being around the good-looking man flattered her and made her feel glamorous. Her friends told her how cute and fun he was. His energy and humor dazzled them.

All evening, he hovered over her, complimenting her and making her feel like a princess being swept off her feet. After they had spent most of the evening talking, he handed her his business card. *Hmmm,* she thought, *a CPA.* The card read "Resolution Trust Corporation."

"So you work for the government?" Mary Jean asked.

"Yes," he said. "I supervise eleven employees and I've got billions of dollars in assets to liquidate. Gotta get back some money for the taxpayers."

Mary Jean was impressed. Here he was a college graduate with additional certification, and she hadn't even finished high school. With all of her pretty girlfriends around her, this very desirable man was most interested in her.

Later that night, he asked for Mary Jean's phone number. She smiled coyly and wrote it on the back of a cocktail napkin.

* * *

Mary Jean Pearle was the only child of Gene Harrison Pearle. Her father was born on March 6, 1923, when Dallas was only the forty-second largest city in the country.

Even as a young man, Pearle was smart and ambitious. He graduated from Southern Methodist University, but in his early life he struggled financially; one summer, he drove an ice cream truck. When he turned thirty-five, his life changed dramatically. His widowed mother, Ida May, died at sixty-three and left him a quarter million dollars—a vast sum in 1958. His only brother, who was two years older, had died during the Second World War and his father, Claude, passed away three years after that. Gene was the sole heir.

Although he suddenly became wealthy, Gene managed to stay levelheaded and did nothing foolhardy with the money. At the time, he sold real estate for Ebby Halliday, a woman who would become a Dallas icon in the real estate world. Pearle had seen many people make their fortunes in real estate and he had the drive and charisma to become one of them. After receiving his inheritance, he continued working in Ebby Halliday's quaint, white, residential-looking structure at Preston and Northwest Highway. All along, he wisely invested his money, purchasing rental properties that provided additional income. Then, he'd use those funds to buy more property. In addition, he invested in the stock market and soon became a very wealthy man.

In 1960, at the age of thirty-seven, he met Dorrace Clark, an attractive, dark-haired divorcee with two teenage sons, Robert and Richard. Pearle was a comfortable-looking man, of average height and stocky build. His olive skin was an interesting contrast to his light brown hair. He had never been married and he was impressed with Dorrace, an ambitious woman who had dreams of opening her own antiques business.

A year and a half after they married, Mary Jean was born, and Gene Pearle, now almost forty, felt blessed to finally have a child, especially a daughter. He was always gracious to women, insisting that they should be treated like princesses, and that's exactly how he would treat Mary Jean for his entire life. She was Daddy's girl. At her birth, her half brother Bobby was fifteen, and Rick was fourteen. Quickly, the little brunette became the star of the family; everyone catered to her. Later, when Mary Jean became a teenager, her brother Rick drove for over three hours to take her to Austin, Texas, simply because she wanted to see a Peter Frampton concert. It was a very grown-up experience for a thirteen-year-old.

The family lived in a long, rambling house in North Dallas, where Mary Jean attended Hillcrest High School. She became close to many classmates, and several have remained lifelong friends. After her third year of high school, she wanted to test her wings and try living in New York City. Since her father denied her nothing, he rented her an apartment in the Big Apple for six months; however, Mary Jean was back home in three. The pace of the huge city was not to her liking, and she yearned to be back in Dallas with her friends, family, and everything else that was familiar.

By now, her mother was well established as a dealer in fine antiques, owning Dorrace Pearle Antiques on Routh Street near the Quadrangle. Mary Jean began helping her mother in the store.

In her early twenties, Mary Jean tried out all the latest fashion trends, even wearing black fingernail polish. Her brothers called her a "fashion junkie" as she tinted her hair red and wore heavy mascara and dark, muddy eye shadow. But when fashions changed, so did Mary Jean.

SEVENTEEN

At the same time John Battaglia was becoming involved with Mary Jean Pearle, Michelle LaBorde was making major changes in her life. Ever since law school, Michelle had dreamed of being a law professor. At the time, her professors advised her to practice law first; because actual experience would allow her to bring more realism to her classes. After practicing for nine years, Michelle was more than qualified to teach.

Her dream came true in August 1991, when Southern University Law Center in Baton Rouge hired her as an associate professor to teach criminal trial procedure, trial advocacy, and many other areas of law. The environs of Southern University are true to its name. The campus sits on a wide bend of the Mississippi River where cargo-laden barges cruise lazily up the river. Live oak trees drip with Spanish moss, giving them a hazy appearance. In summer, the campus is dotted with pink-blossomed crape myrtle trees, painting the landscape pink and green.

Each year, the law school holds continuing education seminars and in Michelle's first year, Southern offered one on family law. The director asked Michelle to speak. She had previously made a conscious decision not to be an advocate on domestic violence issues because she needed to heal herself before she could help heal others. Now she knew her voice had to be heard. She told the director she would speak on "Family Violence." After the seminar, she was enthusiastically received and word soon spread that the new professor was more than a bright mind and a pretty face. The woman had firsthand experience with domestic violence, and she was willing to talk about it.

A previous client of Michelle's was an eccentric man whose name had appeared in the Guinness Book of World Records more than once. One entry cited him for flying his private plane solo around the world. He was also known for his annual holiday party, a huge gala to which the most glamorous and fascinating people in Baton Rouge were invited. Michelle was always on the list. Her life had returned to normal, but in late 1991 she had no steady boyfriend. She dressed casually for this year's party in an understated black dress. Though she tried not to stand out, her dress showed off her trim body and made her hair look all the more blond.

After she had been at the party for thirty minutes, she eyed a tall, very handsome man. He wore a black suit and a black collarless shirt. His black hair was slightly graying at the temples. She asked her friend, an interior designer named Marilyn, about him.

"Oh my God, why didn't I think of this before!" Marilyn squealed. "You two would be perfect together. His name is John and he's *so* Italian. Come meet him."

The description sent chills through Michelle. She

almost bolted for the door, but her friend continued to tell her about the man.

"He's a chemical engineer and was just transferred here from California. Worked there for a couple years. He's been in town only a few weeks and doesn't know that many people. You two will get along famously," her friend said, dragging Michelle across the room.

When Marilyn introduced Michelle to John Ghetti, he asked, "Did you just get here?"

Michelle looked at her watch. "No," she said. "I've been here at least a half hour or so."

"Impossible," he said, taking Michelle's hand. "I would have noticed you before now."

Michelle could feel warmth flow through her body. He locked his eyes on hers and she was instantly charmed. They talked for the next two hours. His huge brown eyes sparkled when he spoke of cooking Italian food for her, and when he smiled she noticed he had the whitest teeth she'd seen outside of a toothpaste commercial.

EIGHTEEN

Flushed with the warm excitement of a new romance, Mary Jean spoke enthusiastically to her parents about John Battaglia. Just a week after meeting him, she took John to her parents' home to meet them. Her mother liked him well enough. She saw him as an attractive, successful young man to show off to her friends. Her father treated him cordially, but if he had been asked, he would probably have said that no one was good enough for Mary Jean.

After Mary Jean had dated John for only a few months, she shocked her family and friends by announcing marriage plans. As the wedding neared the following year, 1991, Mary Jean's brother Rick saw little fissures in Battaglia's personality. Small hints kept popping up that he wasn't the kind, considerate person Mary Jean thought he was. Rick tried to point these out to his sister, but Mary Jean was in love and she couldn't believe that John Battaglia had any flaws. Mary Jean felt that magic had just entered her life.

However, Mary Jean was in denial. John had told her about beating Michelle LaBorde and breaking her nose, but he downplayed the fight to such an extent that Mary Jean believed that it had been an isolated incident. John also told Mary Jean how horrible Michelle had been to him, depriving him of seeing his child, as well as having affairs with several lawyers she worked with. He also complained that Michelle had been a dreadful wife and an even worse mother.

Mary Jean felt sorry that John had had to endure such a terrible marriage. She wouldn't dream of treating him like that. Believing his lies, she let love cloud her mind, and excused whatever he had done. At that point she felt like Cinderella who had just found her Prince.

Having been raised in the Catholic Church, John Battaglia wanted a Catholic wedding. Although Dorrace and Gene Pearle were of a different faith, they consented to his wishes and began planning an elaborate affair, putting deposits on caterers and florists, and buying Mary Jean a beautiful designer gown. As the wedding neared, the Catholic priest who had been counseling the couple refused to marry them. He was convinced that they had issues they had not yet resolved, issues that would cause future problems.

The priest voiced his concerns that John had anger management problems and hadn't reconciled to the fact that he had been abusive to his first wife. He realized that John refused to take responsibility for his actions. On the other hand, the priest saw Mary Jean as controlling. He determined that she had trouble relinquishing power and wasn't allowing John to be part of the decision-making process.

Mary Jean's parents wanted to give their daughter an extraordinary wedding present. For several years, they had lived in a large, two-story red brick home on

Dickason, in an area just north of downtown. They surprised their daughter by presenting her with that house as a wedding gift. The four-bedroom, three-bath home had a large formal living room with an adjoining music room that held a baby grand piano. An elegant European chandelier sparkled over a polished fruitwood table in the vast formal dining room, a room big enough for the grandest of dinner parties. The house even had an elevator.

Mary Jean and John were thrilled. Knowing that she and her Prince Charming would live happily ever after, Mary Jean discounted the priest's misgivings, and the couple decided to marry immediately. They chose April 6, 1991, only six months after they had first met.

Her parents lost all of the deposits they had made on the sumptuous wedding when Mary Jean and John invited a minister from her church to unite them in marriage in the living room of their new home.

On their wedding night, the perfect, considerate man who had always put Mary Jean first and smothered her with compliments suddenly snapped at her over a small disagreement. His language was vulgar and abusive. It was the first tolling of the bell, warning her of danger ahead. As she'd had no experience with abuse of any kind, it was difficult for her to recognize it. Her model of marriage was her parents' loving relationship. In addition to treating Mary Jean as a princess, her father had always treated her mother like a queen.

Mary Jean took another look at her new husband and she saw a stranger.

* * *

After they returned from their honeymoon, Mary Jean rationalized that John's belligerent slip was only an isolated occurrence. She didn't know that when a woman first tolerates abuse, her abuser sees it as permission for future violence. Unfortunately, Mary Jean began to follow a pattern, much like Michelle had. She discounted the seriousness of their problems and went about trying to make their marriage happy.

It was a sad revelation for Mary Jean when she discovered that her Prince Charming snored. She found it impossible to sleep as she lay listening to his nocturnal honking. She slept with her head under her pillow, stuffed foam rubber plugs into her ears, and switched on a sound machine that simulated the crashing of ocean waves, but nothing helped.

Two months following their wedding, Mary Jean was excited to learn that she was pregnant. Now her rest was essential, but she still wasn't getting any sleep. She would nudge John, telling him to turn over. Finally, he picked up his pillow and stomped down the hall to another bedroom. Except on rare occasions, he didn't come back.

On January 9, 1992, Mary Faith Battaglia was born, and Mary Jean was ecstatic. John was equally thrilled and doted on the little blond baby, calling her "Faithy Mouse." He was happy to feed the child and care for her, even changing her diapers. As she got older, he would take her for rides in the car. At home he'd hold her in his arms and sing to her as they danced around the room. Mary Jean was delighted that he was such a loving and gentle father.

However, the new baby didn't deter Battaglia's increasing anger at Mary Jean. Part of his anger may have been that he had to live in a house owned by his wife. With that burden to his ego, he didn't physically abuse her as he had Michelle, but he resorted to verbal domination, criticizing and belittling her. When she didn't immediately lose weight after her pregnancy, he told her she was fat. Knowing she didn't have the education he had, he felt comfortable calling her stupid. He undermined her confidence and tried to make her doubt her own self-worth, despite the fact that she was a smart lady—adroitly running a successful antiques business and handling rental property that brought in more money than he made.

Being married to John was an emotional endurance test. He called Mary Jean every vulgar name she had ever heard. She begged him to get counseling, thinking that he could learn to manage his explosive temper. He refused to go and treated her more harshly. Some of his insulting tirades lasted as long as twenty minutes. At the same time she didn't dare tell her friends or family about their troubled relationship. She would be embarrassed to admit that John had such a violent temper and was screaming at her. Abuse just didn't happen to someone like her.

John and Mary Jean entertained lavishly in their wonderful home. As their friends walked through the front entry, they would never have suspected that John had exploded at Mary Jean only minutes before.

At dinner, twelve guests would sit at the beautiful dining-room table laden with antique china richly decorated with twenty-four carat gold and placed atop matching gold chargers. Sparkling lead crystal goblets and wineglasses, along with hundred-year-old, heavy French silverware adorned with clusters of grapes, completed each setting. A huge bouquet of fresh flowers designed by Mary Jean's favorite florist lent a soft fragrance to the room.

During cocktails and at dinner John would tell funny, animated stories, sometimes about their daughter's cute antics, many times about other subjects. He always kept their friends entertained. Everyone loved John.

The guests would dine on beef Wellington, lobster Newberg, or whatever delicious gourmet dish Mary Jean had prepared. They dabbed at the corners of their mouths with starched, smoothly ironed linen napkins, and thought what a perfectly wonderful life the Battaglias had.

At Christmas, the Battaglias mailed cards to their many friends with a beautiful professional photograph of their family tucked inside. For Faith's first Christmas, John and Mary Jean were photographed sitting in front of their lavishly decorated fireplace. A tall tree sat in the background and John's arm warmly embraced Mary Jean's shoulders. Faith sat on the floor in a red velvet dress, her father wore a dark suit, and her photogenic mother looked exceptionally pretty and alluring in a black velvet dress with a split up the left side. Mary Jean's hair and makeup were perfect, just like the smile on her lips. They looked like the ideal family . . . or so their friends believed.

NINETEEN

Michelle's life suddenly changed. It was like the first warm breath of spring. She felt an inner peace she hadn't experienced in years. When John Battaglia married Mary Jean Pearle and they had a child, he finally stopped harassing her.

Laurie continued to visit her father once a month. During one of the visits, Mary Jean accompanied John in flying Laurie back after a weekend visit, so Mary Jean got to meet Michelle in Baton Rouge. The women eyed each other. Mary Jean was impressed with Michelle's education and her career as a law professor. At the same time, Michelle was busy admiring Mary Jean's designer clothes and beautiful jewelry.

Laurie, now five years old, loved her new baby sister, Faith, and for once she began looking forward to her Dallas visits. Mary Jean and her mother, Dorrace, were warm and thoughtful toward Laurie, treating her as a true member of the family. Frequently, she would return from Dallas with beautiful dresses and pretty shoes. The Pearle family could not have been nicer to her.

Still, Michelle worried about Mary Jean. She knew

what hell being married to John Battaglia could be, and she feared that Mary Jean was suffering the same fate.

Sometimes the two women would talk on the phone to arrange the monthly visits. At one point, Michelle asked, "How's everything going?" She tried to be subtle, but Mary Jean's answer indicated that she understood.

"Great," Mary Jean said. "Our friends tell me I'm very good for John. I calm him down."

That reminded Michelle of the many times she'd tried to put a pretty face on her volatile relationship with John. But she was reassured when, after a visit to Dallas, Laurie mentioned that Mary Jean's brother Rick had been in the army. Rick lived directly across the street from his sister. Michelle knew that John wouldn't face up to a former military man. Maybe Mary Jean was having an easier time of it after all.

In the meantime, Michelle LaBorde began dating the handsome and dashing John Ghetti, to whom she had been introduced at the holiday party. He was stable and loving, and made a good living so Michelle didn't have to apologize for her impressive salary. After dating him for eight months, she married Ghetti in June, 1992.

Ghetti touched a soft spot in her heart when he said he loved children and wanted to start a family immediately. The following year, Michelle gave birth to a son, Kevin Michael Ghetti.

TWENTY

John Battaglia's well-cut suits were his daily uniform for his RTC job. He looked every bit the distinguished supervisor.

However, he continued to complain about productivity. The more he griped, the more his efforts were met with hostility from the administration. He could sense his popularity declining. People began avoiding him. Whispering behind his back, employees discussed what a whiner he was and how easily he blew up.

But while Battaglia pretended to object to the foot-dragging of his cohorts, he would order already closed businesses to be scrutinized a second time using a different accounting formula. Those redundant inquiries floated some businesses on the books for two or three additional years, making John more inefficient than the employees he complained about.

His habit of alternating between being courteous and being disagreeable showed up at work. He was respectful to his superiors but rude to RTC employee Nancy Parker. She'd had polio as a child and walked with a pronounced limp. Battaglia found her an easy target for his fits of anger. One day, after he had snapped at her repeatedly, she promptly sued him for sexual harassment.

In revenge, Battaglia filed a sexual harassment complaint against his female supervisor for using vulgar language. Even after his supervisor apologized and promised to clean up her foul mouth, he refused to back off because Nancy Parker wouldn't drop her complaint.

The conflicts at work should have made John Battaglia be more cautious, but instead they led him to lash out even harder. He complained, accused, and threatened until he lost his job supervising eleven employees—he was demoted to checking invoices from companies contracted to do accounting services for the RTC. In his mind, there had to be some way to get even.

To escape his on-the-job frustration, Battaglia sought diversion at night. On May 22, 1993, he borrowed his wife's car and drove to Deep Ellum. Offbeat restaurants, tattoo parlors, and over sixty bars and clubs, some offering live rock bands, dotted the area. Deep Ellum sat just three blocks east of downtown. Elm Street, the main thoroughfare, ran through the middle of both neighborhoods. After the Civil War, former slaves settled there and, because of their dialect, referred to the street as "Ellum," and from that "Deep Ellum" evolved. It became a little bit like Harlem, with a taste of Bourbon Street, and it was an offbeat place, ideal for outsiders. John Battaglia especially enjoyed the chic cafes that had transformed the old warehouse area.

However, he should have checked Mary Jean's car more thoroughly that night. Her father, Gene Pearle, saw the safety of his only child as very important. A gun enthusiast, Gene gave Mary Jean a Smith

9-millimeter silver pistol to keep in her car for protection. The gun had slid from under the seat and was in plain sight when John Battaglia pulled up to the popular cafe Sambuca on Elm Street. The club's security chief, Calvin Lane, allowed no one packing a gun to enter.

Lane, a handsome black man, didn't have much trouble with unruly patrons, as he stood seven feet, six inches tall and weighed over four hundred pounds. He patrolled the front entry through which patrons passed on their way to the restaurant's parking lot. With his height, he could see everything, and what he saw that night was a gun lying at John Battaglia's feet. He strolled over to Battaglia's car to question him about it.

Battaglia brushed aside the gun's presence, saying it belonged to his wife, but Lane wasn't buying it. He didn't want anyone with a gun to darken his restaurant's door. And he didn't much care for Battaglia's surly attitude.

Sambuca security was only one of Lane's many jobs. He worked trade shows for businesses, where the "Gentle Giant" fascinated people who clustered outside his booth waiting to meet him. Advertisers sought him to push their products, and he had made several TV appearances in *Walker, Texas Ranger*. Someone like John Battaglia wasn't about to bruise Calvin's ego. He waved down the next police car that came along.

John Battaglia was still fuming when Officers Scott Carbo and Daren Roberts strolled over to his car and peered inside. They could easily view the shiny silver gun sitting on the floor, and told Battaglia to get out with his hands up. After frisking him for more weapons, Carbo picked up the gun, checked it, and

found that it was loaded and in fine working order.
When the officers asked to see his permit, Battaglia
should have known better than to mouth off, insisting that the gun belonged to his wife so he didn't
need a permit. He was perturbed at being stopped
in the first place.

The officers arrested him for unlawfully carrying
a weapon, a Class A misdemeanor, and took him to
police headquarters. That was a serious offense for
someone working for a government agency, an offense Battaglia later fought hard to conceal,
knowing it could cost him his job.

By the time he had been delivered to headquarters it was almost 2:00 A.M. The only attorney he
knew that might help him at that hour was Robert
Clark, Mary Jean's half-brother.

Clark drowsily reached for the ringing phone on his
nightstand and listened to Battaglia's tale of woe. He
slowly climbed out of bed and got dressed. He knew
that if he didn't go, he'd have to listen to John grum-
ble, so he drove down to jail and bailed him out.

The next week, Battaglia was sorting through a
batch of invoices from Texas Data Control (TDC), a
company hired to keep data-processing records for
the RTC. It was classified as minority-owned because
it was partially made up of Hispanics. He was
shocked at the figures—$500,000 a month to belch
out reports. He glared more closely at the amounts
and discovered that although the reports were
mailed in batches, the charges were coming in for
each one as if mailed individually—TDC was charging for each page as if it were a separate document.
That alone added up to an additional $900,000 over

the last three years. Battaglia gathered up the evidence and hurried to the RTC's oversight manager, Donald Houk. Houk pored over the documents and labeled Battaglia the "new watchdog over TDC billings." Battaglia glowed at the recognition. He didn't like being told to continue paying the invoices, but he was promised that an inspection would begin immediately. In the next few weeks, John detected no signs of a serious investigation, and TDC continued bilking the government.

By the fall of 1993, John was furious with the snail-paced inquiry, so he wrote Stephen Beard, Director of the U.S. Office of the Inspector General (OIG), stating, "I intended to use my skills to help my country resolve what I perceived to be a national crisis." Then, he outlined his findings, describing TDC as an octopus that was greedily sucking up government spoils. The OIG performed an audit of TDC's billing procedures and agreed with Battaglia. The report caused Battaglia's hopes to soar, especially when the OIG told the Dallas office to seek a refund of $5.6 million from the TDC. It probably didn't hurt that Battaglia threatened to go public with his findings if the OIG didn't address his concerns.

While all that was taking place, Battaglia stumbled across an article about a government employee who had made millions suing a defense contractor— basically a whistle-blower case. Battaglia's hands itched at the prospect.

During the same year, Michelle Ghetti was researching on the Internet and saw that Louisiana Governor Edwin Edwards was establishing a "Violent Crime and Homicide Task Force." This was her

chance, her opportunity to change the laws that had
protected John Battaglia and left her all the more a
victim. She researched the procedures for serving on
the task force and found that some members would
be appointed by state legislators. She had taught the
son of a state senator in two of her law school classes.
Excited, she called her former student and asked to
be put in touch with his father. One phone call later,
Michelle was a member of the task force.

Then, one door after another began opening. She
was the only domestic violence advocate on the task
force, but she soon met Bobbette Apple, Director of
the Office of Women's Services for Louisiana. Many
other bright women who were involved in the issue of
abuse, including a former student, Anne Stehr, became part of her team. She began building a strong
coalition of knowledgeable women who could assist in
her struggle for tougher, more far-reaching legislation.

Thinking about how John Battaglia had received
only a slap on the wrist for repeated protective order
violations, Michelle wrote a law spelling out penal-
ties, giving a specific number of hours, days, or years
of jail time for violations involving violence or injury.

She remembered the time that John was arrested
and given probation with the admonition to keep his
distance from her. Then he showed up at her bedside.
As her most powerful change, she made noncontact
of a spouse a condition of bail. If an abuser still tried
to illegally see a spouse, he was in contempt of court
and immediately sent to jail until his trial.

Knowing how frequently John had slipped out of
his counseling sessions, she established mandatory
therapy as a condition of probation.

Stalking was what John Battaglia did so well and so
often. The courts were reluctant to do much about

stalking because many stalkers border on being mentally ill. But stalking escalates. It's the first rung in the ladder toward violent behavior. She strengthened the law and detailed how stalking would violate a protective order and lead to jail time. Her laws would not affect John Battaglia, but he was her reason for writing them.

Michelle had attended high school with Jay Jardenne, now a well-respected Louisiana state senator. He enthusiastically agreed to sponsor her laws.

It was up to her to get the laws passed. She would leave her classroom and pick up two-year-old Kevin from the baby-sitter. At the state capital, she attended legislative hearings. Standing in the back of the room, she wrote notes to senators asking them to meet with her. With Kevin on one hip, she would hand out packets of her abuse laws to senators and urge their support.

One night, Michelle was lying in bed, tears streaming down her cheeks as she watched police follow O.J. Simpson's white Bronco during his famous chase. She was editing her abuse laws and she considered the Simpson case the worst ever of spousal abuse. *Now maybe people will be more aware.* "God is good," she said to herself, knowing the entire country would be getting a first hand glimpse into the tragedy of abuse.

Her husband, John Ghetti, walked by and saw her crying. "What's wrong?" he asked.

"The timing of this is unbelievable," she said. "With all this media attention on domestic violence, the legislature will pass our laws unanimously."

And they did.

* * *

The year 1994 turned out to be a significant one for Michelle Ghetti.

Wanting more recognition for her laws, she entered the "Mrs. Baton Rouge" Pageant. A pretty face wasn't enough; contestants had to speak on a platform of important issues. She won the title, in part, by making more people aware of domestic violence.

The following September, she stood in the spotlight, acknowledging the applause of six hundred state dignitaries. At a gala banquet at the Centroplex in Baton Rouge, the YWCA named her "Woman of Achievement" for her public service in government and education. She was selected from the group of fifty-five outstanding women especially because of her domestic violence legislation. Now Michelle was living her dream—to help other women suffering the same type of abuse she'd suffered at the hands of John Battaglia.

TWENTY-ONE

January 17, 1995 was sunny and brisk when John Battaglia took three-year-old Faith's hand and led her up the stairs to Baylor Hospital. Her new sister, Liberty Mae, had just arrived. At the nursery window, John held Faith up to see Liberty, and Faith fell in love with her instantly.

As she had with Faith, Mary Jean chose a virtuous name. Judy or Suzy just wouldn't do. The new Battaglia daughter looked exactly like her mother, with big round brown eyes and curly auburn hair.

With so few children in the family, everyone greeted the second Battaglia daughter with great joy.

John Battaglia proudly drove his new daughter home from the hospital. As she lay cradled in the car seat, he kept looking over, talking to her. He was already inventing new baby names for Liberty: Libby Bear, Baby Bear; whatever was warm, sweet, and loving.

As they drove, Mary Jean glanced at her husband. At the moment he showed no signs of being obsessed with his work. Nor did he appear worried about the year's probation and $500 fine he had received six months earlier for gun possession.

Right now he looked like the best father ever.
Mary Jean knew he loved his daughters. She had
never seen him cross with Faith, nor known him to
discipline or even raise his voice at her. He was always so caring. How she craved that same treatment
for herself. She was still enduring his verbal lashings,
and it was getting all the more difficult to pretend
that life with John was beautiful.

Battaglia pulled into the driveway of their Dickason house. Mary Jane realized that it was large
enough for the family plus their three dogs and two
cats, but it had only a small yard for the girls. More-
over, she would never choose to send her children to
the local Dallas public schools.

She mused how wonderful it would be to have a
new home. Somewhere with a big yard, a great
school system, and an address she'd be proud to give
her friends. Her housekeeper rode the bus every
day, but how much better if they could find a place
with maid's quarters. Mary Jean would have to talk
with her father.

Highland Park is a state of mind. It's one of those
places where people happily shell out a quarter million dollars for a fifty-year-old two-bedroom, one-bath
home on a flat square of earth with no view. Now,
many of those cottages are being bulldozed and replaced by five-thousand-plus-square-foot mansions that
tower over their neighbors and sell for millions. Highland Park and its sister city, University Park, are two
incorporated towns, actually landlocked islands in the
shadow of Dallas skyscrapers.

The Battaglias spent weeks scouring the Park
Cities to find their perfect house. Finally they chose

a one-of-a-kind estate that gently graced the rolling hill on a premier street, Lorraine Avenue. Their million-dollar house was built of warm brown bricks with a terra-cotta Spanish tile roof. The tall, two-story home was beautifully positioned on a large lot, shaded by towering live oaks and elms. The garage sat far to the rear of the property, with a two-bedroom guesthouse built as its second story. It would make ideal maid's quarters.

The main house, with more than four thousand square feet, had four bedrooms and four baths in addition to all the formal rooms that the Dickason home had. An extra room, large enough for the pool table, was attached to the family room. An elegant staircase with a wrought-iron banister of hand-hewn leaves and flowers led to the second story. The home would be perfect for Mary Jean's priceless antiques.

In addition to its proximity to downtown, the Battaglias were drawn to Highland Park for its highly touted schools that boasted a number of National Merit Scholars.

In order to allow his daughter to live in "The Bubble," as Parkies called their area, Gene Pearle sold thousands of shares of stock. Mary Jean was given title to the property, paid for by the proceeds from the Dickason house and her father's stock.

This financial arrangement left John feeling like a kept man and all the more the outsider.

TWENTY-TWO

On March 23, 1995, two months after Liberty was born, but before the family moved to their new mansion, John Battaglia filed his suit on behalf of the RTC in U.S. District Court in Dallas, and sent a copy to U.S. Attorney General Janet Reno. The following August, federal prosecutors looked into Battaglia's allegations, and the government astonished everyone by deciding to join Battaglia in his lawsuit. He was positively giddy over the decision and felt exonerated for all of his faultfinding. There was new color to his cheeks and he smiled more frequently. Now his gait through the offices was more like a strut.

The patriarch of Mary Jean's family, Gene Harrison Pearle, died on August 30 of the prostate cancer that had afflicted him for two years. His death occurred only six weeks after he had cashed in a chunk of his assets for Mary Jean's house. Mary Jean was devastated. More than any other person, he was the one she depended on, respected, and loved. With his death, she felt that something inside her had died too. After the funeral, she went home and collapsed in bed. She lay there for weeks, grieving and unable to shake off the depression. Their housekeeper, a young Mexican woman, cared for both daughters, cleaned the house, and cooked the meals. Liberty was only seven months old, and the housekeeper was pregnant.

Concerned about Mary Jean's listlessness, her doctor prescribed Zoloft to fight the depression, but it did little to help. She had trouble eating and sleeping, and within the span of two weeks she lost twenty pounds.

John helped with the children in the evening, but he spent his days talking to attorneys and gearing up for the trial that he was sure would transform him into a millionaire overnight.

The RTC was dissolved on December 31, 1995, but despite the disappearance of his job, there was no stopping John. He met weekly with lawyers for the government and with his own personal lawyer, Robert Clark.

In order to have some income, Battaglia set up a private accounting practice in the offices above Dorrace Pearle's antiques store, but his heart and the majority of his time were invested in working on the case. He didn't mind that he only made $40,000 that year, because he knew that after his suit, he'd have millions.

In August of 1996, John Battaglia contacted Denise McVea, a reporter for the *Dallas Observer*, who took his photo and wrote an article gushing over his patriotic zeal. McVea, taken in by the Battaglia charm, referred to him as "an earnest, amiable fellow," and related all that he was doing for the taxpayers in this country. She mentioned that if he were successful, "he could walk away a rich man." After the article ran, the newspaper published letters that it had received applauding Battaglia's efforts. One woman wrote, "John Battaglia, go get 'em!"

The False Claims Act would allow the U.S. Attorney's Office to sue for triple damages and also seek a $10,000 civil fine for each violation of the statute. Battaglia would be suing for a minimum of $15 million and could possibly pocket as much as a third. He estimated Mary Jean's net worth at $4 million. Now he'd be the richest person in the family. That was power.

The defendant, TDC, was made up of ten subsidiaries; each subsidiary had a minimum of two lawyers representing its interests. In all, there were thirty-seven attorneys embroiled in the fight.

Battaglia was the man of the hour, helping to orchestrate the questions for voir dire and outlining the charges the government would bring against TDC. Washington designated him as their "confidential informant." It was a heady experience to have federal counsel deferring to him and asking for specifics on the wrongs committed by the defendant. The thousands of pages of legal documents were filed under the title "THE UNITED STATES OF AMERICA AND JOHN D. BATTAGLIA."

United States District Court Judge Joe Kendall presided over the case. The well-respected judge would eventually hear literally years of legal wrangling. The complaints and countercomplaints continued into mid-1998. TDC was charged with overbilling and submitting false invoices, and to Battaglia's dismay, TDC countersued the government for more than $8 million.

The trial finally opened on August 8, 1998. Six men were seated as the jury to decide who was telling the truth and how much the winner would get. The trial stretched on for a month before Judge Kendall handed it over to the jury.

After listening to both sides, the jury shocked Battaglia by finding that the RTC was in breach of contract because it had stopped paying TDC's invoices when the legal quagmire began—exactly what Battaglia had urged them to do. Because of the breach, TDC was entitled to recover $8,677,669.28 plus attorneys' fees, interest, and court costs.

John Battaglia never told his lawyers that, over the term of its contract with TDC, the government had requested thousands of reports that the initial contract had not called for. The jury also found that the RTC was in arrears for an additional $7 million for these extra reports, plus interest. In the end, the government was forced to hand over more than $15 million.

John Battaglia was devastated. Not only had his actions embarrassed the federal government, but his folly had also cost the country millions in attorneys' and court fees.

TWENTY-THREE

John Battaglia had to live with the knowledge that he had just wasted five years of his life. He had lost five years of earning a higher salary, and worst of all, he had damaged his professional reputation.

Losing his RTC whistle-blower suit was devastating. Gone were the millions he would have made. He suspected that people were pointing at him, laughing behind his back. After boasting to friends that he was going to show that goddamn scamming subcontractor, he now might have to listen to those same onetime friends belittle him.

With the case finally lost and settled, he took his hurt and anger out on Mary Jean.

When she tried to encourage him and bolster his ego, he would only bellow, "You don't understand! You're just a stupid bitch!"

Past experience had taught her that this was only the beginning of his verbal attack. He would continue yelling, using even more vulgar words, and then scream until he was inches from her face.

One January night in 1999, she didn't want to be in the same room with him, so she left to start dinner.

He followed her. While she sauteed chicken breasts, he picked up a cookie and bit into it. He crinkled up his nose and said, "This cookie's stale."

"Do you have to complain about everything?" she asked.

"Well, it *is* stale," he yelled, and threw it at her, hitting her chest.

Tears filled her eyes. She glanced down at her four- and seven-year-old daughters standing by her side. *This is no way to raise little girls,* she thought. Her daughters shouldn't be brought up thinking this was how men are allowed to treat women. She couldn't count the times she had asked him to stop insulting her in front of the children. She had tried to keep the family together, wanting her children to be raised by two parents. Her divorced friends celebrated holidays in a frenzy of hauling children back and forth between two parents and two sets of grandparents. She had stayed on with a counselor ever since her father's death, and now that same counselor was emphasizing that a loving, single-parent household was better for children than a daily diet of constant turmoil. And tonight, she had had it. John's steady badgering was eroding their marriage like waves pounding a sandy beach, gradually wearing it away until nothing was left.

She stood by the window over the kitchen sink and looked out at the precisely groomed rye grass, the multicolored pansies, and all the beauty that thrived in a Dallas winter. Either she or her family had essentially paid for everything. What right did John have to treat her this way? She turned to him. "I won't live like this!" she screamed. "Get out of here now!"

"Oh, for God's sake. It was just a cookie."

"No, it's more than that. It's your attitude. It's how you think you can treat me and get away with it. I'm sick of you always putting me down." She glanced at her watch. "Pack your things. I want you out of here in one hour."

"Well, son-of-a-bitch," John said, and threw another cookie, this time into the sink.

John Battaglia found it humiliating to be thrown out of his own house like yesterday's trash. Well, not really his own house, he relented. Damn that Mary Jean, and damn all of her family money. She was controlling him with it, and it only made him angrier that she could.

After packing enough clothes for the season, he hugged his daughters good-bye, threw his suitcases into his car, and backed down the long driveway. Then he drove to one of his favorite places in Dallas.

In Deep Ellum, Battaglia passed buildings that were over a hundred years old and had housed many different businesses. In 1884, Robert S. Munger had invented a new cotton gin that revolutionized the ginning business and the first one had been built in Deep Ellum. Other manufacturers soon followed. The area underwent transitions from factories to shops to jazz and blues joints, and now was a vibrant mixed-use neighborhood.

John Battaglia had always liked the area. It reminded him of when his father had worked in New York City and he'd frequent Greenwich Village. It had that same European feel to it: the broken concrete sidewalks, the worn red brick buildings. It didn't matter how casually or tattered anyone dressed. Deep Ellum would be a relief from label-conscious Highland Park.

He passed old buildings painted with graffiti, and others elaborately decorated with psychedelic murals. Then he pulled up to a four-story red brick building that almost touched Central Expressway: Adam Hats Lofts. The place looked fast, hot, and now. He mused that living in a loft would be a cool, bachelor type of thing. He gazed around the area and took note of the young girls strutting down the sidewalk. Most had tattoos and a few were into body piercing. This had to be the farthest place in all of Texas from Highland Park. This was exactly where he wanted to be.

TWENTY-FOUR

In December 1999, Mary Jean Pearle and her daughters were spending their first Christmas without John Battaglia. Decorating her home for Christmas, Mary Jean vowed to make it the most festive year ever. Selecting from her large inventory of decorations, she trailed garlands, lights, and ornaments up the elaborate wrought-iron staircase. The Christmas tree touched the ceiling, laden with one-of-a-kind hand-blown ornaments that were decades old. Every fireplace mantel and mirror was draped in fresh pine boughs and decorated with balls and ribbons. Three embroidered Christmas stockings hung from the fireplace mantel, and poinsettia-crowded baskets added additional color. The entire house sparkled like a jeweled Christmas wonderland.

The little girls were growing up fast. Christmas came shortly before their January birthdays when Faith would turn eight and Liberty five. Although they mainly wore play clothes, Mary Jean loved dressing them in elegant outfits from Neiman Marcus.

In this year's Christmas photo, Liberty wore a red velvet dress with a white organdy scalloped collar. Even though Faith was missing a front tooth, she was beginning to show signs of becoming a beautiful young woman. She looked quite grown-up in a forest-green velvet dress with its massive velvet bow at the waist, especially with her long blond hair cascading over her shoulders.

On Christmas morning, Mary Jean and her daughters sat in their pajamas around the tree, opening what looked like the entire inventory of a toy store. The girls hugged their mother and thanked her for all the toys, books, and clothes. Mary Jean hugged them back, thanking God that they were in her life.

The girls were eager to see their father today because he was bringing his daughter, Laurie, who was visiting for the Christmas holidays. The little ones adored their big sister. John Battaglia wouldn't arrive until 9:20 A.M. to take them to church, so they took their time eating breakfast and getting ready.

At 8:45, the doorbell rang. Mary Jean went to the door and was shocked to see John and Laurie standing there. They were more than a half hour early. It was an awkward situation, but Mary Jean reached out and hugged Laurie while John stood back, looking like a child who hadn't been invited to the party.

Faith and Liberty came running. "Come see what we got for Christmas," Faith said. Then she looked apprehensively at her mother. "Okay if Daddy comes in?" she asked. According to the protective order Mary Jean had received after evicting John, he was not allowed in her home under any circumstances.

Faith's question presented another awkward moment, then Mary Jean said, "Oh, okay. Come on in."

Battaglia entered, and strolled over to the tree. He stood admiring his daughters' gifts, which were all beautiful and expensive—everything that he could not afford. His anger began to grow.

Mary Jean watched Laurie laugh and talk with her two daughters. They really were three sisters, and

Mary Jean had come to love Laurie as well. She gave Laurie a hug and asked, "Would you like to stay for dinner after church today?"

Laurie looked hopefully at her father, who obviously had not been included in the invitation. "Can I, Dad?" she asked.

"If I'm not welcome, you're not staying," he said curtly.

Mary Jean rolled her eyes, realizing that nothing had changed between them. "Well, you were early, but now I better get the girls ready." She turned to go upstairs, and as soon as she placed her foot on the Oriental runner covering the steps, she was shocked to see that her ex-husband was following her. Upstairs, she walked past her bedroom and automatically reached for the knob to pull the door shut.

"What are you trying to hide in there?" he asked.

"I don't trust you."

"You've already taken everything from me," Battaglia accused.

"John, let's not go there."

Her tone was firm and it angered him. In fact, her firmness was what he disliked most about her. He said, "I can say anything I want."

"And so can I," Mary Jean said as she entered her daughters' room. But she began feeling shaky and apprehensive. From the tone of his voice, she could feel his anger building. She knew the signs.

Battaglia lunged at her and screamed, "No you can't!"

Mary Jean saw him coming and pressed her face down on Liberty's mattress to protect herself. He balled his fist and hit her head. Then she felt his fist pound the flesh on the back of her head and she pushed her face deeper into the mattress. But the blows kept coming—five, ten, fifteen—each with a sickening thud. He was hitting her as hard as a man could hit a woman.

"Call 911!" she screamed to her daughters.

She lost her grasp on the mattress and fell to the floor. He reached down and pulled her up by her hair to make her a more convenient target. He began kicking her with the toe of his leather dress shoe; she screamed with each blow. He didn't seem to care where he kicked: her head, shoulders, legs; he just kept kicking. Her silk pajamas were no protection against his aggression.

She was losing strength and afraid to look up for fear of exposing her face to his brutal attacks.

All three girls were in the room witnessing his assault and screaming, "Stop it, Daddy! Daddy, you're hurting her, stop it!" They were all crying. Laurie, the oldest, was screaming the loudest and kept tugging on her father's shirt in a fruitless effort to pull him away. Faith was also trying to separate them. Liberty ran into the bathroom to hide.

Mary Jean tucked herself into a fetal position and shook from pain and fear. Her entire body was under siege.

Suddenly, the pounding stopped. After a few moments, she timidly raised her head and saw that John was no longer in the room.

"Mommy, are you all right?" Faith asked, running to her, crying. "I locked the door as soon as Daddy left."

Laurie stood paralyzed and angry. Her father had abandoned her, and her suitcase was still in his car. She ran to the window to check and saw that his car no longer sat in front of the house.

By now Mary Jean had picked herself up from the floor and was examining the damage. In addition to swollen bruises and cuts, there was a gash in her heel and her shin throbbed. Clumps of her dark hair lay on the floor. She was relieved to hear the sound of sirens drawing closer to her house.

Sixty-six-year-old John Battaglia Sr. had retired to Florida. After he left Dallas, he had worked in New York as a hospital administrator before his retirement.

In June of 1999 he and his second wife, Kathy, established "Children of Chaos," a nonprofit charity for children whose lives had been tragically affected by the Balkan war.

Two days before their son attacked Mary Jean, the charity's website announced that their first truckload of warm clothes, blankets, and medical supplies had left on a plane for Kosovo.

The children of Kosovo and Albania had touched John Battaglia Sr., but he had no idea of his granddaughters' private hell in Dallas. He had again cut off contact with his son.

Officer J. Greer of the Highland Park Police Department arrived at Mary Jean's house within eight minutes. Two paramedics closely followed in an ambulance.

Greer looked at the deepening color of Mary Jean's bruises and said, "Let's get you to the emergency room for a CAT scan and the doctors can examine your bruises. I'll go along and fill out this form there."

"But it's Christmas," she said, almost apologetically.

"Ma'am, you look seriously hurt."

Mary Jean glanced over her sore body. She touched

her right cheek. "Ouch. He really got me here." Then her hand found her swollen jawbone and ear.

The officer grimaced. "I can see from here that your wrist and arm are bruised, and it looks like you've got a puncture wound to your right heel. Ma'am, you need more than paramedics; you need a doctor."

"Can't I bring charges against him anyway?"

"Sure, but you need medical attention."

"I know," Mary Jean said, dejectedly. She glanced at her watch. "I'm having twelve people here for dinner at two. I have almost everything ready and there will be lots of people to help. Just let me file charges."

The officer shook his head. "Okay, okay," he said with resignation. The paramedics pulled out rolls of bandages and peroxide and other disinfectants to treat Mary Jean's abrasions. They couldn't detect any broken bones, and she promised she'd see a doctor the next day.

Officer Greer glanced at the three girls who were hovering near Mary Jean. "Are these your kids?"

She pulled Faith and Liberty toward her. "These two are mine, and Laurie here is a very dear family friend," she said, patting her arm. "They all saw the attack."

The officer began writing a report, and included the girls' names as witnesses. "This is a Class A misdemeanor," he said.

"A *misdemeanor?*" Mary Jean asked. She was shocked. "He did all this and it's only a misdemeanor?"

"It comes under the category of 'assault/family violence.' They handle that a little differently."

"A little less seriously, it sounds to me. Even if it's a misdemeanor, can't a warrant be issued for his arrest?"

"Absolutely," the officer answered. Then, for the

record, he pulled out a camera and took photographs of Mary Jean's bruises.

Laurie slumped down on an eighteenth-century brocade chair in Mary Jean's living room. Tears glistened in her eyes. "I've got no place to go. Mom's visiting my brother in Colorado Springs. What should I do? I don't think I have her phone number."

Mary Jean hobbled over to her and placed her arm around Laurie's shoulders. "One good thing," Mary Jean said. "You get to stay for dinner."

Everyone smiled and that momentarily broke the tension.

By the time Mary Jean's family started arriving for what was to be a festive dinner, all of her wounds had been cleaned and bandaged.

Mary Jean was forced to tell her family about John's attack. They were all appalled. They told her to sit on the sofa and they would take care of dinner. Everyone busily pitched in, trying to make the best of the situation.

Laurie rummaged in her purse and finally found the name of her mother's hotel. Mary Jean called Michelle and explained what had happened. By now it was 5:00 P.M. and there was no way to get a plane to Colorado Springs on Christmas night.

The next morning, instead of seeing a doctor, Mary Jean drove Laurie to the Dallas/Ft. Worth airport and bought her a ticket to fly to Colorado Springs to be with her mother and brother. Laurie had tears in her eyes when she hugged Mary Jean good-bye, but she was looking forward to spending the remainder of the holidays with her family.

However, Christmas 1999 would forever live in Laurie's memory and change her relationship with her father. She wanted nothing more to do with John Battaglia.

TWENTY-FIVE

There was no question that Mary Jean would immediately file for divorce. A judge who thought John needed a cooling-off period prevented him from seeing his daughters for thirty days.

Mary Jean would soon learn that divorcing John would not be easy. He became a master at obstruction, complaining about every proposed property settlement and visitation schedule that Mary Jean's lawyer suggested. Battaglia didn't want to be told when he could see his daughters; in fact, he didn't want to be told anything by Mary Jean. At one time, he offered to go away for $250,000. Later, he told people Mary Jean said she wouldn't even give him $10,000. In his mind, he was only being jerked around.

John Battaglia began a pattern of vicious phone calls, another direct violation of Mary Jean's protective order. In May of 2000, he left a message on his children's phone: "Mary Jean, you better quit interfering." Then, addressing his daughters, he said, "I'm sorry for whatever may be coming down the road for you. It may be very bad."

Mary Jean's hands shook as she made a copy of John's latest call to give to the Highland Park Police.

Mary Jean received a subpoena to appear in County Criminal Court No. 10, on July 12, 2000 at 9:00 A.M. Thirty-six-year-old Judge David Finn would preside over the hearing on John Battaglia's misdemeanor assault charge for beating Mary Jean on Christmas Day. She relished the idea of confronting John about the attack. Finally, John would get what he had coming. However, shortly before their court date, the phone rang.

"Mary Jean?"

She recognized John's voice and it set every nerve on edge. "You're not supposed to be calling on this line," she told him.

"I know, but you'll be glad to hear this. I've been thinking about the divorce. That last visitation schedule is one I could live with. The money settlement, too. Although I don't like it, I'll go ahead and sign our final divorce papers. My attorney has it all set up. Meet me in the family court at eight-thirty Wednesday morning."

"But that's the day we have the hearing for your assault charge."

"I know. This will only take a few minutes; then we'll both head over to the hearing."

"I'm concerned there won't be enough time," she said.

"How long does it take to sign your name? You already have the papers. You know what they say. I thought you'd be happy to get this behind you."

"Well, I will be glad when it's over." She thought

another moment and said, "Okay, I'll meet you in court at eight-thirty."

The temperature had already reached ninety degrees by 8:30 A.M. that Wednesday when Mary Jean promptly entered the 330th Family District Court. She gave her name to the clerk and told him why she was there. The man appeared confused.

The clerk checked over the docket and said, "We don't have anything for a Battaglia today."

"Didn't my husband's lawyer, Mr. Yturri, arrange a final divorce hearing for this morning?" she asked.

The clerk checked the docket again. "No, ma'am. Don't have his name down here either."

Mary Jean flashed hot with anger. John had fooled her. She asked to use the phone to call Judge David Finn's court. By the time she got the number and found the person she needed to speak with, it was ten minutes to nine. "I'm coming! I'm coming!" she screamed into the phone. Then she ran to the parking garage.

John Battaglia looked crisp and professional in his summer suit as he sat beside his lawyer in Judge Finn's courtroom. He waited patiently, but complained in a voice just loud enough for the judge to hear that he was concerned that Mary Jean wasn't in court yet, for he had business appointments waiting.

The hands on the courtroom clock reached nine and Judge Finn called the court to order. "Is the defendant ready?" he asked David Yturri.

"Yes, we are, Your Honor."

"Is the prosecution ready?"

The prosecutor, Assistant District Attorney Megan Miller told the judge that they needed a few more minutes. "Mary Jean Pearle has called and is on her way," she explained.

"Well, if this was important enough to her," Finn stated, "she would have been here on time."

"It's extremely important," Miller said. "She was directed to a different court. She'll be here momentarily."

Judge Finn waited ten minutes, then raised his gavel to dismiss the assault charges against John Battaglia.

"No, no, wait!" Miller jumped up and pleaded. "The state can't prove this offense without the testimony of the complaining witness."

"So?" the judge said.

Assistant DA Megan Miller looked around to make sure Mary Jean wasn't rushing down the hall; then she said, "We're forced to announce 'Not ready, sir.'"

A broad grin spread across Battaglia's face. He and his attorney dashed out of the courtroom before Mary Jean could arrive.

Only a few minutes later, a tearful Mary Jean Pearle hurried into the courtroom. "John told me to meet him at another court to sign our divorce papers," she complained to Miller.

The assistant DA turned to her. "I am so sorry. The judge was going to dismiss all charges against John if we didn't declare that the state wasn't ready. John would have gotten off scot-free."

Mary Jean rushed to the judge, crying, "You can't dismiss this! John Battaglia beat me up in front of the children. I'm scared to death of the man!"

Prosecutor Miller was by her side. "John Battaglia is too dangerous for us to wait the mandatory six months to refile," she told Finn. "We need some break on this."

"Okay," Finn said. "I'll let you refile in six weeks." Then he slammed his gavel and asked for the next case.

Judge David Finn may not have been aware that he had an audience that day. Representatives from a court watch group sponsored by The Family Place had witnessed the drama play out.

Megan Miller went back to the volunteers to answer their questions. "We cannot believe what just happened," one woman said.

"I know. That was awful," Miller responded. "Judge Finn should have given Mary Jean an opportunity to be heard. She wasn't late on purpose. The only thing the judge is allowing is for us to refile in six weeks, and believe me, we're going to refile."

TWENTY-SIX

For months, John called Laurie begging her to return his calls. She was still furious with him and couldn't erase the memory of Mary Jean screaming and cowering with fear.

Although Laurie refused to answer, Michelle recorded each call. His voice was soft and pleading, but his calls were annoyingly frequent. Sometimes he'd call while Laurie was standing near the answering machine, and she would just walk away when she heard her father's voice. Most of his messages bemoaned the fact that he hadn't heard from her. Was she trying to punish him? He accused her of violating the Ten Commandments by not honoring her father. Then he tried bribing her. Did she want her allowance? If so, she had better call. He would frequently bring up religion—questioning if there were a special place in heaven for rude children and accuse her of violating God's laws. In one call, he said, "After all, your father hasn't murdered anyone . . ."

The second hearing for Battaglia's Christmas attack was reset for August 16, 2000, in Judge David Finn's court.

Mary Jean had steeled herself this time, but was

afraid that John would find some way to weasel out
of his court date. She set her alarm for 6:00 A.M.,
early enough to avoid any last-minute problems. She
would be in court No. 10 at 9:00 A.M., come hell or
high water. She had her navy-and-beige silk suit
hanging outside her closet door, her navy heels on
the floor nearby. She wasn't going to waste a moment worrying about a last-minute hitch.

Well before nine, Mary Jean was seated with the
prosecution, ready to present her side of the case.
John opted to take his chances with the friendly
judge and waived a jury trial. He was also fearful of
bringing in his three daughters to testify, especially
when one wouldn't return his phone calls. He entered a plea of no contest.

With everything established ahead of time, the
procedure went swiftly. Judge Finn immediately
found John Battaglia guilty and fined him $1,000
plus court costs. John had to pay a total of $1,182.48
to Mary Jean within thirty days. His sentence was set
at 365 days in the Dallas County jail and, with knee-
jerk speed, it was reduced to two years probation.
Due to complaints he received from the first assault
hearing, the judge added eighty hours of community
service, in addition to monthly alcohol and drug
testing. He also included a monthly meeting with a
probation officer to whom John would pay a fee of
$40 each month.

Two weeks after the resolution of the assault, Mary
Jean received her long-awaited divorce decree. She
had agreed to pay John $75,000 and let him visit the
girls each Wednesday and every other weekend as
well as several holidays throughout the year. Still,

John Battaglia in 1962 with his mother, Julia,
who killed herself ten years later.

Handsome and
intelligent, John
Battaglia worked
as a professional
model.

John Battaglia and his first wife, Michelle LaBorde.

In May 1985, John Battaglia became a Certified Public Accountant.

John stalked Michelle in his new Jeep Cherokee.

The Battaglias rented this Lake Highlands home before their first child was born.

John adored playing with his first daughter, Laura Julia.

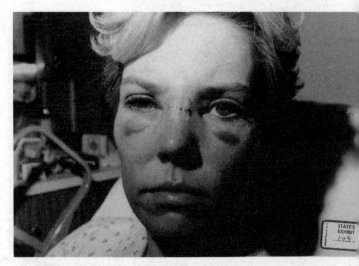

Following their 1987 divorce, Michelle was hospitalized
after John attacked her.
(Photo courtesy Dallas County District Attorney's Office)

John met Mary Jean Pearle in 1990 and they were married the following year. In 1992, Faith was born.

Mary Jean's father bought her this luxurious house in 1995.
(Photo courtesy Michael Kittrell)

Liberty, almost five, and Faith,
shortly before her eighth birthday.

John and his two
girls in 1997.

After Mary Jean sued for divorce, John moved to the Adam Hats Lofts, which would become the murder scene.

Christmas 2000, the last Yuletide holiday for Liberty and Faith.

Police broke into Battaglia's loft and found fifteen guns, including rifles, shotguns, and pistols.
(Photo courtesy Dallas County District Attorney's Office)

The .38 revolver that John used to shoot his daughters sat by his phone, from which he called Mary Jean.
(Photo courtesy Dallas County District Attorney's Office)

The automatic Glock was used for the final execution shot.
(Photo courtesy Dallas County District Attorney's Office)

Dallas Police Officer Dane P. Thornton
was the first officer on the scene.

ME Death
Investigator
Gigi Ray
photographed
the crime
scene.

Police set up a stakeout of Battaglia's Ford truck and waited to arrest him. *(Photo courtesy Dallas County District Attorney's Office)*

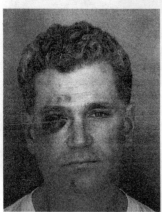

John suffered bruises and a black eye from fighting the police during his arrest. *(Photo courtesy Dallas County Sheriff's Office)*

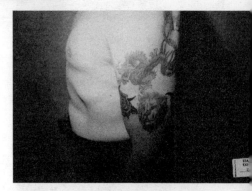

John had red and yellow roses tattooed on his arm in memo of his daughters, whom he had just murdere *(Photo courtesy Dallas County District Attorney's Offi*

District Attorney Bill Hill ran for re-election against Judge David Finn, whom Mary Jean exposed for trying to dismiss beating charges against Battaglia. (2002)

Because of Faith and Liberty's murders, Texas State Representative Toby Goodman sponsored a bill in the legislature forcing judges to look carefully at allowing unsupervised visits where parents have a history of abuse. *(Photo courtesy Rep. Goodman)*

The Frank Crowley Courts Building in Dallas, where John Battaglia's capital murder trial began on April 22, 2002

John Battaglia sat through months of voir dire before his murder trial. At times he appeared only mildly interested. (Photo courtesy Richard Michael Pruitt/Dallas Morning News)

Judge Janice L. Warder of the Criminal District Court presided over John Battaglia's trial.

Chief prosecutor, Dallas County Assistant District Attorney Howard Blackmon, led the fight to find John Battaglia guilty of capital murder and send him to his death.

Assistant D.A. Keith Robinson helped prosecute John Battaglia.

Assistant D.A. Pat Kirlin served on the team of three prosecutors in the Battaglia trial.

The hard-working lead defense attorney Paul Johnson tried to save John Battaglia from the death sentence.

Mary Jean Pearle wore pictures of her slain daughters during the trial.
(Photo courtesy Richard Michael Pruitt/ Dallas Morning News)

During the punishment phase of the trial, Michelle LaBorde Ghetti testified against John Battaglia, explaining how one of his beatings put her in the hospital. *(Photo courtesy Richard Michael Pruitt/Dallas Morning News)*

After Battaglia received the death sentence, Dallas County
Sheriff deputies escorted him to the penitentiary
and death row. *(Photo courtesy WFAA)*

Mary Jean Pearle had her father's casket exhumed,
then buried three feet deeper to accommodate
his granddaughters' casket on top.

under no circumstances could John come into her house or phone her. The Tom Thumb grocery store in Highland Park Village was officially designated as the exchange point for the visitations. Any departure from those strict guidelines would constitute a violation of his probation.

John Battaglia found a loophole in his probation agreement. If he paid his fine early, Judge Finn would waive the eighty hours of community service. However, his meeting with the court was scheduled after the payment date. He asked Mary Jean to let him pay her directly and sign a notarized statement that she had received the payment. She found it easier to do that than to argue with him. He could easily pay since Mary Jean had just written him a check for $75,000.

After an eleven-month estrangement, Laurie consented to visit John for Thanksgiving because she missed her sisters. She wouldn't resume monthly meetings but she did promise to come back at Easter.

John Battaglia's probation slate stayed clean for only three months. On November 30, his monthly urinalysis tested positive for marijuana. Mary Jean assumed that this violation of his two-year probation would not be taken lightly. She had hoped that Judge Finn would revoke Battaglia's probation and place him in jail. On November 30, prosecutors filed a motion to revoke Battaglia's probation, but inexplicably never sought a hearing. Mary Jean assumed a hearing would be scheduled for January 2001—the normal time period. However, on December 4, John posted a $500 bond. During the next two and a half months, John had not missed a date with his probation officer, and had passed a subsequent drug test with flying colors. The court's only recourse was to withdraw all charges against him.

Mary Jean seethed over John's latest escape. He was the Teflon man. Being on probation didn't seem to faze him. He never suffered any consequences.

In February 2001, John Battaglia was hired as the chief financial officer of the Arcturus Corporation, a small oil and gas exploration company that was located in a suite of nicely furnished offices in a downtown high-rise. It was a job he had dreamed of. In addition, he decided to keep his private accounting firm with its 120 clients, even if it meant working sixteen-hour days.

Laurie was in Dallas for the Easter break on April 17. Since all three girls were at Battaglia's loft Saturday night, John allowed Laurie to have dinner with Mary Jean on Easter.

Many Easter presents were wrapped for Faith and Liberty, and Mary Jean didn't want Laurie to feel left out. She slipped a fifty-dollar bill into an Easter card and put it by Laurie's place at the dinner table.

That evening, John Battaglia left Mary Jean a message on the children's answering machine: "The next time you give my daughter fifty dollars, why don't you tell her how you screwed her out of her fucking college fund? You fucking pig. How do you feel, pig?"

The next day, Mary Jean played the message into her handheld recorder to make a tape for the Highland Park police. The police went to the town judge to obtain an arrest warrant the same day.

A week went by, and the warrant had still not been executed. Mary Jean took a copy of the tape to the Dallas County district attorney's office, where a probation officer told her that he would immediately begin the process to have Battaglia arrested. However, he went out of town for a few days, leaving the papers on his desk. A second week went by, and the Dallas County Sheriff's Office, who would be serving the warrant, had still not received anything with John Battaglia's name on it.

Finally, on May 1, Highland Park police filed the warrant with the district attorney's office—two weeks after Mary Jean had presented it to them.

TWENTY-SEVEN

On the last Saturday in April, the late spring afternoon was comfortably warm as seventy-nine-year-old Lucinda Monett and her younger friend, Linda Murphy, motored up Douglas Avenue, one of Highland Park's main thoroughfares. Highland Park in April resembles a giant bouquet of brilliantly colored azalea blossoms. The flowers grace yards and common areas and attract Sunday drivers from all over the city.

The women were returning to their North Dallas homes after a stint of volunteer work at a book sale to benefit the Dallas Public Library.

As they passed Lorraine Avenue, Linda cried out, "Stop, there's a lemonade stand!"

Lucinda scowled at the thought of stopping. She had been standing on a concrete floor since early that morning, selling musty used books. She was anxious to get home, take a bath, and relax.

"You can't be serious," she groaned. "You really want to buy lemonade from two little kids? Who knows how long it's been sitting out there in the sun?"

"Nonsense. If you ever see a lemonade stand that's run by children, you have to stop," Linda replied. "My kids used to sell lemonade when they were young and it really bothered me when people would whiz by."

Lucinda shook her head of gray hair. She had twisted it up that morning, but now it mostly hung in tendrils down her neck. A look of dismay crossed her face as she pulled to the curb. She glanced at Linda, hoping she would change her mind before she rolled down her window.

The same mercantile blood that coursed through the veins of the Lorraine Avenue mansion owners flowed through their children as well. The importance of making a profit was learned at an early age, and most of the children in the neighborhood took turns manning a lemonade stand. Today, two girls who looked like sisters smiled up from folding chairs before a card table covered with a white tablecloth. A hand-lettered sign advertised "Lemonade and Cookies."

Linda rolled down her window and called out, "How much for two lemonades and cookies?" Then she saw something so sweet, it would always stay with her. The older girl affectionately placed her arm around her little sister's shoulders and ushered her to the car.

"It's fifty cents for each Dixie cup," the older sister said. "That includes a cookie, but they're not great. Store-bought," the girl apologized.

"Great. We'll take two cups and all the trimmings," Linda said, pulling a dollar from her purse.

Still arm in arm, the two girls walked back to the table. Then the older girl poured lemonade into two paper cups while the younger one placed two sugar cookies on paper napkins. Carefully, the girls brought the refreshments to the car, moving slowly so they wouldn't spill lemonade or drop a cookie on the grass.

The women accepted their refreshments, then stayed in their car, sipping lemonade, nibbling on cookies, and admiring the neighborhood's architectural beauty.

"Hope the cookies are okay," the older sister called out.

"They're just fine," Linda assured them. "The lemonade's good too."

The girls smiled shyly at the compliments.

When the women finished their refreshments, they brushed cookie crumbs from their clothes and crumpled up napkins, sticking them inside the paper cups.

The girls were back to take the trash and thanked the women for buying their lemonade. All the while, the older sister tenderly kept her arm around the little one's shoulders.

That loving image would be burned in the women's minds. A few days later, they would see those faces smiling at them again from the front pages of *The Dallas Morning News*.

TWENTY-EIGHT

Wednesday morning, May 2, dawned fresh and bright following a night of soaking rain. At seven, John Battaglia's first thought was to get some exercise before going to work. He figured he'd clean up afterwards, so, without shaving, he dressed in an old pair of shorts and a red-and-white-striped shirt.

He rolled his bicycle onto the elevator and took it down to the basement garage where he lifted it into the bed of his truck. He took off for White Rock Lake.

As he arrived, a gentle breeze was blowing sailboats across the lake. People all around him were enjoying the spring morning. He could have taken the trail around the lake, but chose a shorter one and began pedaling on the path to North Dallas that terminated at a park near the LBJ Freeway.

Thirty-five minutes later, he arrived at the park, sweating and panting. He sat on his bike, trying to catch his breath, while he watched a woman, Cindy Joungwaard, wrestle her two white Samoyeds out of her car. John Battaglia walked his bike over and told her that she had two good-looking dogs. He then proceeded to walk along the trail with her, talking while he rolled his bike.

"I saw your bumper sticker. I'm a Stars fan too," Battaglia said, referring to the Dallas Stars hockey team. "I've met a lot of the players."

"Yes, we're Stars fans," Cindy replied. Her responses were brief. She was anxious to put some space between herself and this overly friendly stranger. The more he talked, the more he gave her the creeps.

"But, Eddie Belfour is a loser," Battaglia continued, refering to the team's goalie. "Getting arrested at the Mansion hotel for trying to drag a girl into his room."

"Oh, I think there's more to the story than that," Cindy replied. "We know the people at the Mansion. My husband used to live there, and my daughters like to go there for dinner. Now they're boycotting the place because the Mansion had the police arrest Eddie."

Battaglia barked, "What are you talking about? That guy shouldn't be allowed to play on the team!" Then, in a more conciliatory tone, he said, "Must be nice if your husband was living at the Mansion. What kind of work does he do?"

Cindy wanted to end the conversation right there, but she was finding it difficult to get away from the man. She eyed the terrain for a spot to take her dogs—someplace where he couldn't go with his bike. But last night's rain had muddied the areas not covered by the trail, and she didn't want to steer her dogs off the path for fear their muddy feet would ruin the interior of her car.

"My husband is with a company that bought several savings and loans," she said offhandedly.

"Hey, I used to work for the RTC. I investigated all those crooks. Which savings and loans were they?"

Cindy couldn't remember the names of the previous businesses, but she told Battaglia that her husband was now with Bluebonnet Savings and Loan. Once those words had escaped, she wished they were back in her mouth.

"Oh, I know those. They were Commodore, North Park, Mesquite. There was a whole bunch of them," Battaglia said.

Cindy nodded, realizing he was right. "Where'd you start your ride?" she asked, trying to change the subject.

"Back at the lake. Seven point two miles. I don't live around there, though, I have a loft in Deep Ellum. Now I've got to ride back to the lake where I parked my truck."

That was the most hopeful news Cindy had heard, but he didn't seem to be in any hurry to leave. She was telling him things that she'd only discuss with close friends. Why was she talking to the man?

She was becoming more unnerved by the minute, and at one point nodded toward her larger dog and said, "He's been trained as an attack dog." Battaglia glanced at the dog, but only seemed mildly impressed and not at all alarmed.

Cindy looked back at her car, realizing that there was a lot of mud between her and her vehicle. Then she looked over at Mr. Know-it-all and thought, *to heck with the interior.* She plowed her dogs through the mud and ran back to her car.

She had no way of knowing that, later that night, she'd hear about this stranger on the news.

The exercise had let John forget his problems temporarily, but now around ten, he was showered, shaved, and back in his office.

Two days earlier, his probation officer, Debra

Gibbs, had warned him that his file had been sent for a possible probation revocation. John knew it meant that law enforcement was looking at him seriously; Mary Jean had probably called her pals in Highland Park and reported his last phone call to her. He could be arrested anytime and sent to jail. He had managed to squeak through the charge of smacking Mary Jean with only probation, he had slid smoothly past the marijuana charge without even a slap on the wrist, and now he was going to lose it all over one phone call. Didn't that beat all?

He made several calls to mutual friends of his and Mary Jean's. He told them how manipulative Mary Jean had become, and how she was trying to have him arrested so he would lose his business. Could they believe she'd be so mean? "Please," he begged, "give her a call and talk some sense into her."

John Battaglia paced his carpeted office. He had taken off his suit coat; his shirt was spotted with perspiration. Consumed with his impending fate, he continued to try to reach people who might intercede for him and plead his case to Mary Jean.

Before he left for lunch around noon, he picked up the phone and called Michelle Ghetti. He did not expect her to be home since she'd be teaching, but he was frantic to reach someone. When her machine prompted him to leave a message, he said, "Why are you and Mary Jean conspiring to put me back in jail? You know you are both ruining my life. Not only that, you're ruining my career and you're ruining my relationship with the girls. Can't you two see that?"

He nervously ran his fingers through his hair before continuing. "It never fails. Nobody ever thinks about my needs or me. Just like Laurie's Easter trip, nobody checked to see when it would be convenient for me to get her to the airport. Nobody ever thinks about my feelings."

He switched to another subject. "Just wondered if you've heard about Mary Jean's lesbian friend," he said with a devious chuckle. "She's been in a custody battle over her children and has lost custody. That's what she deserved. Maybe that's what Mary Jean needs. To lose the girls." He paused for a second, then said, "That would teach her a lesson.

"So, Michelle, do me a favor. In your Christian way, please talk with Mary Jean and get her to drop the charges so I won't go to jail."

Battaglia placed the receiver in its cradle, then contemplated who else he could contact.

Spent and exhausted, at 3:00 P.M. he decided to go to the source of his possible arrest and called Highland Park police detective Katherine Justice. Mary Jean had reported John to the tall brunette so many times that Mary Jean and the detective had become good friends.

Detective Justice was in her office and immediately took Battaglia's call.

"I understand you plan to arrest me tonight," he began.

"Have you been talking with your probation officer?" she asked.

John ignored her. "You probably plan to do it in Highland Park Village when I'm with my kids."

"No, no. You will not be arrested tonight. I can promise you that. No way. I know this is your night with the girls, so you just go. We can straighten this out later."

"You *say* you're not going to arrest me, but you might. This sounds like some kind of setup to me."

"John, listen. The papers were only filed yesterday, so there hasn't been enough time to process an arrest."

"I don't know what to believe," he told her.

"You just need to talk to your probation officer and we can get this straightened out like we did last time. You can turn yourself in tomorrow, but I promise, you won't be arrested tonight."

John Battaglia's most constant companion of late was a lovely, willowy blonde named Kelly. Five-foot-nine with long hair, she looked like a model. She owned an antiques store where she sold eighteenth-century French furniture—coincidentally the same kind of business that Mary Jean and her mother owned, although smaller.

With the threat of an arrest over his head, Battaglia was unsure if he'd be allowed his normal Wednesday night visit with his children. Since he wasn't allowed to call his ex-wife, he asked Kelly to call Mary Jean shortly after five, and make certain the plans were still on for the evening.

When Kelly called, she hesitated and apologized for bothering Mary Jean, and then related Battaglia's request.

Mary Jean replied, "Sure, I still plan to take them over to the shopping center around six. Just have John call them on their phone and they can make plans."

Battaglia must have been standing nearby. In only moments the girls' phone rang and Mary Jean could

hear her ex-husband's voice coming over the speakerphone in Faith and Liberty's room. Faith answered
the phone with "Hey, Dad," and Mary Jean heard
her ex-husband say, "Hi, girls. How's it going? Do
you still want to go for dinner tonight?"

"Sure," both girls said. "How 'bout Mi Cocina?"
Faith said, suggesting a popular Mexican restaurant
in Highland Park Village.

"I don't know," her father replied. "After the kind
of day I've had, I'm really not too hungry. In fact, I
may be arrested in Highland Park Village and, if I
am, I probably won't see you for about a year."

Mary Jean strolled into her daughters' room and
saw a look of disbelief in their eyes; she felt disgusted
that John would say that to the children. Then, dropping the arrest scenario, he made arrangements to
pick up the girls at 6:00 P.M.

Faith looked sad as she glanced out at the huge
tree that sometimes scratched her window at night
when the wind blew. After gazing for a few moments,
she turned to her mother.

"We won't see him for a year?" she asked.

"No, it's all right," Mary Jean said. "He's just saying
that. It'll be thirty days or so."

Tears welled in Faith's eyes. "Why do I have the
worst daddy in the world?"

Mary Jean's heart sank. Although she had to agree
with her daughter, she tried not to show her feelings
for the child's sake.

"Oh, Faith, you really don't," Mary Jean said, then
wondered how many times she had defended John
for the children's sake.

Faith reflected for another moment, then said,
"You're right. The worst daddy is the one in University Park who killed the mommy in front of his three

children. My daddy is the second worst," she said, remembering the fairly recent murder by CPA Tim Richardson whose three small children watched him violently slice his wife Mary to death with a pair of scissors.

Mary Jean felt terrible when she heard her daughter's words. Why was John allowed to inflict such emotional pain on this family?

"You need to get dressed," she said. But she was as uninspired to get her child ready as her daughter was to go. She could see Faith's apprehension. Mary Jean had already slipped on a new pair of beige linen pants and a matching silk blouse. That would do for the meeting she had to attend after she dropped off her girls. Something springlike might have been more fun, but tonight she was in a very beige kind of mood.

"Where's Liberty?" Mary Jean asked, as she pulled out a pair of blue denim shorts and a pink-printed, short-sleeve pullover for her youngest daughter.

Faith shrugged and said she'd help her mother look. After they checked the house, they went outside. Liberty wasn't at the swing set or the area around the swimming pool or in the front yard. They went back inside and climbed the stairs, all the while calling Liberty's name. In the girls' bedroom, they checked the closet. No Liberty. Mary Jean bent down and raised the gingham dust ruffle to Liberty's bed. She spotted two frightened brown eyes staring at her. When she took Liberty's hand and pulled her younger daughter from under the bed, the little girl was trembling; her eyes full of fear.

With the girls safely buckled into the car, Mary Jean backed down her driveway and steered onto

Lorraine. At Preston Road she took a left and passed the prestigious Dallas Country Club. She barely glanced at the grounds that resembled green velvet or the geraniums, roses, and phlox that spilled along pathways and climbed up stucco walls. Her heart was so heavy that she paid no attention to all the spring flowers in bloom.

At exactly 6:00 P.M., Mary Jean turned left into the Highland Park Shopping Center, designed by a Southern Californian architect, who had given the cream-colored stucco buildings a lacy Moroccan motif, and the terra-cotta tile roof a definite Spanish flair.

Mary Jean looked for John Battaglia's truck. It wasn't in front of the grocery store. She drove through the parking lot, past a Bentley and two Rolls Royces, but couldn't find him. Not really wanting to let him have the girls tonight, she toyed with the idea of leaving, but she didn't dare give him an excuse to lose control and retaliate with another barrage of expletives, or worse. She swung her car in a larger arc through the center, passing exclusive specialty stores—Escada, Hermes, Christian Dior and other pricey boutiques—but she could not find him. She felt her heart beat faster. Since his vicious attack, Mary Jean had been very careful. She was convinced that John wanted to kill her. She was not the only one who felt that way. Her attorney was also concerned, and had insisted that Mary Jean choose a very public place for dropping off the children. Above all else, she was never to be alone with him. Ever.

At 6:25 P.M., to both her relief and chagrin, she spotted Battaglia's truck. She pulled up one row away from him and told her daughters, "Okay, sweeties, here you go." They both climbed over the seat and gave her kisses and tight hugs before reluctantly

getting out of the car. She watched them shuffle un-
enthusiastically to Battaglia's large truck. As he
stretched across the seat to unlock the door and
open it for them, she happened to catch his eye. He
frowned and glared at her. It was the most hateful,
belligerent stare she had ever seen. She watched as
Liberty showed him the laminated book she had
made in school; then piled several Beanie Babies on
top of it before climbing into the truck. Faith shut
the door and Battaglia put his car into gear. He circled by Mary Jean. As he passed, Mary Jean caught
Faith's lonesome stare. Without smiling, Faith gave
her mother a final wave good-bye, moving her right
hand in an arc in front of her sad face.

Mary Jean watched them leave. Before Battaglia's
black pickup had pulled onto Mockingbird Road, she
felt an overwhelming sadness, and tears glistened in
her eyes. She had never felt so alone. Those girls were
her life. She drove aimlessly away from the shopping
center, but she couldn't rid herself of the vision of
Faith's halfhearted wave and melancholy expression.

Tonight, Mary Jean was to attend the USA Film
Festival Board meeting. The organization raised
money for the arts, and she enjoyed working on it.
She would see many of her friends there. Her
thoughts wandered to the galas she had helped orchestrate, which brought back pleasant memories of
meeting the actors and actresses who came to town
for the benefits. It was a happy, upbeat organization,
but she felt neither happy nor upbeat. Tonight she
didn't want to be around people who expected her
to be cheerful and outgoing and positive. Tonight,
she was none of those things.

Since Mary Jean wouldn't be home from the
board meeting until ten or ten-thirty, her good

friend, Melissa Lowder, had agreed to let John Battaglia drop off the girls at her house after dinner. Melissa's house was several blocks from Mary Jean's and was on Mary Jean's way home. Mary Jean decided she would feel better if she stopped and talked with Melissa instead of going to the meeting. Once she made that decision, Mary Jean accelerated up Preston Road, raced down University Avenue, and then pulled into the driveway of Melissa's two-story beige brick home.

John Battaglia would later tell a *Dallas Morning News* reporter what the children had said to him that night.

John exited Avon Cleaners with his plastic-covered laundry and dry cleaning slung over his shoulder. As he opened the truck door, a store across the street caught his eye.

"See that place over there?" he asked the girls. "It's got tents and stuff. Maybe there's something we could use for our campout next weekend."

Liberty and Faith looked at each other but said nothing.

"What's wrong? Cat got your tongue?"

Faith gave her father a despondent glance. "I don't think we're going camping," she said quietly.

Battaglia audibly groaned. "Okay what is it this time? What's your mother up to?"

The girls looked hesitant to speak. Liberty said, "You tell him," then turned to look out of the truck's window.

Faith cleared her throat. "Daddy, you know what you told us on the phone tonight? That you'd be in jail?"

John's muscles tensed. "Well, maybe it won't happen that soon."

"Mom says you could be in jail for a month or so."

That damn Mary Jean. She'll do anything to make my life more miserable than it already is.

Battaglia looked off into the crowded street, ignoring his daughter's statement. His mind started racing. "How about getting some barbecue?" he asked. "We haven't done that in a long time."

The girls nodded.

So Mary Jean's intent on keeping me from my girls, he thought. *Well, I'll just show her who's boss.* His mind moved into fast-forward and began spinning out of control.

"If I'm gonna eat barbecue I can't do it this suit. Let's run by the loft and I'll change into something casual."

The entrance to the Adam Hats Lofts was utilitarian and somewhat factorylike. The building had retained much of its original character from when the Ford Motor Company had constructed it in 1913 to build Model Ts.

Faith and Liberty had rollerbladed in the lobby, which looked like a whimsical playground—one wall was painted deep purple, and that purple color continued vertically to all four floors. Another wall was gold and others were white, lending more vivid contrast to the dramatic colors.

Ford had built a metal, four-story, open spiral chute to fling automobile parts to various sections of the plant. Now the decorative curly structure was painted bright yellow on one side, orange on the other. It playfully twisted and turned around a shiny black pole.

The lobby soared open to all four floors, and overhead, exposed skywalks resembled the pieces of an Erector Set.

John and his daughters took the elevator to the fourth floor, past more walls painted vivid colors in an attempt to give the building warmth.

Tall ceilings soared above their heads, and held heavy, exposed utility pipes that gave the building a high-tech look.

As they neared his loft, John Battaglia said, "Wait till you see my new place. It's bigger and nicer than the one I had on the third floor." John pushed open the door to reveal a 1600-square-foot space whose open plan made it feel even larger.

Faith squealed, "Yuck, it's a mess! There's boxes and stuff all over the place."

"Sure, I only moved in yesterday."

Liberty glanced around, then said, "I bet you'll make it real nice, Daddy. Your other place looked good."

"It will be great once I find a place for all these books."

Stacks of John's books crowded the bases of century-old support columns. The loft's brown-stained concrete floors echoed hard and unforgiving, magnifying every footfall.

Two walls held floor-to-ceiling windows. The loft sat on the side of the building closest to the roaring eight-lane Central Expressway. Even the hum of the air conditioning couldn't muffle the noise of cars and semis clamoring their way south to Waco or north to Denton. The cars were so close that anyone in the loft could make out the faces of passengers.

The western window framed a picturesque view of downtown Dallas with its crowded collection of skyscrapers. A walk-in closet, laundry room, and bath lined the wall to the right, with the kitchen straight ahead, close to the window with the view.

Despite the gorgeous panorama, the loft's stark aura was as cold as a tomb.

Faith and Liberty kicked off their shoes, as they always did when they entered their dad's loft. The feel of the cool, rough surface of the floor was a drastic contrast to their own home's thick carpeting and highly polished oak floors, which felt like silk under their feet.

"How long's it gonna take you to change?" Liberty asked her dad.

"I won't be long." He glanced at his watch. "It's just seven now," he said, as he headed for his closet.

A few minutes later, he came back wearing a snow white T-shirt and creased blue jeans. "Before we go to dinner, I want to talk to your mom and check out this story you've been telling me. I need to get to the bottom of why she's trying to put me in jail."

"You can't do that," Faith said. "You're not supposed to call Mom."

"Well, then, how about you calling her? If she's not there, just leave her a message to call you back."

Faith hesitantly picked up her father's portable phone, punched in her mother's number, and waited for her familiar message. When she heard the beep, she said, "Hi, Mom. Call us back. Okay? Call us back."

Battaglia, disappointed, said, "Guess I've got to think of something else." He leaned over and placed his elbows on the kitchen's white Formica countertop. "Would either of you please tell me why your mother wants me in jail? I mean, really. What have I done to her? I don't go inside her house and I don't call her on the phone.

"How about you, Faith?" her father said. "Since you left the message, why don't you try to see what she's up to when she calls back?"

Tears filled the little girls eyes and she lowered her head. "Okay, if I have to."

"On second thought, your mom may be out till late. Let's talk to Grandma." Battaglia punched in the number for Dorrace Pearle. After a few rings, she picked up. "Hi, Dorrace. It's John."

"Oh, er, hello, John," Dorrace said, obviously surprised to hear his voice.

"I need a favor," he began. "The girls have a question for their mom and I don't want to break the rules and call her. So would you give her a jingle and let her know that they want to talk with her?"

"Well, I guess I could."

"Just have her call them over here at the loft."

"Okay, John. I'll call her right now on her cell phone."

As Mary Jean strolled up the sidewalk to Melissa Lowder's house, she passed a large elm on her left that had a graceful fern hanging from one of the lower branches; behind it stood a beautiful magnolia tree. Overall, it was a lovely place for a single mother of two. Mary Jean had met Melissa when their older daughters were in kindergarten, and for the past five years they had remained good friends.

They had socialized as married couples, but now both women were divorced, which added another commonality to their friendship.

Just as Mary Jean started to climb the stairs leading

to Melissa's front porch, her cell phone rang. She glanced at the caller ID and saw it was her mother's number, so she punched the receive button.

"Mary Jean, it's Mom," Dorrace said. "I just got a rather strange call from John. Said the girls wanted to ask you about something and would you please call them at his loft."

"Oh darn. What's he putting them up to now?" She paused for a moment, then said, "On second thought, judging from the last time I saw them, they probably want to come home. Okay, I'll call down there. Thanks."

Mary Jean crossed Melissa's porch and rang the doorbell. Melissa greeted her with a broad smile, then gave her a warm hug. "I'm surprised you're here. I expected to see you much later," she said.

"My plans have kinda changed. Right now I've got to call John. Which phone do you want me to use?"

"There's another line in the kitchen," Melissa told her. "The kids are in there finishing up their dinner, and I'm just doing some paperwork back at the desk in my bedroom. Come back when you finish."

Mary Jean went to the kitchen and chatted with Melissa's son and daughter for a few minutes, then around seven-twenty she picked up the phone at the kitchen desk and punched in the number for Battaglia's loft. She hoped one of her girls would answer so she wouldn't have to speak to her ex-husband.

John Battaglia said hello and it grated on Mary Jean to hear his voice.

"Hi, John," she said lightly. "Mom called and said the girls wanted to ask me something."

"Yeah," he said, and Mary Jean could hear the

echo-like sound that always accompanied his punching the speakerphone button.

"Ask her!" John's voice pounded. *"Ask her,"* he repeated in a louder, harsher voice.

"Mommy?" Faith stammered. She was noticeably crying and her voice sputtered out in short sobs. "Why do you want Daddy to have to go to jail?"

Mary Jean could feel her body temperature climb. "Oh come on, John, don't do this to them."

Then Mary Jean heard the screams that will forever haunt her. Faith's voice cried out, "No, Daddy, don't! Oh please no, Daddy. Don't do it. No, no, no!"

Suddenly, over the piercing cries of her daughter, Mary Jean heard the blast of a gun. Her bewilderment at John's question abruptly changed as she grasped the situation. *Oh my God, he's shooting the children!* "Run, babies, run!" she screamed. "As fast as you can, run for the door!"

Everything was happening quickly. Mary Jean began to shake and her eyes filled with tears. She was overcome by a feeling of complete helplessness. If only she were there, she could try to wrestle the gun away from him, but she could do nothing but hang on to the phone—her lifeline, but also her connection to the nightmare. She continued to hear shots. Five? Six? She couldn't tell for sure. They came so rapidly that they sounded like one continuous explosion. Then, all went quiet. Mary Jean pressed the phone closer to her ear. In only moments, John's voice came back on the line. He spoke in a loud, threatening, mocking tone. "Merry fucking Christmas, Mary Jean!" he yelled. Then the line went dead.

* * *

Mary Jean's screams brought Melissa running.

Melissa was breathless when she reached the kitchen. "What on earth's happening?" she asked Mary Jean.

"John just shot the kids!"

"No!" Melissa said, her eyes wide. Her hand flew to cover her mouth.

"I heard shots," Mary Jean said through her sobs. "Oh, God, call 911."

Melissa grabbed the phone as Mary Jean ran to her car to get Battaglia's address to give to the police. When she returned, Melissa was already talking with the 911 operator. "I've got the police," she called to Mary Jean. "I'm talking to Highland Park right now."

Melissa turned back to the operator. "Mary Jean Battaglia just got a call from her ex-husband who lives on Canton. He's called her while shooting a gun at her children."

"Okay," the operator replied.

"You should have a file on him. Can you pull that up?"

The operator told Melissa that she had a lot of information on John Battaglia, and asked for Mary Jean's address and phone number. Melissa explained that Mary Jean was now at her house. The operator told her under no circumstances should Mary Jean return home. She was to stay at Melissa's.

Melissa could hear the operator giving instructions to a dispatcher. She told Melissa to hold on a second while she called other officers. Melissa listened to her relay a message: "I need to have you call in as soon as possible," the operator said.

Oh, oh, Melissa thought, *she's only leaving a message. She hasn't gotten hold of anyone.*

By now Mary Jean had returned to the kitchen, and reached for the phone. "Oh, please, let me talk to them." Melissa immediately handed her the phone.

"Hello," Mary Jean said.

"Hi, this is Highland Park. I understand what's going on."

"Oh, thank God," Mary Jean yelled. "He killed the children!"

"Okay, I understand," the operator said calmly. "And we understand the problem with him." It was like the two women were having completely different conversations. The operator continued, "We know where you are right now so we have a number where we can call you."

Mary Jean responded as if she hadn't heard the operator and began crying harder. She said, "He's at two-seven-zero-zero Canton."

"Canton?" the operator said.

"He's in Apartment 317," Mary Jean sobbed, giving the wrong number.

"Ma'am, ma'am. Calm down just a minute. Okay?"

"I am. I am. It's two-seven-hundred Canton."

"Canton? Is that in Dallas?" the operator asked.

Then Mary Jean corrected herself. "I think it's Apartment 418. He just moved to an apartment upstairs. He was going to be arrested tomorrow. I was talking to my baby, then he shot the gun off," Mary Jean's sentences ran together as she rambled in a high, incoherent pitch.

"Ma'am, I understand. You have to calm down just a little bit so I can understand you. Okay? Now is that in Dallas?"

"Yes. It's on Canton down in Deep Ellum in the Adams Hat Building."

"Okay. This is what I'm gonna do," the operator

said. "I'm gonna call the Dallas Police Department, have them go over there."

"He killed my children!" Mary Jean screamed.

"Ma'am, I'm gonna have Dallas go there. So, I need to hang up with you, okay?"

"I'm going down there," Mary Jean said before the operator interrupted her.

"No, ma'am."

"I've got to!"

"No, ma'am. You cannot go there."

"Yes, I've got to! I've got to. He shot my children!"

TWENTY-NINE

Faith had stood facing the speakerphone, wiping her eyes against the back of her hand. When she heard her mother's voice, her father had hissed, "Ask her. *Ask her!*"

Faith continued sniffling as she questioned her mother about wanting to put Daddy in jail. Before her mother could reply, she heard the click of a gun behind her. She turned to see a .38 revolver in her father's hand. He had just flipped off the safety.

She could hear her mother's voice in the background saying, "Oh, come on, John . . ."

When Faith saw the gun, she began shaking violently.

Without emotion, John Battaglia raised the gun and pointed it directly at his oldest daughter. Her eyes grew wild and she screamed, "No, Daddy, don't! Oh, please no, Daddy. Don't do it. No, no, no!" She sobbed and begged for her life as her father began to squeeze the trigger. Looking her in the eye, Battaglia fired the first shot. It ripped into her right shoulder, sliding through soft tissue. She screamed, both from physical pain and the emotional anguish of knowing that her own father was shooting her. The shot spun her around and she collapsed onto the floor. Battaglia fired again and the second shot entered her torso, severing her spinal cord and instantly paralyzing her. She was facedown by the kitchen sink. Her hand cushioned the side of her face.

When Mary Jean's voice had shrieked from the speakerphone, "Run, babies, run," Liberty had sprinted toward the front door, her only escape from the loft.

Battaglia had to chase her, running from the kitchen, past the laundry room, to his bedroom area, shooting at her wildly as she ran. Liberty's little legs couldn't take her fast enough as her father closed in. She screamed when her father caught her only fifteen feet before she could reach safety. His first shot grazed her head, slicing off three inches of flesh a quarter inch deep. She shrieked and raised her hand to her throbbing head, but the little girl kept running. His shots less accurate on this moving target, Battaglia's next bullet tore into her right arm, inflicting another wound as it exited. Terrified, Liberty opened her mouth to gasp for air, and tears rolled down her cheeks. The next bullet punctured her side and the one after that severed her spinal cord.

He went back to the speakerphone and wished Mary Jean a Merry Christmas. Then he turned off the phone.

In a sick, psychotic haze, he picked up his Glock, a semiautomatic that held up to fifteen bullets. Ironically, Mary Jean's father, Gene Pearle, had given the pistol to him to protect his family. It was a blessing that Gene would never know his gift had been used for such a heinous act.

Battaglia first walked back to Faith. Blood streamed from her wounds, but he had to make sure. He had to know that Mary Jean would never have her again. Pressing the gun to the back of her head until it indented her scalp, he pulled the trigger. Her body jumped as the bullet entered her head. Black gunpowder burned her flesh, and the bullet exited through her forehead, leaving a quarter-sized hole.

Moving over to Liberty who was spread eagle on the floor, he administered the same execution-style shot. The bullet entered behind her ear and exited by her nose, taking a tooth with it.

Battaglia hadn't bothered to pick up the casings, hide the guns, or wipe off his fingerprints. He placed the Glock on the nightstand in plain view.

The 911 operator quickly called the Dallas police dispatcher and explained that she was calling from Highland Park. "We have a sort of a domestic situation," she began.

"Okay," the dispatcher replied, assigning it a second-level urgency.

"The husband is actually gonna be at an address in Dallas and he has possibly, he does have a gun, and, uh, the wife believes he has possibly shot his children."

"Oops," the dispatcher responded.

The operator told the dispatcher that this was the only information they had from the mother, and gave the Dallas police the address and loft number, adding that it was apparently near Deep Ellum. Then she mentioned that police had a huge file on the man.

"The wife still lives here in Highland Park. He has visitation rights with the children. He has the children now. She has called me and is panicking. She talked to him on the phone."

"Right," the dispatcher responded.

"He shot off his gun. She thinks that he shot the children."

"God," the dispatcher groaned.

"I'm trying to get hold of one of our supervisors to let him know, too, but I wanted to go ahead and get you guys going."

"Do you know the name of the apartments?" the dispatcher asked.

"No, I don't," the operator replied, forgetting that Mary Jean had said the Adams Hat Building, which was similar to the name of the lofts. The operator spelled out Battaglia's name, told the dispatcher that he was a white male, and gave his date of birth; then she repeated, "But like I said, we have had several problems with him. Several domestic disturbances."

The dispatcher asked if they should go ahead and get an ambulance to the lofts.

"Uh, ya know. I, I don't know," the operator replied.

"Okay."

"If he actually has, ya know, shot his children or not. I mean, she's panicking because she is the mother."

"Right. Sure."

Then, with a change of heart, the operator said, "As long as we have an officer going, ya know?"

The dispatcher finished her sentence, ". . . go ahead and get an ambulance over there?"

"Okay, thank you," the operator said, and hung up.

John Battaglia walked into his bathroom and opened the medicine cabinet. After rummaging around and pushing a few prescriptions aside, he found a bottle of tranquilizers. Grabbing it, he popped open the top and shook out the collection of pills. He threw them into his mouth and cupped his hand under the water spigot, gulping them down.

Somehow he had managed to stay clean throughout the killings; his clothes bore no trace of blood.

Battaglia slammed the loft's door shut and hurried along the hall to the elevator, taking it down to the garage.

He felt he'd had no choice about what had happened in his apartment. Mary Jean had finally forced him into it. She was always using the Highland Park Police as her own private little police force. It irritated the hell out of him to see them jump every time she called them to report his phone calls or whatever else he had done. Well, he had finally shown her.

With an arrest warrant possibly coming down on him for probation violation, the police could come pounding on his door any day now to haul him away. It was particularly frightening that his attorney had told him that jail time was a definite possibility, because previously, his attorney always had managed to get the charge reduced or the bail lessened, and he would escape his problem. In fact, he had made a game out of it.

If he were arrested, he'd be fired as the chief financial officer of Arcturus, and lose his own private business. He had finally realized how fast this could happen when Faith reminded him tonight that he wouldn't be around next weekend. That realization felt like somebody had socked the wind out of him, and forced him to act.

That damn Mary Jean. This was all her fault.

In the musty garage, he climbed into his truck and drove away cautiously, doing his best to avoid attracting attention. He heard no sirens, no commotion. At least for the moment, he was safe.

* * *

Driving only a couple of blocks, he pulled up to July Alley, a local bar he frequented. He walked in and nodded to the bartender, then sat at a table near the window. He didn't want company. He frequently sat alone, only this time it was by choice. He ordered a Tanqueray and tonic. While he waited for it, he pulled out his cell phone and made a call. When his drink arrived, he chugged it down, ice cubes clinking as he drained the last few sips, then ordered another. He watched young people in jeans pass by on the sidewalk. He remembered being that age, but he couldn't remember being as happy as they seemed. Then he wondered, had he ever been happy?

He gulped down his second drink and motioned for the check. He pulled out a ten-dollar bill to cover the tab, thought *what the hell,* and threw down another five for the tip.

Now fortified, he wanted company. But before he could play, he had some work to do. He retrieved his truck from the parking lot and turned onto Main Street, then drove toward his new office. He had one last piece of unfinished business.

THIRTY

Mary Jean saw the road ahead through a blur of tears. Her hands had been shaking ever since she left Michelle Lowder's house. She couldn't imagine the 911 operator telling her not to go to her girls. Nothing could have kept her away.

A block from Michelle's house, Mary Jean tore past the massive, gothic style Highland Park Presbyterian Church. At Hillcrest, she barely slowed to turn right.

It was shortly after seven-thirty, and the sun was setting, but the light blue sky, already tinged with pink, was still bright enough for Mary Jean to see by. She raced through the next red light and down the street that bordered Southern Methodist University, quickly passing its large brick dorms and student center.

Almost everyone drove a cautious thirty miles an hour in the Park Cities because of diligent policing, but Mary Jean's driving twenty miles over the limit had not alerted any police, although she would have welcomed their presence.

She pictured the red brick lofts where John lived, imagining the street clogged with police cars and ambulances. *Maybe he just shot up the apartment,* she tried to reassure herself.

While trying to focus on the road, she punched in her mother's phone number. She had already told her about the tragic phone conversation with Faith, and now left a message saying where she'd be. Dorrace would contact the rest of the family. Mary Jean knew they'd be devastated and want to be with her. She passed one more church and said yet another prayer. "Oh, God, let there be a miracle. Let them somehow still be alive." Every thought of her daughters brought a new flood of tears. Mary Jean was surprised that she had any more tears to shed. At the light on Mockingbird, she careened left and soon approached Central Expressway where she could drive even faster. "I'm coming, girls," she yelled. "I'm coming!" Then she broke down all over again, her shoulders shaking and her stomach churning from fear.

It had only been five minutes since she left Melissa's house, but it seemed like an hour, and it would be another ten minutes before she'd reach the lofts. She increased her speed, all the time screaming and cursing. *This wasn't really happening.*

In the distance, the glass and granite skyscrapers of downtown Dallas emerged before her. Lights were coming on in the tall buildings and they twinkled like jewels. Soon in the midst of the mirrored glass walls, she pulled her car into the downtown exit. She felt like she was flying and standing still at the same time: the speedometer said she was flying, but in her mind, everything seemed to be going past in slow motion. At times, she'd sniffle, blow her nose, and try to take deep breaths; then the enormity of the situation would hit her anew and she'd break into wailing sobs. She cried with her whole body, leaning over the steering wheel and shaking.

Patrol Officers Zane Murray and Ray Rojas were on their nightly patrol, scouting the Dallas streets in the

Central Business District. They listened to their squad car radio spit out offenses and request various officers to handle them. A Code Six-X came in from Highland Park, indicating that people were fighting.

"I need someone from the Central Business District," the dispatcher said.

The officers knew that no one regularly patrolled that area. According to their computer screen, the apartment where the fight was supposed to be taking place wasn't far from where they now were, so Murray switched to another channel to get more information.

"Mother thinks kids were shot," was the first line he read on the new computer channel.

"Oh no," Rojas said. "Sure hope that's not right."

Murray radioed the dispatcher that they would take the call. He hit his lights and they were on their way.

Mary Jean turned onto Canton Street, and gasped. She was alone. There wasn't one police car, not one ambulance. Nothing. A sickening rage filled her. *Doesn't anybody care? For God's sake what's going on?*

Long ago, she had memorized the number for the Highland Park Police. Now she punched it in and asked that they connect her with their 911 operator so she could talk with the same person.

"This is Mary Jean Pearle," she said when the operator answered.

"Yes," the woman replied.

"I'm getting ready to come up on his apartment. I don't see any police cars. I wonder what's going on?"

Mary Jean parked by the entrance and kept her phone to her ear. She stepped out of her car and ran to the building's front door. She jerked on the handle. Then she saw the electronic door lock.

She listened to the scolding voice of the Highland Park dispatcher. "Ma'am, I told you, I do not want you to go there. I have the Dallas Police Department going over there because Highland Park can't. Ma'am, it's not safe for you to go there by yourself. Okay?"

Mary Jean couldn't speak because tears were choking her throat. "I'm so scared of him," she managed before breaking into more loud screams.

"I understand," the operator said.

"Please help me. I've already come here."

"Ma'am, do not go inside that apartment. You need to stay in your car."

"I tried to get inside, but the building's locked."

"Ma'am, I promise we have the Dallas Police Department going over there."

"Have you told them he's killed my children?"

"Yes. I told them the whole situation."

"Can you call them back. Will you?" Mary Jean's breath was labored as she pleaded.

"Yes, but I'm keeping you on the phone because you are not going in that apartment."

"Please call them back," she pleaded. "Please, they might still be alive—still in there. Oh, my God!"

"Ma'am?"

"I see a policeman going the opposite way."

Mary Jean hurried out of her car, waving her arms frantically and screaming, "Stop! Please help me!" but the police car drove on.

Forlornly, she sank back in her car and continued her conversation.

"Listen," the 911 operator said, "Katherine Justice, our detective here? She's gonna call your cell phone so I need you to hang up with me."

"Okay," Mary Jean said.

At that moment, Mary Jean saw the policeman

again. He had been going the opposite direction, but had made a U-turn, and was now parking behind her.

She jumped out of her car to talk with the officer, telling him everything she had screamed at the 911 operator. While the officer was getting a resident to open the building's door, two more policemen pulled up. She cried hysterically as she yet again had to explain her phone call with her daughter. The officers had to concentrate because it was difficult to understand Mary Jean through all her choking sobs. After questioning her, they rushed inside the building.

John Battaglia signed in with security then took the elevator to the fifty-third floor of his downtown office building. He rushed down the hall and unlocked the door to Arcturus.

He hurried to his office and sat down before his computer. He pulled up his investments and began printing them, one by one.

At 7:50, he picked up the phone and called Baton Rouge. Again he reached only a machine. When he spoke, his voice and manner were very calm.

"Hey Orie, this is Ba-ba," he said, using the pet names he had invented for his daughter and himself. "I'm putting your money, a check, in an envelope for you along with some documents that show other accounts I have money in. This is your college money. Put it in an account and invest it. Save it for college, okay? Love you, sweetheart. Talk to you soon."

Mary Jean's cell phone rang. It was Detective Katherine Justice.

"Mary Jean?" the detective said. "I can't hear you sweetie. What's going on?"

Mary Jean again reiterated the horror she had experienced earlier. Each time she had to tell the story, she became all the more devastated.

"Are the police there?"

"Three of them."

"Okay, tell them John has an outstanding warrant," Justice said, giving the police a reason to approach the loft.

"I can't," Mary Jean said, "They're already in the building now, opening it up."

"They're gonna be okay," the detective tried to assure her.

"I can't believe this," Mary Jean sobbed.

"You talked to them, right?"

"Yes, and Faith was going, 'No, no, daddy, no, don't do it. Don't do it!' And then the gun went off. I heard them screaming.

"Oh my babies. I can't believe this," Mary Jean said. "I didn't think he'd do it. Oh my God!"

"But they're okay?" Justice said.

"No!" Mary Jean screamed, "they're *not* okay. I think he killed them in there!" Her cries could be heard from a block away, but her words were scrambled and Katherine Justice had trouble understanding her.

"Calm down. Calm down. Till the police come out. Okay? Take a deep breath."

"Okay. He, oh Katherine . . ."

"Take a deep breath. You're doing good," the detective tried to persuade her.

"I know, baby, oh my God, please don't let it be, please Jesus. But he fired like five or six times—unless he killed himself too."

Mary Jean looked around. "I want an ambulance here. Maybe they're still alive. I doubt it, but maybe."

"That's right. Think positively."

"I was thinking, no he couldn't have done it. Just couldn't have. But, I'm also trying to kind of prepare myself, ya know? It's just what you normally do."

After more sobs, Mary Jean murmured, "Faith, Faith, Faith. I can't believe he would kill that angel. But he just wouldn't be shooting it off for kicks."

"I don't know," Justice said. "I don't know him like you do."

"I don't either, but nobody shoots a gun off for kicks, you know? But I appreciate you talking to me baby 'cause I've gotta talk to somebody right now. My mother and my brother are on their way."

Just to keep Mary Jean talking, the detective continued to ask her details of what led up to the shooting: the meeting at the shopping center and how she came to phone the girls. The minutes ticked by, but there was no sign of the police returning with any kind of news.

"Oh this is so hard," Mary Jean said. "This is so bad. You always wonder what people go through when something like this happens to them, ya know? You never think it will be you."

"Yeah," the detective agreed. "And we thought we were doing the right thing, ya know?"

"I know. I never thought he would do this. I never, never thought he was this bad. Hold on."

Katherine, who could hear another voice in the background, asked, "Who's there with you?"

"My friend, Melissa Lowder. She just showed up."

The detective was relieved to learn that another person was with Mary Jean.

Mary Jean choked out words. "Oh. Oh, I'm so scared."

"You calm down now. Okay? As much as you can."

"I will," she said. "Oh my God, an ambulance is pulling up now."

"Calm down. That's standard."

Mary Jean gasped, trying to gain control. "John told the girls that maybe he'd be arrested up at Highland Park Village. If so, he wouldn't see them for about a year."

"No, no," Justice said. "I know he talked to his probation officer, 'cause he [John] called me today." The detective described her conversation with John. ". . . I promised him we weren't going to arrest him tonight."

"God if only we had," Mary Jean sighed.

"Well, the papers. I told him the papers had just been filed yesterday."

"It doesn't matter," Mary Jean said, still crying. "This whole thing is so awful crazy. But you've been so nice talking to me. I just don't know what to do. I don't want to go up there. I don't know what it's like if you see your kids' heads splattered all over the place." Her voice came out in staccato bursts as she gasped for breath between each word. "I don't know if it's better to see it or not."

"You don't, okay?" Katherine assured her.

"Do they teach you that in your stuff?"

"Yeah. Think about that, okay?"

Mary Jean gulped. "Oh God. A guy came out. I've gotta talk to him."

The detective could hear conversation in the background, and then she was shocked by a piercing scream.

There was a long, numbing pause before Mary Jean was back on the phone.

"They're dead!" she yelled.

"Mary Jean?" Katherine said, in disbelief. Then she heard a policeman tell Mary Jean to get into the car. Melissa's voice could be heard, "I know. I know. I know. Honey, I know," she said sympathetically. "Sit right here. Okay, right here."

"Mary Jean, Mary Jean," Katherine pleaded, hoping Mary Jean still had her cell phone with her. Then she heard her voice come closer to the mouthpiece, but she was sobbing terribly.

"They're dead," Mary Jean said, her voice eerily different, sounding in shock.

"No!"

"He's not in there with them, though. He just killed them."

"No!" the detective yelled, unable to hide her horror.

"I hope he hasn't gone to kill my mother."

"Your mother's not there?" Detective Justice asked.

"She's on her way."

Then the detective listened to chaotic background conversation until she could finally discern Mary Jean's voice.

"I don't want to see them," Mary Jean said to someone. All the while Katherine was trying to get her attention.

"Mary Jean. Mary Jean. Do you want me to come down?"

"I can't hear a thing you're saying with all that's going on down here," Mary Jean replied. "What?"

"I said do you want me to come down there?"

"Yes, I need you bad, babe. I need you bad."

"Okay," Katherine told her. "I'm on my way."

THIRTY-ONE

A second ambulance pulled up to the front of the Adam Hats Lofts; the frenzied sirens and flashing red lights heightened the tension of the scene. The ambulance doors opened and two paramedics jumped out and rushed toward the building.

When the paramedics entered Loft 418, they pulled on latex gloves and headed first to Liberty. One man crouched down and carefully reached for her wrist, praying he'd feel the faint beating of a pulse. Nothing. The man was in his forties and had children at home only a few years older than the one that lay before him. He momentarily turned away from the body, fought for composure, then asked where the second girl was.

As police heard about the shootings over their radios, one by one, squad cars began to line the street.

Cars carrying investigators from the Physical Evidence Section (PES) and Crimes Against Persons (CAPERS) were on their way.

When the crime scene was secured at 8:32 P.M., Officer Zane Murray picked up his cell phone and called the Dallas County Medical Examiner's Office. The busy ME office is open 365 days a year, and will even perform autopsies on Christmas Day if necessary.

Glynda Ray, known as Gigi to her family, friends and coworkers, was one of two investigators manning the 3:00-to-11:30-P.M. shift. She took Murray's call.

The attractive brunette was in her forties, and her upbeat, energetic demeanor gave no hint that she dealt with death on a daily basis. Highly qualified, Ray held a master's degree in criminal justice in addition to being a board certified medico-legal death investigator.

"We have a Signal 27 [dead body] at 2700 Canton," Murray began. The call was handled as official police business, and Murray was trained to stay neutral regardless of his personal feelings.

"What kind of Signal 27?" Ray asked.

"We have two little girls shot by their dad."

The death investigator sighed as she recorded the address and other information Murray relayed. A few minutes earlier, Gigi had received a call from a Channel 11 reporter who informed her of a shooting at the lofts. She listened carefully to Murray because the media received their information from scanning police radios and frequently had inaccurate data. The reporter assumed that "a shooting" meant only one victim.

She phoned Professional Mortuary Service, a company that the county contracted for transporting victims back to the medical examiner's for autopsies. The company would provide her with a van and two people, "her crew," as she called them. They would meet her at the scene.

Even though the police had requested ambulances, they were only present in the unlikely case that the victims were still alive.

Ray's kit always stood at the ready; it contained her Polaroid, a 35-millimeter camera, and a flash unit. She quickly went through the aluminum case, making sure her gloves, sacks for bagging victim's hands, and all the other equipment she would need were there. Always dressed for action, she wore a pair of comfortable slacks, a cotton shirt, and rubber-soled shoes.

She climbed into her white Chevy Lumina with the black, round Dallas County Medical Examiner logo on the door.

By 8:55 P.M., Gigi Ray was within a half block of the lofts. She could see the string of emergency vehicles and throngs of news media roaming the area. Photographers hoisted cameras on their shoulders, and reporters brandished microphones at anyone who would talk. The large white news vans had huge, extendible masts sitting atop their roofs, stretching almost to the fourth floor, which were used to transmit microwave signals back to the newsrooms.

At the loft entrance, Gigi identified herself to the young policeman manning the door. Entering the lobby, she asked a nearby officer if the next-of-kin were present. He nodded toward Mary Jean Pearle who was now sitting on the floor, calmly making calls on her cell phone. Gigi wasn't surprised that Mary Jean was so composed. She had seen that in other cases. Mary Jean might have been in a state of shock, or just exhausted.

Hurrying over the hexagon-tiled entry, the investigator found the elevator and was soon on her way to the fourth floor.

She stepped off into a swarm of activity. Uniformed police officers stood at each end of the hall, shotguns at the ready. They had the dual task of protecting people if John Battaglia decided to return, and of quizzing residents as they re-entered their lofts. Many residents stopped and asked questions. They listened to the officers, shook their heads in disbelief, then walked on more thoughtfully, more somberly, back to their lofts.

Ray's job was to be the eyes and ears for the medical examiners. She would write a detailed report of the scene for the doctors who would perform the autopsies the next morning. As she approached the entrance to Battaglia's loft, she joined a group of blue-uniformed officers standing in the hallway discussing the scene.

"How's it going?" she asked the first officer she encountered.

He shook his head. "It's a real cluster-fuck. They're still trying to figure out whether or not to get a search warrant."

She glanced inside and saw the body of one of the little girls lying in blood. She decided to wait for the arrival of PES before entering the loft.

Taking out a tablet and pen, she asked the policeman who had information for the medical examiner.

He nodded toward Zane Murray, the officer who had called her earlier. Murray was young and hyper and wanted to be out chasing Battaglia. But as one of the first officers on the crime scene, he was posted there until he received further orders. He filled Gigi in on what they knew about the murders. Murray was particularly worried about the way the 911 call had been handled. Since it had first been aired as a domestic disturbance call, officers had continued to take care of other calls until they learned that children had been shot.

As Gigi began writing her report, she could sense that everyone was concerned about Battaglia's whereabouts. All through the hall, officers had turned on their two-way radios, which periodically squawked with voices reporting the search efforts.

The absence of a warrant did not shackle the medical examiner. The bodies were under Ray's jurisdictional authority, and she could remove them without a police warrant as soon as she arrived on the scene. However, she opted not to do that because she worked hand in hand with CAPERS and PES, who had yet to take their pictures and gather all the details. Their jobs were based on teamwork and they had a deep mutual respect.

Once the people from the Physical Evidence Section arrived, they and Gigi slipped cotton booties over their shoes, pulled on latex gloves, and went inside.

First, the investigators did a walk-through of the scene. They would normally search to see if there had been a struggle and if blood was located anywhere else in the loft. Then, PES painstakingly went through and identified each piece of evidence with a yellow numbered placard before taking photographs.

THIRTY-TWO

Officer Dane Thornton remembered Mary Jean telling him that Battaglia had moved from Loft 316 only a couple of days before. If Battaglia had kept a key, that would be an ideal place to hide from the investigators and still stay close to the scene.

Thornton asked another officer, Sgt. Phil Carrillo, to accompany him. Both officers hurried down one flight to the third floor.

They knocked on the door of Loft 316, stepped back, and waited. There was no response. Thornton had a track record of ten motorcycle crashes while in pursuit of escaping motorists and bank robbers, which made him a legend but had also taken a toll on his body. Carrillo immediately volunteered to break down the door.

Carrillo raised his foot and swiftly cracked the jamb on his first attempt. Yelling "Police!" they dashed inside, guns at the ready and eyes darting into the yawning space. The layout was essentially the same as Battaglia's new apartment, only smaller.

The loft appeared empty, but the officers followed the same procedure they had upstairs to search the large walk-in closet and other smaller areas that could conceal a person. Without bodies, packing boxes, or furniture to hinder their search, they were able to secure the loft quickly and check it off their list of concerns.

Just to be on the safe side, they left an officer at the door in case Battaglia decided to return.

Mary Jean Pearle had been at the lofts for more than an hour. Now sitting on the lobby's floor, looking drained, she held tightly to her cell phone, which connected her to a support team of family and friends. Then she thought of Laurie Battaglia and immediately became frightened for the girl's safety. She quickly punched in Michelle Ghetti's phone number.

When Mary Jean heard Laurie's voice answer, she had trouble speaking. She swallowed hard, then said, "Honey, can I talk to your mother?"

"Hi, Mary Jean," Laurie replied. "How are the girls?"

Laurie's question stabbed her heart and she fought for composure. "Laurie, I need to speak to your mom."

In the background, Mary Jean heard Laurie calling Michelle. Soon Michelle picked up the receiver and said with a wry laugh, "Well, what's going on now?"

"Is Laurie off the phone?" Mary Jean asked.

They waited a few moments until they heard Laurie hang up her extension.

Then Mary Jean blurted, "John just shot the girls."

"That's not funny," Michelle said. "Don't make a joke out of something like that."

"It's no joke, Michelle! Just tonight! A little while ago John shot the girls in his loft while I was on the phone with Faith."

Michelle stifled a scream and ran outside so Laurie couldn't hear. "Oh, my God!" she cried. "This can't be happening!" She broke into loud, uncontrollable sobs. She fell into a wooden chair on her patio, unconsciously beating on its arm. "I can't believe it. That's so horrible!"

"He's still on the loose," Mary Jean warned. "The police haven't found him so that's why I'm calling. I'm worried that he might be heading to Baton Rouge to do something to y'all."

"Oh, dear Lord," Michelle murmured. She stifled a sob and thought how considerate Mary Jean was. Here, in the middle of her tragedy, she was thinking about them.

"Oh, Mary Jean. I am so, so sorry," Michelle managed. "That's just dreadful!" She wiped away the tears streaming down her face, then said, "I've got to decide what to do here. I'll call you back in a little bit."

Michelle immediately phoned her sister, Lisa Holmes who jumped in her car and hurried to Michelle's.

While she waited for her sister to arrive, Michelle sat in her den and took a deep breath, trying to calm herself. She recalled her concern about what John might do to Laurie—and now he had inflicted that wrath on those two sweet little kids. She had no idea how to tell her daughter, but she knew she had to get herself under control first.

Michelle somberly went into Laurie's room and revealed the devastating news. Laurie screamed and screamed, then broke into heart-wrenching sobs. She fell into her mother's arms. Michelle held her shaking daughter, but it was impossible to comfort her. Laurie had lost part of herself. She had lost her sisters.

* * *

Michelle was so relieved to hear her sister's car pull into her driveway. Lisa Holmes rushed inside and threw her arms around her sister and niece. They all held each other and cried.

Michelle had returned home only twenty minutes before Mary Jean phoned. She had driven Laurie home from her church youth group and had picked up fried chicken on the way. They had just finished eating when Mary Jean's call came in.

Sometime after her sister arrived, Michelle noticed that she had received three messages from John Battaglia. Now, after Mary Jean's call, she was more than anxious to hear them.

She played back the first message and listened to John's plea for her to ask Mary Jean to drop the charges so he wouldn't have to go back to jail. "Back to jail?" Before tonight, Michelle hadn't spoken with Mary Jean since Easter, so she didn't understand what John was talking about. But knowing what she knew now, his words, "Maybe that's what Mary Jean needs. To lose the girls," haunted her. She checked her recorder; he had left that message at noon.

A call came in later at 7:20 P.M., and another at 7:50. She saw that Battaglia had placed his last call to Laurie from his office, so she fast-forwarded to that one. Knowing what her ex-husband had done right before he left his message, she felt sick at the sound of his voice. But she couldn't help being shocked at how calm he sounded.

"Hey, Orie," Battaglia said. "This is Ba-ba . . ." Michelle listened to him describe how he was sending basically all of his money to Laurie. "This is your college money. Put it in an account and invest it. Save it for college, okay? Love you sweetheart . . ."

Michelle stared at her recorder. She had the chilling thought that he was about to commit suicide.

The most logical places police thought to look for Battaglia were his two separate business locations. First, they checked out his office on nearby Fairmount Street. Six months after his divorce, he had been evicted from the office above Dorrace Pearle's antique store. Always staying close to maintain vigilance on his ex-wife, he had moved his private CPA practice to a small, two-story building only a few blocks away.

The property manager unlocked the door to Battaglia's second-story office for the police. Shouting "Police!" they entered the small room. Numerous crayon drawings decorated the walls, but there was no indication that John Battaglia had been there. Police stationed an officer at his business just in case.

John Battaglia also worked for the Arcturus Corporation, which was located on Ross Avenue in a distinctive downtown high-rise. Because of an open space near the top floors, it was sometimes called the "key building."

In addition to two patrol officers, a tactical officer accompanied Dane Thornton to the Arcturus Corporation. The building's security officer met them in the lobby, where the police explained their mission. The uniformed security man reached for his roster and saw that John Battaglia had signed in an hour earlier at 7:40 P.M. The police wondered out loud if Battaglia could still be up in his fifty-third-floor office.

The security officer accompanied them to the elevator that whisked them up to the Arcturus Corporation's floor. He unlocked the door to the reception area. The police drew their guns and went inside. Starting at one end of the floor, they began securing each room in every office, looking behind doors, opening closets, and checking the large, built-in cabinets. They reached the office that belonged to John Battaglia. In the corner on top of a file cabinet sat a photo in which he knelt, smiling, with both arms around his daughters. The terrible irony of the picture struck everyone. Thornton picked up the photo to use for identification of the suspect.

The computer's screensaver cast a glow over the room, but one touch of the mouse revealed that he had been on the Internet. The screen message read, "John has not sent or received data for twenty minutes." The police had no idea how long he had stayed in his office. Before entering, they had spent almost seven minutes securing the area; it was possible that he could have passed them on another elevator as they were climbing toward his office.

The four policemen and the security officer dashed out of the office and ran to the elevator. Battaglia had eluded them, but they were getting closer.

THIRTY-THREE

When Officer Zane Murray was released from guard duty at the crime scene, he and fellow officer Ray Rojas were assigned to search the rest of the Adam Hats Lofts building. Adrenaline pumping, they first headed for the roof. Opening a trapdoor in the fourth-floor ceiling, they pulled down the overhead stairs that would take them to the attic and, eventually, the roof. They found the door opening to the outside, and cautiously peered around the roof before taking their first steps onto the tar and gravel surface. They saw many possible hiding places. Two large advertising billboards sat at perpendicular angles, lit by spotlights anchored to the roof. A large metal water tank stood on stilts, probably a relic from the days when the building had been a Ford assembly plant.

In order to give cover, the officers searched with their guns drawn and their backs to each other. The area was large and the probability high that someone could be watching, and change hiding places as the officers moved from point to point. Using their flashlights, they thoroughly checked around the water tank. They scrutinized the billboards but, with so much light from the spotlights, those would be unlikely hiding places. After several more min-

utes of fruitless searching, they concluded that the
roof was secure.

The loft residents had begun to file out of their
apartments. Some had heard the commotion in the
streets, and those facing Canton saw the spinning
lights on the emergency vehicles. Because of the
building's thick concrete walls, others had heard
nothing and only learned about the shootings when
they turned on the ten o'clock news. Every television
channel's lead story was the murder in the Adam
Hats Lofts.

One first-floor resident, Sandy Wilhert, a young,
pretty blonde, had been watching the news at ten
and "freaked out" when she heard what had happened in her own building. In 1997, she had been
the first resident to sign up for a loft and had always
felt safe. She ran outside and grabbed the first officer she saw to find out what was going on.

As the officer gave her a synopsis of the murders,
she felt a chill run through her body. She remembered those cute little girls skating in the lobby over
the past several months. They had seemed like
sullen, unhappy children; they looked like they
didn't want to be there. She had felt sorry for them.

"I've seen a lot," the weary officer said, as he tried
in vain to stop the tears forming in his eyes. "But,
God, this is so horrible!"

They watched a man try to enter the lofts with two
dogs he had taken out before all the commotion
started. Now the dogs barked and howled, refusing
to enter the building.

"We're looking for Battaglia's car," the officer told
Sandy. "I think he drives a small black sports car."

She didn't know anyone named Battaglia, but when the officer described him, he sounded like the man who had a reserved space next to hers in the basement parking garage. But that man drove a truck.

More residents began milling around. They grumbled that a background check was supposed to be run on anyone who wanted to rent a loft. What kind of guy was this? The management had allowed a murderer to move in?

Sandy kept thinking about the good-looking man who had the parking space next to hers. He was perfectly nice, but not chatty or overly friendly. She didn't see him in the mornings, but rather after work hours when he was dressed in clean-pressed jeans and a T-shirt. He kept his shiny black truck so clean she could see her face in it.

She told the policeman that the man they were looking for sounded like the one who parked next to her, but that he didn't drive a sports car. She gave a description of his truck, and agreed to accompany the police to the garage.

Down in the dimly lit basement, they found only a grease spot where Battaglia usually parked. Officers fanned out and began peering into large dumpsters and rummaging through the garage. It became apparent to Sandy that the officers had no idea where Battaglia was.

The police left one officer in the parking garage while the others went back upstairs to speak to Mary Jean.

With so many officers on the scene, communication became confused, and information was needlessly duplicated. The officer Sandy had talked with didn't know that Mary Jean had already told the police that Battaglia drove a silver and black F-150 Ford 4x4 truck. An all-points bulletin was radioed throughout the city, advising every officer to be on the lookout.

The thought of her friends and family in potential jeopardy had alarmed Mary Jean all evening. She kept thinking of friends whom John Battaglia would also know. As they entered her mind, she would give police their names and addresses.

Dallas police scoured the city. They went to Melissa Lowder's house to make sure that her children were safe, and left an officer there with the baby-sitter. They drove to the house of another of Mary Jean's friends, Karen Rogers, who was just returning home. Police escorted her baby-sitter to her car.

Other officers rushed to Mary Jean's house on Lorraine in case Battaglia had gone there and was hiding, waiting to torment her further. As they entered to search her home, they met her live-in babysitter, Anna Castillo, in the front entry. They had the sorrowful task of breaking the news that the two children she loved and cared for daily had been murdered. Anna had a daughter who was one year younger than Liberty; they had been best friends. Anna had felt like a second mother to Faith and Liberty, and hearing of their deaths sent her into screaming, sobbing hysterics.

One of John Battaglia's friends, Candy Bristol, had been irritated with him the last time they went out, but he was hoping she'd have cooled down by now. Three weeks ago, they had been at a bar where several men were overly friendly to her. She had cuddled up to her admirers with smiles and conversation, and afterwards John had let her know just how he felt about being ignored. Hopefully she had forgiven him and would be willing to be with him tonight. He turned his truck toward Candy's house. She lived over by lower Greenville, an area well supplied with bars and places to have a good time.

Battaglia knocked on Candy's door but there was no answer. He then drove his truck down her alley to check for any lights in the back of the house. Could she have seen him at her door and be ignoring him? So intent was he on trying to see inside her house, he drove straight into Candy's trash cans, crushing all of them.

He cursed under his breath, quickly got out of the alley, and pulled onto the street. There were plenty of girls. Another friend, Missy Campbell, lived in an apartment in the lower Oak Lawn area.

Battaglia parked in front of Missy's tattered building. He had dated Missy several times. He liked her tousled blond hair, which made her look sexy, like she had just tumbled out of bed. Or better still, like maybe she was ready to tumble in. She was different, but he needed a diversion. By social class, lifestyle, or any other measure, she was nothing like the women he would find in the Park Cities, but that's what he wanted. She never locked her door. Friends were always welcome. If anyone had had too much to drink or too many drugs, they knew it would be perfectly all right to crash at Missy's.

John Battaglia knocked briefly, then opened the door.

"Anybody here?" he called as he glanced around the sparsely furnished apartment. He heard nothing. He started to walk through the living room, but felt his stomach begin to lurch and tighten. He felt dizzy and disoriented from the tranquilizers he had taken before his drinks, and rushed to the bathroom. The last thing he remembered was hitting the hard linoleum floor.

It was after ten when Missy Campbell shoved open the door to her apartment and went inside with her date, Bobby Phillips.

She went to the refrigerator and grabbed two cans of Coors, popping the tops. Taking them back to the living room, she sat down with Bobby on the sofa and they began to chat. After a few minutes, Bobby excused himself to use the bathroom.

Missy heard him talking in the bathroom, and wondered what was going on. He couldn't be hallucinating; he was the straightest person she knew. He never used any kind of recreational drugs.

"Missy, come here!" he yelled. "You've got some guy passed out on the floor in here."

She ran to the bathroom and found John Battaglia stretched out between the tub and the toilet. She bent down and shook him. "John, John, wake up," she said. "What the hell's wrong with you?"

John groaned as Missy shook his shoulder. His eyes fluttered open momentarily; then he slipped back into his stupor. Missy continued shaking him until she had his attention.

"John, what's happened? You were out cold."

John Battaglia's eyes squinted in the bright, sterile light. He shook his head, trying to clear it.

Missy and Bobby pulled him to his knees, then got him on his feet. They half-pulled, half-dragged him to the living room and plopped him down on the worn couch.

Battaglia managed a sleepy grin. "I took some pills," he confessed. "They were downers, but they didn't do a damn bit of good."

"You look pretty fucking down to me," Missy said.

"What I need is to wake up. I could use a little speed," John told her. He reached for the pipe that he had shoved in his pants pocket. It was wrapped inside a plastic baggie and had a grainy substance stuffed into the bowl. "Be a doll and light this shit for me," he said.

Missy picked up a lighter and held it under the bowl of his glass pipe. Her date saw what was happening and left, slamming the door loudly behind him.

Battaglia watched the gravel-like powder sink down in the bowl as it gradually melted into oil. He could have taken the methaphetamine through a needle, but that hurt. Snorting didn't get him high fast enough, so smoking was his favorite option. He sucked deeply on the pipe, and the smoke rushed into his lungs, coating the membrane, then into his sinus cavities and quickly to his brain. He had been resting his head on the back of the sofa, and now he sat up, looking more alert. He pulled again on the pipe and exhaled with a smile. "That's better," he said. He was happy and lightheaded when he handed the pipe to Missy for a drag.

"You know what I want to do?" he asked.

Missy shrugged.

"I want to get a tattoo. I'll get one for you too. Sound okay?"

Missy smiled. "Hell yes, that'd be okay. I've been

wanting a pretty little yellow butterfly. Right there," she said, pointing to her right shoulder.

John Battaglia had met Missy through her brother, Gary, shortly after he moved to Deep Ellum. Her brother owned a bar, and John had become friends with him there. Gary introduced John to his sister because he thought she needed the stability of an educated, nice-looking guy. In Gary's view, Battaglia was a real solid citizen—and he had such a calm manner. It impressed Gary that Battaglia spent a lot of time with his kids. John frequently had his children at his loft and talked about them all the time. Gary thought he was a great dad.

Gary also knew that Battaglia wanted a different lifestyle after he split from his wife. His sister may have been more than John had bargained for; after he started running around with Missy, John got caught up in drugs again.

John Battaglia finished his pipe and fumbled for the keys to his truck. "Before we get the tattoos, let's go get some fucking cocaine," he suggested.

Michelle Ghetti called a friend with the Louisiana State Police to see if he could check the airlines; she wanted to find out whether or not John was on a plane heading to Baton Rouge. Her friend put her in touch with Sergeant Brooks of the Baton Rouge police, who set up a patrol of her house and contacted the Dallas police, who began checking the airlines.

Michelle and her children packed a suitcase and went to her sister's to spend the night. Michelle wanted to hear John's messages again, and Laurie showed her how to retrieve them while away from home. Michelle listened to all three, but she misunderstood Laurie's directions. Trying to save the messages, she hit the wrong number, and erased every one.

Michelle, her sister, and Laurie had almost memorized John's messages and wrote out everything they could remember. Michelle called Mary Jean's cell number; Mary Jean told her that an officer wanted to talk with her. Michelle told the officer that Battaglia had called her three times that day. The officer was particularly disturbed when Michelle said that Battaglia had called Laurie at 7:20 P.M., right after he had murdered the girls. The officer questioned why John was trying to contact his only living daughter.

THIRTY-FOUR

Shortly before midnight, John Battaglia parked his truck in a lot near Cafe Brazil, and he and Missy opened their doors and floated out onto the parking lot and into the Pharmacy Bar for drinks before buying an eight ball of cocaine. John was flying on tranquilizers, speed, and alcohol, and Missy wasn't far behind. Anyone trailing him that evening would have surmised that he was trying to commit suicide.

As they strolled over to Elm Street Tattoo and Body Piercing, John said, "I want to get two big roses on my left arm. One for each of my little girls."

"Why?" Missy asked.

"So I'll always have them with me. Nobody can take them away if they're tattooed on my arm."

Missy glanced up at John's glassy eyes and thought he made no sense. *Must be the cocaine talking,* she thought.

Battaglia pushed open the door of the tattoo parlor, which the management insisted be kept hospital clean. The place looked like a beauty shop, with half-walls constructed between booths for privacy. An adjustable chair in each booth rotated to any position, allowing a tattoo to be pricked onto any area of the body the customer requested.

Tattoo artist Madeline Eltran greeted them.

"Hi guys," she said. "We're about to close. What can I do for you?"

"We'd like a couple tattoos," Battaglia answered.

"It's almost midnight. How about coming back tomorrow?"

"Tomorrow won't be good," John said firmly. "I've got to get the tattoo tonight. I'll be in jail tomorrow."

"What for?" Missy asked, looking startled. Then, remembering his history, she guessed, "Probation violation?"

"Something like that," Battaglia said.

Madeline glanced at her watch.

"I'll make it worth your time," Battaglia told her. "I'll throw in extra for the overtime. What say?" He grinned a silly, cocaine-induced smile. "It would mean a lot to me." He pulled out three one-hundred-dollar bills.

"Oh, all right," Madeline said. "What did you have in mind?"

Battaglia walked over to a wall where dozens of design templates hung for customers to choose from. "I like this big rose," he said, pointing to a flower with a three-inch diameter. "I'd want a couple, but I'd like them strung together. You know, with something like black barbed wire? You don't have any wire here."

"No problem, Madeline said. "I could sketch in the wire. That's easy."

"Easy for an artist," John said, giving her a wink. "How about one red and one yellow?"

Madeline nodded, and guided him to a rack that held hundreds of vials of ink in every imaginable color.

"They're fragile. Just point and I'll put them in my tattoo gun."

Battaglia was familiar with the procedure. He had gotten three other tattoos from the place. Madeline picked up a gun that looked like a tiny, handheld sewing machine. She inserted a vial of bright yellow. One touch of the "on" button and the ink-filled needle would begin pulsating up and down.

After choosing the red he wanted, John staggered over to Madeline's booth, pulled off his T-shirt, and sat down.

Madeline admired the lion's head on his left shoulder and said she would start the roses an inch under the lion. She swabbed his arm with alcohol, then pressed the rose template against his skin and traced the flower in two different places. She picked up a fine felt-point pen and began sketching barbed wire. The complete design filled the space between the lion on his shoulder to a point right above his elbow.

John glanced at the design and announced that it was "perfect!"

Madeline pulled on Latex gloves. "This might smart a bit," she said as she picked up the gun.

After all that Battaglia had ingested, he didn't feel a thing.

Madeline continued to chatter as she worked. She often talked to put her clients at ease, but John wasn't the least bit nervous. In fact, he was a very willing talker himself. He told her about being a CPA, about having been in the Marines, and about every other facet of his life. Periodically, Madeline would wipe away the pinpoints of blood that accumulated as she continued injecting the needle.

While John got his tattoo, Missy strolled over to the templates and chose a dainty butterfly. Madeline looked over and smiled. "That will be easy," she told Missy, then went back to decorating John's arm.

* * *

The death investigator, Gigi Ray, found Battaglia's loft emotionally cold and sterile. Certainly not a place for children. On the other hand, it seemed like the home of a very egotistical man. Most of John Battaglia's clothes were designer. In fact, the entire loft was about him.

Ray took out her Polaroid and began snapping photos to accompany her report. She took a close-up of each girl, then paced a few steps back and shot again to include more of the surrounding area for the doctors to use as reference for the autopsies. After that, she pulled out her 35-millimeter camera and took slides that would show the overall appearance of the room. She shot a photo of the bunk beds, and realized that Battaglia had been building bookcases for the girls to use as a room divider. She found that puzzling. If he had long-range plans that included his daughters, why had he just murdered them? She continued taking pictures, capturing the spent bullets and the massive gun collection.

It was her job to pronounce the victims dead. She didn't need to touch these children or check for a pulse to know that they were dead. In fact, rigor mortis was starting to settle in. She had written in her report: "21:30- Pronunciation." She found the whole scene extremely disturbing.

Ever since then, the loft had been buzzing with investigators. The entire fourth floor was jammed with officers milling around the hall and clustered near the entrance. The whole place was growing crowded and noisy. Cell phones rang. Officers called in their reports. Others, working long past their shifts, left messages that they would be home much later that night. Michelle Ghetti called twice from Baton Rouge. Ray called her supervisor back at the ME's office to tell her that she'd be late because the search warrant had not yet arrived.

The PES cameras recorded everything in the loft, especially the girls, all Battaglia's weapons and the exact placement of the guns.

By midnight, Ray could see how difficult it was for the police to work with the little bodies lying only a few feet away. It was old hat for PES, but those who didn't deal with death on a daily basis were keeping their distance from the bodies, walking along paths as far away from them as possible. Their faces looked tired and strained as the evening wore on. She felt it would be easier for police to work if the bodies weren't there, so she talked to Detective Elton Fite from the Child Abuse Section about removing them. He agreed that there was no need to wait on the search warrant's arrival.

She studied both girls. She knew that all the blood and other trace evidence might be lost if the bodies were simply picked up and placed on gurneys. She decided to first wrap them in clean white sheets, then put them in crash bags.

The bags were stored in the trunk of her car. Ray hurried out of the building, and inhaled deeply as the cool air touched her skin and gave her a respite from the loft's claustrophobic atmosphere. However, once she stepped outside, the media quickly came to life and watched to see where she was going. When she retrieved two crash bags from the trunk of her car, the media made hurried calls on their cell phones and ran to their vans to report the deaths of *two* children, as opposed to one. Ever since the media heard the initial report from scanning police radios, they believed there had been only one victim.

Ray ignored the frenzy and dashed back inside. When she returned, she told her crew there was a problem. "The victims' grandmother is down there and reporters won't leave her alone. There's no way we can get through that crowd with the children's bodies."

One officer mentioned that there was a garage in the basement.

"Good, let's do this," Ray said. "When we put the girls in the bags, we can take them down in the elevator to the basement." She turned to one of her crew, "Dick, you bring the van into the parking garage from the street and we'll load up there."

Gigi Ray unzipped a black crash bag, opening it almost flat. With latex-gloved hands, she helped the crew pick up Liberty and place her on a sheet. After so much time, full rigor mortis had set in. She was so stiff that her arms and legs held their frozen position as she was raised from the floor. She looked like a statue of a child sprayed with red paint. A PES investigator took her photo. Ray watched and nodded, thinking, *a jury would be swayed by that.* After the sheet was wrapped securely, the body was zipped into the crash bag. Then they went to the kitchen to get Faith.

THIRTY-FIVE

Detective Katherine Justice pulled off her glasses and rubbed her tired eyes. She couldn't imagine how Mary Jean was holding up.

Mary Jean's mother tolerated a number of reporters' questions, but she'd periodically come by to talk with her daughter. They both would cry; then they'd dry their eyes. They would try to discuss something else, but the tears would invariably return.

Justice said to Mary Jean, "It's still not safe for you to go home since John hasn't been caught. How about my taking you to a hotel over on Mockingbird and maybe you could get some rest? Anything would be better than this."

Mary Jean nodded. They decided that Dorrace, Melissa, and the detective would accompany Mary Jean to the hotel.

The all-points bulletin had reached every officer within earshot of a radio. For four hours, more than one hundred police officers had been looking for John Battaglia and his silver and black Ford pickup. They drove up and down the streets in the Central Business District, then broadened their search to cover the entire city of Dallas. Everyone's computer screen displayed a description of Battaglia and his truck.

On that clear Wednesday night, visibility was good, but there was no sign of Battaglia.

Possibilities multiplied in the minds of police. John Battaglia had money. He could be on his way to Mexico, Canada, or just about anyplace he wanted to be. In the hour between the time he had allegedly killed the children and when the search began he could have run out to the Dallas/Fort Worth airport and boarded the next plane leaving for anywhere. By now the police had searched the huge airport parking lots, but his truck had not been spotted. Detectives pored over passenger departure lists, but his name wasn't on them; still, he could have used an alias. When the Baton Rouge police alerted them to the possibility that he was on his way to do away with his last living daughter, they again searched the passenger lists to Baton Rouge. It was as though John Battaglia had disappeared into thin air.

Around midnight, Senior Corporal Lowell Bryant, a plainclothes detective and a thirteen-year police veteran, was making yet another sweep of the area surrounding the lofts, an area that police had been patrolling all night. He was in his unmarked police car and dressed in civilian clothes. As he crossed the intersection of Elm Street and Malcolm X, the officer's eyes widened as he spotted a black and silver truck sitting in the parking lot near Cafe Brazil. He checked to see that the license plate matched. Somehow, he knew it would. After all the miles police had put on their cars tonight, the truck was only blocks from Battaglia's loft. Bryant picked up the portable mike to his radio and called headquarters to relate his discovery of the truck, and its location. His heart raced knowing how close he was.

Bryant pulled into another parking lot, catty-corner to the one Battaglia's truck was in. He parked behind some trees, turned off his lights, and waited.

The news flashed through the ranks like lightning. Officers Zane Murray and Ray Rojas had been working the case for almost five hours. Once they heard that Battaglia's truck had been spotted, they jumped in their car and took off.

One by one, officers began arriving at the parking lot. They stayed hidden so when Battaglia came for his truck, they wouldn't have a chase on their hands. They discounted the idea of checking out nearby businesses because the APB said that he was armed and dangerous and they didn't want to start a shoot-out in a place where innocent bystanders could be hurt.

More police raced in from surrounding districts, many whose shifts had ended hours earlier. Once they were this close to Battaglia, it was too important and too exciting to go home. The gruesome crime scene and the murdered children lying in the loft had ignited the officers' determination to see John Battaglia arrested tonight.

Officers Murray and Rojas parked in the rear of the lot, waiting and watching Battaglia's truck. The lot began filling with blue-and-whites discreetly parked in the rear, but anyone looking for police could have easily spotted them.

They continued waiting.

As the minutes ticked by, they began to wonder if Battaglia had parked his truck and caught a ride with someone else. Maybe this was a ruse, a clever ploy to distract the police and make them think that Battaglia was nearby.

Just before 2:00 A.M., police saw a dark figure emerge from one of the shops and walk toward the truck. They could see his white shirt and dark pants. But police had no description of Battaglia's clothes, so they didn't know what to look for.

The next event would leave them no doubt. The figure took out his remote control and hit the button to unlock the truck. A brief taillight flash accompanied a high-pitched beep. This was definitely their man.

"Armed and dangerous" played in the officers' ears, and they drew their guns.

"John Battaglia you are under arrest," shouted Officer Murray. Lights came on from the encircling squad cars; the parking lot lit up like a football field. By then, Battaglia had opened the door to his truck and appeared to be rummaging inside.

The officer yelled, "Show me your hands!" Several others approached the truck, including Bryant, who had been the first to find Battaglia's vehicle. Each officer aimed his pistol with both hands, his feet spread wide in firing stance.

John proceeded as if he hadn't heard them.

At this point, Battaglia was completely surrounded. With a nod from Murray, four officers circled behind John. His head and shoulders were still inside the truck and he appeared to be searching for something. The officers who had slipped behind him yelled again for him to show his hands. John spun around and doubled his fist, hitting the first officer on the chin.

Battaglia appeared to be deaf and blind. There were at least twenty-five blue suits surrounding him, in addition to plainclothes detectives. The police encountered this kind of behavior most commonly when the suspect was either drunk or stoned. One officer speculated that Battaglia wanted a "suicide by cop" because he didn't have the guts to shoot himself.

Battaglia's punch was their license to attack. With Battaglia still swinging, the four officers jumped him and returned his punches. Four sets of arms swung angrily at Battaglia and he fought them as if he hoped to get away. The sounds of grunting and shuffling were heard through the flying dust. Then all four went down with him onto the dirty pavement. Even as he lay on the ground, the police yelled, "Show me your hands," but Battaglia stubbornly kept them pinned to his sides. The police had no idea if he were concealing a knife or gun. Bryant sat on top of Battaglia, who was still struggling. Quickly, the officer placed his right arm around Battaglia's neck, squeezing with his bicep and forearm. With his other hand, he grasped the carotid arteries that supply blood to the brain. He squeezed tighter. Battaglia tried to reach up and pry off the officer's arm so he could catch his breath. In that brief moment, another officer was able to grab Battaglia's hands and slap cuffs around his wrists. Then two officers jerked him to his feet.

John Battaglia's reddened face showed the effort he had put forth. His right eye began swelling, and blood oozed from minor cuts on his face. He bent his head soberly as officers led him toward a squad car.

Crime scene investigator James Vineyard searched

the truck. He spotted a pistol lying on the front seat near the armrest and assumed Battaglia had been reaching for it. Checking the gun, he found it was loaded.

Once Battaglia was securely locked in the squad car, police spent a few minutes filling out forms, writing in times and jotting down details while every aspect of the arrest was still fresh in their minds.

While reports were being written, John Battaglia sat in the backseat of the car. He appeared unaware of the video camera mounted up by the rearview mirror. The drugs had possibly blurred his mind, as he gave no indication that he knew what was going on. He was photographed yawning, looking out the window, and appearing mildly disinterested in the activities taking place. He watched a couple dozen police mill around. Then he yawned again.

Missy Campbell turned her right shoulder to get a better look at her new yellow butterfly while she talked with her tattoo artist.

"You do such pretty work," Missy told Madeline. "I've always wanted a butterfly. Then when John suggested . . ." She stopped talking and frowned.

"Hey, where's John? I wonder what's keeping him. It shouldn't take him so damn long to get cigarettes."

"He's probably outside smoking," Madeline suggested. "He's paid for everything so you can leave."

"Guess I'll go outside and see what the hell he's doing," Missy said as she walked out the door.

The squad cars still had their lights on when Missy stumbled into the parking lot. She squinted, then shaded her eyes with her hand. Seeing all the police made her dizzy and disoriented. She found John's truck, and saw two policemen systematically combing its interior. But John was nowhere in sight.

Two officers approached her. "Can I do something for you?" Officer Jay Clinton asked.

"What's going on?" Missy asked in bewilderment.

"May I help you, ma'am?" Clinton repeated, unwilling to give her information without knowing her identity.

"I'm looking for my date. He just came out for cigarettes a while ago. Should have been back by now. That's his truck there."

"John Battaglia?" one officer said.

Missy looked shocked that they knew his name.

"He's over in that squad car," Clinton told her, pointing. "We just arrested him for murder."

Missy frowned in disbelief. "That's impossible!" she said. "I've been with him all night."

"Were you together around seven this evening?"

Missy paused for a moment, then said, "No, I didn't see him till after ten. Who are you sayin' he killed?" she asked timidly.

When the officer told her that he was charged with murdering his daughters, Missy's mouth opened in disbelief. Then the reality of the situation sank in, and she screamed and began crying hysterically. She covered her face with her hands, and her entire body shook. She didn't want to believe what the police were saying. It just couldn't be true. Then John's words came back to her, *I want to get two big roses tattooed on my left arm. One for each of my little girls. . . . So I'll always have them with me. . . . Tomorrow won't be good. . . . I'll be in jail tomorrow.*

THIRTY-SIX

A young officer strolled over to a very distraught Missy Campbell. She sat crying on the concrete parking lot, her yellow sundress wrinkled and dirty.

"Ms. Campbell, we need your help," the officer told her as he offered a hand to pull her up from the broken concrete. "You're not a suspect, but we'd like to ask you a few questions. We need some idea of what you and John Battaglia were doing tonight."

Missy had trouble speaking through her sobs. "I need to talk with my brother first."

"Tell you what," the officer said. "We'll drive you to headquarters where you can make a statement and also call your brother."

Missy agreed, and when the police took John Battaglia to headquarters, she was in the squad car directly behind his. She sank deeper into the fabric of the car seat and wept during the entire trip downtown.

Officer Casey Clark transported Battaglia to police headquarters, while Ray Rojas sat next to the suspect in the backseat. After the squad car pulled out of the parking lot, John leaned forward and pointed to the police computer. "What kind of software do you have on that?" he asked. The officers glanced quizzically at each other as they answered his questions, but no one spoke about the murders.

As they pulled up to headquarters, Battaglia said, "Isn't this the same place Ruby came when he shot Lee Harvey Oswald?" The officers told him it was. Shaking their heads over his demeanor, they led him inside and down the hall for fingerprinting. Detectives from CAPERS would soon be there to see if he would talk.

At headquarters, the police helped Missy out of the car and ushered her into an office where she gave a statement somberly outlining the evening partying with John. Then she sat whimpering in the waiting room until her brother arrived.

Missy Campbell shared her Oak Lawn apartment with her brother Gary, who also happened to be her best friend. She knew that she could call him at any hour and he would be there for her. She had phoned him right before she gave her statement to the police. On the phone, Gary first asked her if she was stoned. When she finally convinced him of the murders, he was as shocked as she was.

Arriving at police headquarters, Gary walked down the hall past darkened offices, and entered the waiting room where Missy sat on a tan plastic and chrome chair. She had pulled her feet onto the seat of the chair and was hugging her ankles and crying with her face buried in her knees.

"Hey, sis," Gary said.

She looked up, somewhat relieved, but her face was wet and her eyes were swollen. He took hold of her shoulders and pulled her up. Then he hugged and tried to soothe her, but her grief was beyond comforting. Her brother guided her to his car and opened the door for her. She sat in a stupor, still suffering from the nightmare.

"Wanna talk?" he asked.

She raised her head and stared out the windshield.

"It would make you feel better," Gary suggested.

"I just can't fucking believe it," she began. "It freaks me out!"

"Did John say anything about what happened? You know, about the girls?" Gary asked.

"Not one goddamn thing. He was the same old, good-guy John. Happy, talkative, laughing all the time. He sounded so normal, so much like himself. He acted like he was having such a good time. Gary, I can't believe this shit, he was even telling jokes!"

"He didn't mention his kids?"

"Not anything about shooting them. And you know how much he loved them. None of this crap makes sense. He was never a big drinker. Never raised his voice. Never fought anyone. What he's being accused of just doesn't fit worth a damn."

"He hated his wife," Gary said. "She was really rotten to him. Tried like hell to keep his kids from him. John said she used the kids like pawns to get back at him."

"Yeah, but I can't imagine him hurting his girls," Missy said. "John always seemed so even tempered. So fucking cool all the time. Whenever a fight broke out, he'd leave. Never wanted anything to do with that crap."

"Remember how he'd bring his kids along when we'd go to the lake?" Gary reminded her. "It was like he couldn't get enough of them." He smiled at the thought. "I can still see him driving that black Mustang convertible and the kids' hair blowing around and everybody laughing."

"He's the last person in this fucking world I'd suspect of killing anyone," Missy said. "It's like he's two different people."

"Yeah," Gary said. "John must have snapped. Just goddamn snapped."

Mary Jean had not slept all night. Visions of her daughters' faces burned into her mind. She could still see Liberty hiding underneath her bed, not wanting to go to her father's. She could still feel the touch of Liberty's little hand as she pulled her out.

Faith's sad face and her somber expression wouldn't leave Mary Jean's memory. *Why? Why? Why?* She had had so many chances. She could have just said no when Kelly called to ask if the girls would still be meeting with John. She berated herself for not listening to her children. They didn't want to be with their father that night, so why hadn't she just told them they could stay home? In the back of her mind were the court visitations ordered by their divorce decree, but there was also that warrant for probation violation that would soon be served. She knew that this might have been his last visit with the girls for a very long time.

Also, Mary Jean realized that John had never hurt the girls. He had never even spanked them or raised his voice to them. What ominous sign could she have seen that would have hinted he could kill them? In her grief, she pounded her pillow with her fist while she cried continuously. She was consumed with guilt.

She had delivered her children into the hands of their killer.

Mary Jean had asked Detective Justice to call her when they caught John, but it wasn't until after 2:00 A.M. that the detective tapped on her door to tell Mary Jean that John Battaglia had been arrested. Mary Jean fell into the detective's arms and hugged her and cried. She went through all of the evening's emotions all over again. But the news gave Mary Jean some comfort; at least she felt safe. John was finally locked up where he should have been years ago, if only the system had worked.

Katherine left and Mary Jean went back to bed. Although she was exhausted from the evening's nightmare, she could not sleep. She looked at her watch as the first gray traces of light filtered through her hotel window. Five A.M. She needed to get home. She wanted to walk into her comfortable house, see her daughters' room, touch their clothes, and see their photographs. "Oh God," she moaned loudly, "what am I going to do without them? They were my hopes, my dreams!"

THIRTY-SEVEN

As soon as Mary Jean told Detective Justice that she wanted to leave the hotel, the detective and Melissa Lowder drove her home. When they came to Lorraine, her beautiful home still looked the same to her, except that there were no little girls running across the broad lawn or up the long driveway. That brought more tears.

She got out of the car and walked into her foyer. Her baby-sitter, Anna, came running to her, crying hysterically. The women hugged one another and cried.

The police had stayed with Anna until John Battaglia had been arrested, and then left her to curl up with her five-year-old daughter and sob the rest of the night.

Mary Jean entered the kitchen and noticed the flashing red light on her answering machine. Before she had left to take the children to meet John, she had listened to and erased all of her messages. She assumed these new calls were from friends who had heard about the killings. Today, Thursday morning, *The Dallas Morning News* opened with the front-page headline: FATHER SOUGHT IN SLAYING OF DAUGHTERS. The newspaper included an interview with Dorrace Pearle at the lofts. She told reporters about John's phone call, and the tragedy that followed. The paper had gone to press before John was apprehended, but morning radio and television news shows broke the news of his capture and the details of the murders. Suddenly, John Battaglia became Dallas's most hated man.

Mary Jean hit the "play" button and listened to the first message. She froze when she heard Faith's voice. "Hi Mom. Give us a call, okay? Give us a call."

That sad reminder brought another avalanche of tears. Mary Jean walked into her den and collapsed on her sofa. She couldn't listen to any more messages.

After several moments, she stood up and wearily went to the stairs and pulled herself up by the banister. She wanted to go to her daughters' room. Maybe she would feel a little closer to them in those familiar surroundings. She stood in the hallway outside their room and took a deep breath to brace herself. She neared the door, and, for a moment, she could only lean against the doorjamb as she took in the scene. She blotted her eyes with Kleenex and realized that she had cried almost continuously since she had first heard her daughter's voice on the phone, screaming for mercy.

She glanced at a heap of white, fuzzy teddy bears—so many that they were piled into a pyramid on the floor. It was difficult to look at the blue-and-white checkered gingham quilted spread and dust ruffle. She thought of the many times she had entered this room to wake her girls, and she remembered watching them sleep, tucked under their pristine, checkered sheets.

Her eyes wandered to their collection of dolls, but she was immediately distracted. A light flickered on their answering machine. She wondered why there would be a message. Then she thought that a little friend may have called to tell her she was sorry about the girls.

Absently, she made her way over to the machine and pushed "play." Horror swept over her when she heard John Battaglia's voice.

In a smooth tone laced with mockery he said, "Hi, girls. I just want to tell you how very very brave you were, and I hope you are resting in a better place now. I wish that you had nothing to do with your mother. She's evil and vicious and stupid!"

Mary Jean's friends came running from the kitchen when they heard her screams.

As parents dropped off their children at Bradfield Elementary School, the flag was at half-mast for Faith and Liberty. Parents and students gathered in hushed clusters, trying to make sense of the tragedy that *The Dallas Morning News* had reported as its front-page story.

All the frills that Highland Park schools possessed had no magic to soothe the grief everyone was experiencing. Earlier, the staff had called the parents of Faith and Liberty's classmates to let them know that professional counselors would be available.

Paul Johnson was fighting the Thursday morning traffic on Highway 30 from his home in Mesquite— a thriving southeast Dallas suburb—to his office on Market Street near downtown. When the criminal defense attorney's cell phone rang, his plans changed. He'd be going to the Crowley Court Building instead. Judge Janice Warder of Criminal District Court No. 1 wanted to talk to him.

At home, over his morning coffee Johnson had scanned the newspaper and read that police were looking for a John Battaglia, whose ex-wife had accused him of killing their two young daughters. The front-page article was hard to miss, and now the judge wanted to talk to Paul about it.

He pulled into the multileveled parking garage at the Crowley Courts Building and took the elevator up to the sixth floor.

Judge Warder had presided over the First District Court for twelve years, and now she had been assigned the Battaglia case, along with a list of prospective court-appointed attorneys. All judges dread having their cases overturned on appeal, and "inadequate legal counsel" is one of the first areas scrutinized by an appellate court. The judge wanted the best defense counsel she could appoint, so she called Paul Johnson.

Johnson entered Judge Warder's small, well-furnished office. Just like the day's leading story, Paul Johnson was hard to miss. At a trim six-foot-six, the blue-eyed, sandy-haired man cut an athletic figure. He had spent two years in junior college on a basketball scholarship, and then transferred to Southern Methodist University. After graduation, he stayed on for his law degree at the SMU Law School.

Judge Warder outlined the case, mentioning that after his arrest Battaglia had refused to talk without an attorney present. *That was promising,* Johnson thought, *at least the guy understands his rights.* The judge asked Paul if he wanted the case.

When Paul had first read about the murders, he thought that the media had already tried John Battaglia and found him guilty. Doing anything on John Battaglia's behalf would take a monumental effort. But Johnson never backed away from a challenge, so he agreed to become Battaglia's lead defense attorney.

Judge Warder also chose Paul Brauchle to assist Johnson. That afternoon, both attorneys went to the Lew Sterrett Justice Center to talk to their new client. The tall brick center, located next door to the Crowley Courthouse, was fenced with razor wire and had tiny slits for windows.

A guard brought John Battaglia from his cell to an austere-looking meeting room that held a small wooden table and four chairs. Johnson grimaced when they first saw him. Battaglia's eye had appeared red in this morning's newspaper, but was now black, and he had additional bruises on his face.

The lawyers had reviewed the legal documents regarding John's spousal assaults, and they were anxious to ask him about them. A man with a history of wife beating was not the best defendant to bring before a jury.

The three men sat at the table, and John Battaglia downplayed the attacks to his defense team. Refusing to say that he had beaten his wives, he insisted these were trumped-up charges brought by women with axes to grind. However, John had trouble explaining police photographs of Michelle's swollen face and Mary Jean's bruises.

* * *

Over the next few weeks, the lawyers learned about their new client. Battaglia talked willingly about his mother's suicide that doctors said was caused by depression. That interested the attorneys. Killing two little girls would be hard to defend, but now they had a basis for such bizarre action. They discussed that Battaglia possibly suffered from some kind of mental illness. His hyper, then calm demeanor led them to believe that he was bipolar. Now they had to set about proving it so they asked the New Jersey Police to send them all of his mother's mental health records.

County Family Court Judge David Finn didn't receive Mary Jean's long-sought revocation request against John Battaglia until Thursday morning, the day after the murders. After trying to release Battaglia the year before, Finn quickly signed the revocation and issued an arrest warrant. Since John was already locked in jail, the signing was completely unnecessary and tainted with political overtones. People who knew of Mary Jean's attempts to stop her ex-husband's constant harassment wondered what Judge Finn was thinking. Did he remember Mary Jean Pearle standing in front of him less than a year ago, crying and begging the judge not to dismiss the beating charges? Did he remember that she had said she was scared to death of the man? Did he remember John's smirky grin when he rushed out of his courtroom?

After John Battaglia's arrest, his father, John Sr., flew in from Florida. Paul Johnson would learn in short order that John Sr. was a defense attorney's worst nightmare. A loose cannon, John Sr. thought he knew better than anyone how to run the case. Since John Sr. had been estranged from his son for much of his life, he decided he was going to make it up to him now by helping with his defense. He would be a man on a mission.

Paul Johnson laid down his demands to both Battaglias. There was to be no communication with the media: no newspaper interviews, no TV tapings, nothing!

A flutter of activity began once the news reports on Battaglia hit the streets. Battered women's shelters around the city reported a fourfold increase in calls from women in situations similar to Mary Jean's. And women already in shelters sought counseling.

An outpouring of condolences from friends and a multitude of strangers started flooding Mary Jean's mailbox. When the envelopes no longer fit inside her mailbox, the post office began delivering them in white plastic boxes. The sheer brutality of the killings—and the inexplicable callousness with which Battaglia arranged for Mary Jean to listen to her daughters being murdered—appalled the entire city.

THIRTY-EIGHT

There is no task more stressful than planning a funeral for a child. It's completely out of the normal order of how life is supposed to be. Now Mary Jean Pearle had to plan a funeral for two children. She had decided on a single white casket, unable to separate her girls for all eternity. They were each other's best friend, and it only seemed fitting to keep them together.

It had been six years since Mary Jean had lost her father. Not a day went by that she didn't think of him, and many of her friends thought that she hadn't entirely reconciled herself to his death. She still consumed Zoloft, the antidepressant the doctors had prescribed at the time her father died.

The day before the funeral, she startled friends by announcing she would place her children's casket on top of her father's. Hillcrest Cemetery didn't find this extraordinary, but unfortunately Mary Jean had to have her father's casket exhumed, then buried three feet deeper so that Faith and Liberty's casket could rest on top of his. She found solace that the three people she loved so dearly would be together.

* * *

On a cloudy Saturday morning on May 5, at ten-thirty, hundreds of grim-faced mourners marched quietly into Our Redeemer Lutheran Church in North Dallas and filled it to overflowing.

The clouds had burst open the night before as if shedding giant tears, and humidity added an oppressive weight to the air.

Seeing the coffin deepened everyone's grief. Every mother could identify with Mary Jean's loss. Every father wondered at the black heart of a man who could commit such a heinous act against his own children.

Michelle Ghetti flew in for the funeral with her daughter, Laurie. Michelle wept constantly, feeling especially guilty for not insisting on jail time for Battaglia and for having allowed him to plea bargain his way out of assaulting her. Mary Jean entered the sanctuary holding on to Laurie, and Michelle and Dorrace followed close behind. They moved somberly down the church's center aisle.

Mary Jean had chosen the most fitting song for a child's funeral. The walls of the church echoed with the familiar strains of "Jesus Loves Me" as the entire congregation sang from the printed program.

Robert Clark, Mary Jean's oldest brother, acted as family spokesman. Standing behind the pulpit, he described the many accomplishments of his nieces' short lives.

As the mourners exited the church, they had no idea that John Battaglia Sr. and his wife were watching from across the street. The elder Battaglia wanted to save Mary Jean the grief of seeing her ex-father-in-law. Then the two, who were also in

mourning, followed the long entourage of cars leading to the cemetery. They carefully stayed a discreet
distance behind.

At the close of the graveside service, the minister
was offering his final prayer when the clouds that had
plagued the services all morning miraculously separated, and sunshine beamed down on the gravesite. It
was like heaven was opening to welcome the little girls.

Mary Jean Pearle did not want to leave her daughters. Almost everyone had left the sprawling green
cemetery, but she stayed with her mother and two
close friends on the gently sloping hill.

"I can't say good-bye to them," she moaned. "I
don't want to go."

As the day warmed, the scent of flowers intensified
and became overpowering. Finally, Mary Jean moved
closer to the coffin and placed her hand on it. With
tears streaming down her face, she began pounding
on the casket as she spoke to her girls, "Your daddy's
gonna pay," she promised. "As God is my witness, I
will make this right for y'all." Then her friends
helped her into a waiting limousine.

After Mary Jean left and the casket was lowered
into the ground, John Battaglia's parents came from
behind the stand of trees where they had been waiting and silently observing. Garbed in black, they
both cried as they placed white lilies on the girls'
grave. They stood for a few moments, arms around
each other, then quietly left.

* * *

The deaths of Faith and Liberty raised many questions, and fingers pointed directly at law enforcement and the courts. Why did it take two weeks for an arrest warrant to be issued? The highly touted Highland Park police took it on the chin for dragging their feet. Their first lame excuse of wanting to gather more evidence against Battaglia before arresting him was followed by a second lame excuse that they didn't know his work address. However, his work address was listed in the Dallas phone book. In addition, the alarmingly slow response to the 911 call was partially due to the Highland Park operator who had originally told Dallas police that it was a "domestic situation."

Everyone was second-guessing Judge David Finn for not having revoked Battaglia's visitation rights after he had demonstrated so much previous violence.

All the criticism boiled down to one fact. Domestic abuse was not taken seriously enough.

Karen Rogers was one of Mary Jean Pearle's best friends. The two women had been close ever since they met at Hillcrest High School. An exquisitely beautiful woman with porcelain skin and sculptured features, Karen didn't need any beauty aids, yet her grandmother, Mary Kay Ash, happened to be the world-renowned creator of Mary Kay Cosmetics.

Karen had dated Stan Graff, who also became a good friend of Mary Jean's. Karen and Stan were two of Mary Jean's many friends who were outraged that John Battaglia had been allowed unsupervised visits with Faith and Liberty.

They were well aware of the hell John had put Mary Jean through during their marriage, and now the grief and the unfairness of it struck them all.

They couldn't understand why a judge would allow a father who was both physically and verbally abusive to see his children without supervision.

For the memory of Faith and Liberty and for all abused children, they were going to do something about it.

A ripple effect began.

Stan Graff owns Graff Chevrolet in Grand Prairie, Texas, a growing community between Dallas and Fort Worth. The five-foot-ten, sandy-haired man is more apt to tell you that he "just sells cars" than admit he owns the entire dealership. Mary Jean had thought enough of Graff to choose him as one of her daughters' pallbearers.

Graff, a take-charge type of person, contacted Bob Holmes, a Dallas attorney, and told him, "We have a flawed system that everyone is frustrated with, and if everyone feels that way, why don't we change it?"

Holmes eagerly agreed to help.

The next day, Holmes called Bill Carter, who represented Fort Worth in the state legislature. Carter told him that the Texas legislature had a premier expert on family violence—Representative Toby Goodman. Goodman had practiced family law in Texas for over twenty-eight years and currently chaired the House Committee on Juvenile Justice and Family Issues. Attesting to his popularity, he had never lost a bid for reelection.

Goodman, a thoughtful, patient man, was gray-haired and fatherly looking. In the House of Representatives Goodman sits directly in front of Carter, so it was convenient for Carter to give Goodman a thumbnail sketch of the situation and ask him to contact Stan Graff.

The next morning, Goodman wasted no time calling Graff from his office. The representative was willing to listen to anyone wanting to safeguard the rights of children. Graff discussed the problem and wanted to know what Goodman could do about it.

"That upset me too," Goodman replied. "John Battaglia should never have been permitted unsupervised visits with his daughters. There's this presumption that a child benefits from maximum contact with both parents, and in a perfect world that would be true. However, a recent government study found that children in homes where spouses are abused are 1,500 times more apt to be abused than in homes with no spousal abuse."

Representative Goodman didn't hesitate. While sitting at his desk and still on the phone with Graff, he picked up a pen and a yellow ruled tablet and started drafting the language for a new law. Goodman found it easy to be enthusiastic about such a bill, and he'd put teeth in it too.

In Austin, Texas, the Texas House Chamber is an imposing room that seats 150 house members, plus a Speaker and the press. A gallery wraps around the room on the mezzanine level. On May 9, exactly one week to the day after the Battaglia murders, the Speaker of the House called on Rep. Toby Goodman to explain Senate Bill 140. Every Senate bill must have a House sponsor, and State Senator Moncrief had asked Goodman, because of his expertise, to sponsor his bill. The Moncrief bill involved children left adrift after a divorce. Goodman, logically, had written his

"Battaglia" visitation law as an amendment to the custody rights bill. The amendment stated:

> *It is not in the best interest of a child for a parent to have unsupervised visitation with the child if credible evidence is presented of a history or pattern of past or present child neglect or physical or sexual abuse by that parent directed against the other parent, a spouse, or a child.*

Goodman went on to tell the assembly that his amendment was stated in such a way that the court must look at any abuse issues before the judge signs the order. He moved for the passage of the bill. Not one question was raised from the floor, nor was any discussion called for. It passed by voice vote and the speaker's gavel echoed throughout the massive chamber.

The same result for the bill and amendment held true in the state Senate the following week. All members concurred by voice vote, and Senate Bill 140 was sent to Governor Rick Perry, who promptly signed it.

It became law on September 1, 2001. From that date forward, a parent's history of abuse with either a spouse or their child must be considered in a judge's decision to grant unsupervised visits with their children. All because of Faith and Liberty.

THIRTY-NINE

Two weeks after the murder of his daughters, John Battaglia shuffled into court with the baby steps that his leg irons would allow.

Before his indictment hearing, his court-appointed attorneys, Paul Johnson and Paul Brauchle, filed a motion seeking to dramatically restrict publicity about the high-profile case. The motion asked Judge Janice Warder to ban photographs of the indictment hearing. The judge said she would allow only two cameras in the courtroom.

The defense had good reason to want cameras banned. As Battaglia was brought in from the Lew Sterrett Justice Center, he looked every bit the criminal. Razors had been forbidden, and his unshaven face had a scrubby appearance. His hair also looked wild and unkempt. There was no trace of the Kim Dawson model he had once been. His longer hair showed more gray, making him look older.

Battaglia's rough white cotton jumpsuit, light years away from his expensive suits, was wrinkled and baggy. The jail-issued orange slip-on shoes made him look like a court jester.

Judge Warder read the indictment charging him with two counts of capital murder. When she stated that his punishment, if found guilty, could be a life sentence or the death penalty, Battaglia only nodded and stared blankly.

She glanced at his attorneys. "Does he understand?" she asked.

"He does, Your Honor," Paul Johnson said.

It had been rumored that his attorneys would put forth the defense that John Battaglia was bipolar, and therefore mentally ill. His lethargic persona at the hearing may have been caused by the mood-altering drugs he had been given in jail.

On the same day, Judge David Finn raised Battaglia's bail to $4 million, of which one million was to be in cash.

John Battaglia Sr. insisted that he be involved in his son's defense.

Since the older Battaglia openly assumed that his son was guilty of the murders, he asked to accompany Paul Johnson to talk with the DA, hoping to convince him to not seek the death penalty.

At the courthouse, both Johnson and Battaglia Sr. met with chief prosecutor Howard Blackmon. Blackmon told them that no decision had yet been reached.

"We're still weighing our options," Blackmon said. "We don't rush these decisions."

Johnson knew it was a long shot.

Two weeks after the murders, Steve McGonigle of *The Dallas Morning News* talked with John Battaglia Sr.

John Sr. had earlier told Paul Johnson that he felt he could use the media to generate sympathy for his son and sway public opinion. Paul pleaded with him not to, feeling that the case should be decided in the

courtroom. Johnson knew that the media would
only sensationalize the story and show the Battaglias
in a worse light.

The elder Battaglia met with Steve McGonigle anyway. The reporter asked if he had seen his son.

John Sr. nodded. "It wasn't a monster I found in
jail," he told McGonigle. "It was my kid, and he was
in a lot of pain . . .

"No one incited John like Mary Jean," John Sr.
continued. "She just loved to push his buttons. He
really became despondent over Mary Jean's attempts
to put him in jail. He believed that could have cost
him his visitation rights. Guess he felt that there was
no place to go. He felt that Mary Jean had pushed
him in the corner and he'd never see his girls again."

Continuing to press for sympathy, John Sr. told
McGonigle about John's early life, his mother's suicide, and the fact that John had been an altar boy
and a Boy Scout.

Paul Johnson read the two-page article and gritted
his teeth.

District Attorney Bill Hill had been questioned extensively about which penalty he would seek—life
imprisonment, or death, for John Battaglia.

The DA had a policy of conferring with the victims'
relatives before deciding. Mary Jean had already made
her wishes clear. "Your daddy's gonna pay" meant that
she wanted their killer to get the maximum.

On May 30, DA Bill Hill announced his decision
saying, "The circumstances of the case . . . plus John
Battaglia's past violent behavior call for the state to
seek the death penalty."

FORTY

Mary Jean appreciated the widespread support from friends and strangers, but she didn't want any more media attention. *The Dallas Morning News* and dozens of other newspapers clamored to interview her, and television channels across the country were determined to get her on camera. To insulate her from the media turmoil, she hired a public relations/media specialist. Mary Jean was able to talk to friends about her tragic loss, and even found it therapeutic, but she had no desire to take her grief public. It would require an extraordinary situation for her to give an interview.

Judge David Finn—the same David Finn who had turned a deaf ear to Mary Jean when she begged him not to dismiss her assault charge against John Battaglia—provided her with just such a situation.

Thirty-eight-year-old Finn had grand ambitions. He wanted to unseat the incumbent district attorney, Bill Hill. Both the police and DA Hill's office had been recently shaken by controversy surrounding a mountain of drug arrests. The contraband evidence for those arrests, which had been seized by the police and secured in their evidence locker, was later discovered to be pulverized Sheetrock—a powder that looked remarkably like cocaine. Even though police had taken custody of the evidence and were responsible for testing it, Police Chief Terrell Bolton tried to blame the district attorney, whose office had indicted scores of the alleged drug traffickers. When someone discovered the sham, the district attorney was reluctantly forced to dismiss seventy-six drug cases for lack of evidence.

David Finn saw this as his opportunity to strike. He resigned his judgeship, called on friends both in and out of the legal field, and put his campaign together.

In February, David Finn participated in a political debate against Bill Hill. He smiled as he shook hands with Jose Luis Vega and Jacinto Mejia, two of the men the DA had been forced to release from jail. The men had been invited, and the reason for their presence became clear when they stepped to the microphone and asked Bill Hill to apologize for arresting them in the first place.

Everyone knew it was an obvious ploy to embarrass the district attorney, but he refused to fall into David Finn's trap, telling the crowd, "I don't base my decision on what defense attorneys tell me, but on what the facts are." Bill Hill had already called in the FBI to investigate the case.

Gallantly, David Finn strode to the microphone and, reading in Spanish, apologized to the men and their families ". . . because Mr. Hill won't."

The Republican party conducted a poll and found that a runoff vote would probably be necessary because the race between the two Republican candidates was too close for either to gain a majority.

* * *

Mary Jean Pearle read about the debate in the newspaper and decided she had had enough of David Finn's attempt to pass himself off as the standard of common sense and compassion. As it would turn out, Finn had miscalculated her ability. He may have seen her as a helpless victim in his court, but he should not have underestimated a woman whom the legal system had failed—a woman who had only grown stronger with every injustice she suffered.

She decided to call a press conference, and Channel 8 (WFAA), an ABC affiliate, was only too happy to oblige. On February 18, Mary Jean Pearle met in a private home with members of Republican Women For Family Safety. Some of these women were the same ones who had been in Finn's court the day he tried to dismiss the charges against Battaglia.

Nightline News anchor Gloria Compos introduced the special report by saying, "One of the most brutal cases of domestic violence in Dallas last year may turn political. John Battaglia's ex-wife has never addressed the media before, but tonight she points an accusing finger squarely at the judge in the case, who now hopes to unseat the DA."

Mary Jean's attractive face filled the screen. She looked smart in a navy pin-striped suit and white blouse. A small diamond cross dangled from a chain around her neck.

"I'm here tonight because I believe that Judge David Finn let my children and me down," she said in a poised, calm voice.

The announcer, Jeff Brady, told viewers that, "These women are not attorneys, but monitor domestic violence cases." The next face on the screen was that of a pretty blonde, Patti Ransome, the group's spokeswoman. She reported that while monitoring the Dallas county family court system, they found that among all the judges they observed, Mr. Finn was the only one doing a bad job.

The camera zoomed in on David Finn's handsome face as Jim Brady interviewed him. "I gave the state everything they asked for," Finn said. "They wanted one year in jail, probated for two years with conditions, and that's exactly what I did. I don't know where they're coming from." However, Finn was discussing his decision from the previous August when John Battaglia was in his court for the *second* time for his Christmas Day beating.

The announcer moved the audience back to the issue and pointed out that Hill supporters claimed Finn dismissed the Battaglia case when his ex-wife didn't appear in court on time. Finn retorted that the prosecutors themselves requested the dismissal, but of course he didn't mention that he had forced them into it by threatening to find Battaglia not guilty of the charges.

Mary Jean returned to the screen and brought up the aborted hearing over the marijuana test. "That would have been in January, 2001, and then John killed my little girls four months later. So I believe that if he had been in jail he wouldn't have been able to kill my daughters on May second."

David Finn glanced down at the newcaster's desktop. He looked like he was about to cry. "I didn't know anything about the Battaglia probation situation until the day after the fact," he said. Finn's statement followed the one he made earlier in the telecast boasting that he had given Battaglia two years' probation.

The announcer concluded, "Just how much weight one awful domestic violence case carries in the minds of voters may be the deciding factor of who fills the Dallas district attorney's office for the next four years."

On March 12, 2002, voters went to the polls. DA Bill Hill soundly defeated David Finn by a percentage of 59 to 25.

FORTY-ONE

The task of selecting the jury for John Battaglia's murder trial began on January 11, 2002 at the Frank Crowley Criminal Courts Building. The ten-thousand-square-foot jury room was filled with people who, for the most part, didn't want to be there. Several hundred sat on padded folding chairs, while latecomers sprawled on the gray tweed carpet.

Assistant District Attorney Harold Blackmon, the dark-haired lead prosecutor of John Battaglia's case, stood on a wooden platform. Speaking into a microphone, he admonished a crowd of almost eight hundred not to read or watch anything about the case. Prospective jurors clutched an eighteen-page questionnaire that asked them about every viewpoint they held. With a jury pool of that size, it would seem relatively easy to find twelve qualified people. However, that was not to be the case.

Another month passed before prospects culled from the initial throng were brought in, one by one, and quizzed in the courtroom where the trial would take place. The presiding judge, the two defense attorneys, and two of the assistant district attorneys, along with the defendant, were present for every minute of every day of voir dire.

By mid-February, the trial of Andrea Yates, the mother who had drowned her five children, was moving rapidly through a Houston court. That jury had been assembled in two days, and the trial was well underway. By that time, the Battaglia case had acquired only half a dozen jurors.

John Battaglia looked impressive. His attorneys obviously had cleaned him up for the show. He wore a black suit over a crisp white shirt with a patterned dark tie; his hair was short and dark. The handsome man did not resemble the ragamuffin brought in for the indictment; this man looked more like an executive at a board meeting.

Seeing him dressed as he was answered many questions. Why did two fine women agree to marry him? Why did judge after judge place him on probation instead of sending him to jail when his violations began piling up?

The assistant DAs spent a great deal of time quizzing prospects on their opinions about the death penalty. The prosecution couldn't afford to place one anti-death sentence person on the jury.

When questioned about the ultimate punishment, some prospects stated aggressively that they would be able to consider it. Others weren't so sure.

At that point, either Assistant DAs Patrick Kirlin or Keith Robinson would proceed to paint a picture that would make even Stephen King shudder.

They'd begin, "I don't want you to have regrets down the line when you pick up the newspaper someday and see that Mr. Battaglia over here was executed. This is Texas, after all; we don't just talk about the death penalty, we do it.

"After the defendant's appeals are over, they will take him to the Walls Unit in Huntsville. On that last day, he'll get to see his friends and relatives—the very same people who will sit in the chair you're sitting in now and who will beg you to show mercy for their loved one. Then, after he eats his last meal, they'll come for him. He may drop down to his knees and pray for forgiveness. He may scream, yell, and fight those dragging him to the death chamber, all the while proclaiming his innocence and saying how he was railroaded, or he may go somberly with head bowed."

Then, to increase tension and paint a realistic picture, the prosecutors would spell out how the defendant would be restrained on a gurney with six straps across his body, and how needles inserted into both arms would drip two poisons into his veins. They described how one poison would stop his breathing while the other shuts down his heart.

"When his lungs collapse you'd hear his last gasps for breath before death overtakes him." In the quiet courtroom, the assistant DA would pause and wait a few seconds to let that sink in.

Some interviewees swallowed hard, as did Battaglia the first couple of times he heard the rendition. A few prospective jurors would still say they could grant it. But many who had been staunch death penalty advocates at the start changed their minds after they heard the draining description. Regardless of the variety of their replies, the vast majority of prospects were excused, one after the other.

Voir dire had begun in the winter. By spring, only eight jurors had been seated.

* * *

While voir dire lumbered on, *The Dallas Morning News* reporter Steve McGonigle found John Battaglia Sr. willing to again grant him an extensive interview, complete with a photograph of himself. As the court searched for jurors, John Sr. shocked his son's defense attorneys by admitting in print that John had probably shot his granddaughters. He softened his words by trying to give reasons. "John was obsessively bitter toward his former wife over money and custody issues and feared losing access to the children." The father also said, "A psychiatrist found that John suffers from bipolar disorder. In addition, he has depression and an antisocial personality disorder that he may have inherited from his mother."

John Sr. discussed the irony that his granddaughters' slayings and his son's arrest had forged a closeness between father and son that had eluded them for most of John's forty-six years.

Now the lawyers also had to ask prospective jurors if they had read *that* article as questioning continued.

That type of newspaper story on Battaglia made choosing a jury all the more difficult. For example, shortly after the interview with John's father came out, a prospective female juror strutted into court to take her place on the witness stand. Her bright red-and-yellow dress had already made a statement, but it paled in comparison with her words.

Assistant DA Patrick Kirlin asked if she knew about the case, and it was evident that the woman had disregarded any admonition that jurors not read or watch the news. The woman charged ahead, speaking quickly and directing her answers to John Battaglia.

"I've read about it and heard about it. You had your girls in your loft or whatever," she said, facing the defendant. "I think this had been a continuous thing. You were on the phone with your ex-wife. You were taking care of your two young daughters. They were little, not big, little. You got pissed off at your wife and shot your daughters. Not one of your daughters, but two, both of them. Then the police find two dead bodies in your loft, and I don't think anyone else came in and did that. And your wife heard the shots on the phone. So you're guilty."

When Kirlin asked if she had formed an opinion of the punishment her answer was predictable. She raised her voice and pointed her finger directly at John Battaglia. "You, sir, are a monster! And *you* deserve the death penalty!"

Kirlin broke from procedure and, without any discussion with the judge or defense, excused the woman.

As the third month of voir dire approached, John Battaglia sat comfortably, watching and listening to the jury process. Battaglia would chat amicably with his lawyers while the prosecution detailed every needle prick of lethal injection. Sometimes his laugh would ring out at the very moment his possible death was being vividly portrayed.

Around 3:00 P.M. one Friday as the afternoon was growing tediously long, another prospective juror, a gray-haired woman, slowly made her way to the witness stand. She was not quick to give answers to the prosecutor's questions; she took her time, and her replies showed reflective thought.

Assistant DA Keith Robinson asked her what she already knew of the case and a dark, troubled shadow colored her face.

"When I first heard about this, I couldn't help but think about the responsibilities of a father," she began. "A father is a little child's protector, the person who can be looked up to and trusted. As a child, I always felt secure in my father's arms." She glanced over at John Battaglia. "I can only imagine what this man's little girls were feeling in those last terrible moments of their lives. What fear filled their little hearts."

John Battaglia had never showed any remorse or emotion since killing his daughters. Even now, his demeanor remained one of pleasant interest. But his interior emotions betrayed him. A red blotch appeared above his starched white collar. It elongated and crept up his neck, then onto his face until it pooled near his cheek.

Like a marathon racer finally closing in on the finish, the voir dire proceedings sprinted to a rapid close on Thursday and Friday during the first week of April. In those two days, two jurors were seated—the twelfth, and one alternate.

The last juror was not to the defense's liking. He was a law-and-order type with family members who were prosecutors and police. While the assistant DAs beamed, the defense team formally objected to the seating of the twelfth juror, thus establishing their first point for appeal.

FORTY-TWO

Death investigator Gigi Ray had taken the weekend off from the medical examiner's office for a little R&R, a necessity for someone in her profession. She and a friend had driven south to the historic town of Fredericksburg, nestled deep in the Texas hill country. With the bustle of the Metroplex behind her, she could unwind in the quiet serenity with nothing more on her mind than the nightly hum of cicadas.

Gigi returned home April 21, the night before the trial began, on a warm Sunday evening. As she carried her small travel bag down the hall, she noticed the blinking light of her answering machine. She pushed "play" and heard the voice of her coworker Scarlett Long.

"Gigi. The DA's office has been trying to get hold of you. You're to call Paul Johnson." Then she left a number.

Gigi glanced at her watch. Five-thirty. She figured that she wouldn't get hold of Johnson at this hour, especially on a Sunday, but she punched in his number anyway.

Paul Johnson was sitting on a chaise longue next to Paul Brauchle on Brauchle's patio. The air was thick with cigar smoke as they reviewed the Power-point presentation one of their psychiatry experts would detail at the trial. They had spent the entire day with the doctor in Fort Worth.

"Have you heard from that ME investigator yet?" Brauchle asked.

"Gigi Ray? I left a message with her office. Called them late Friday. They were under the impression that Gigi wasn't needed at the trial. I told them she wasn't, but we wanted her at the evidentiary hearing. Since the hearing's right before the trial, I'd hate to have to run around getting a subpoena and delay the trial. They told me she was out of town for the weekend."

The lawyers continued talking, then an hour later, Paul's cell phone rang.

"Mr. Johnson, this is Gigi Ray with the ME's office. I was told to call you."

Johnson gave Brauchle a knowing glance. He placed his cigar in the ashtray and picked up a pen. "Yes, Gigi. Just wanted to check with you about a few things before the trial starts. What did that crime scene look like when you first got there?"

"Well, one of the officers told me it was a real-'cluster-fuck.' It didn't seem like anyone knew who was in charge.

"I thought there was going to be some kind of problem with the search warrant because the officers kept discussing it. Some were saying that they didn't know if one was needed in the first place. Is that what they're trying to say, that there's a problem with the warrant?"

"That's what *we're* saying," Johnson told her, his pen flying as he scribbled notes of everything Gigi was telling him.

Johnson heard Gigi take a deep breath. She said, "Now wait a minute. You *are* the DA, aren't you?"

"No, I'm not. I'm the defense attorney."

There was a long pause before Gigi replied.

"I was told you were the DA."

"Well, ma'am, I can promise you I didn't characterize myself that way. I'm the defense attorney and I haven't told anybody anything different."

"I think this conversation has to end," Gigi declared. "I need to call the DA and let him know that you want me at the evidentiary hearing."

"I can understand that. Guess I'll see you in court tomorrow."

Gigi sat on her couch, totally bewildered. She needed to call Scarlett Long immediately. The calm from her peaceful weekend had evaporated and now her stomach was churning. Scarlett was so dependable. How could this have happened? Well, it didn't matter; Gigi had major fires to put out and some big players to call.

First, she called Scarlett at work to verify her message. When Scarlett heard about the phone call, she felt miserable for having misinformed Gigi. Second, Gigi called her boss, Bill Lené, and explained the problem.

Since none of the prosecuting attorneys had ever called her and she hadn't heard the names of anyone from the DA's office who were working on the case, being told to call Paul Johnson hadn't seemed suspicious to her at all. She called a court investigator and he contacted chief prosecutor Howard Blackmon.

Blackmon phoned Gigi and was very upset that she had given such information to Paul Johnson, the head of the enemy camp. She could hear the disapproval in his voice as he expressed fear that the evidence could be in jeopardy. Blackmon told her to show up for the next day's hearing because Johnson could simply get a subpoena and force her to be there, but he wanted Gigi to meet with him first, thirty minutes before the hearing.

Paul Johnson was at home, basking in the afterglow of his phone call with Gigi Ray. The ME's death investigator had given him invaluable information. With her testimony he could prove that the evidence from the loft had been collected without a search warrant. He could possibly get all evidence found in the loft thrown out of court. It was the shot in the arm that his case needed.

He strolled into his den, dropped down on a black leather recliner, and flipped on the television. After a few minutes of news, there was an announcement that they would be airing videotape of an exclusive interview with John Battaglia at the Lew Sterrett Justice Center. Johnson sat up straight and frowned. This wasn't good news.

Soon John Battaglia's straggly-bearded face filled the screen. The piece had obviously been taped three or more months ago, before voir dire had begun. John's dark gray hair hung in long corkscrews that shot in every direction and matched his long sideburns and four-inch-long gray beard; he looked like a gnome. Paul knew that razors were banned in jail, but they did have stainless steel mirrors. Didn't John know how he looked?

The Channel 8 newswoman interviewed Battaglia. When she asked him about the murders, John told her he thought that he was putting his girls to bed. He was doing something good for them. He explained that the doctors had diagnosed him as bipolar, and claimed that if he had been treated earlier, none of this would have happened. John frequently laughed and grinned at the camera. He said, "All I needed was a pill. Isn't that something?"

Johnson clicked off his set. He had been working on Battaglia's case for almost a year—some days for just an hour, at other times for the entire day. John Battaglia and his father had not taken one bit of his advice. In addition, two of John's brothers were cooperating with the DA.

On that busy Monday morning before trial, Gigi Ray fought her way down the wide corridor at the courthouse to meet with Howard Blackmon. Lawyers were easily spotted in the courthouse. Their dark suits and soft leather briefcases set them apart from the swarms of casually dressed people who were there to pay fines or support a loved one at a trial.

Once Gigi was in Blackmon's office, she insisted that her photos of the dead children, combined with the mother's testimony of the phone call, would be enough to convict John Battaglia. But by the time Gigi left to attend the hearing, Blackmon was still not convinced.

Judge Warder's Criminal District Court filled quickly that April 22 morning in anticipation of Battaglia's trial. The court held sixty-five people in churchlike pews. The gray carpet and cloth-covered walls lent a soft, insulated tone that contrasted sharply with the violence of the case that would be heard. People began jamming together, sliding closer to make room for latecomers.

Paul Johnson opened the evidentiary hearing by calling Gigi Ray to the stand. Out of her normal work garb, she looked more feminine in a blue jumper and coral blouse. After she was sworn in, Johnson wanted the court to hear a full recounting of their previous evening's phone conversation. By asking, "Do you remember telling me that . . . ," he was able to force Gigi to reiterate everything she had related on the phone, including the fact that one officer had called the scene a "cluster-fuck."

Reading from Ray's investigative report, Paul Johnson asked, "Did Detective Fite give you permission to remove the bodies before the warrant arrived?"

"He said there wasn't any need to wait for the warrant."

"Okay, the girls' bodies were removed prior to the search warrant. Can you tell me how PES had pictures of their bodies if no one went inside the loft prior to the arrival of the search warrant?"

"All those people were in there with me," Gigi answered.

Johnson's six-foot-six frame was imposing and as effective now as in his basketball days. In only a few steps, he was at the witness stand, towering over Gigi. It was an intimidating move, but Gigi remained calm. Johnson gave her a stack of seventy-seven crime scene photos to sort through, and he stood beside her while she thumbed through each one.

"Did you take that photo?" Johnson asked, pointing to a picture of the Glock smeared with hair and tissue residue.

"I don't know. Could have. I did take a photo of

that gun, but the police did too. I take slides at my scenes. If this picture was made from a slide, it could possibly be mine."

Johnson now realized that he hadn't requested that pictures be made from her slides. "Do you have a complete set of the photos you took?" Johnson asked.

"The original set of slides is back at the ME's office."

Paul Johnson asked the judge's permission to allow Ray to call her office and ask someone to bring over her slides.

Prosecutor Howard Blackmon stood up. "Your Honor," he began, "the Medical Examiner is separate from PES. Her jurisdiction is the bodies and one was in plain view right from the front door."

Paul Johnson answered that he knew Ray could go in and photograph the bodies and the evidence, but because she did that before a search warrant arrived, he wanted to see if the police were doing it at the same time.

Gigi was asked to stand in the back of the room while they waited for the slides to arrive.

In the meantime, Johnson called Dallas police officer Elton Fite of the Child Abuse Section to the stand, and he was sworn in. The trim officer was dressed in a sports coat and slacks—exactly what he wore as a plainclothes detective, and probably less intimidating to children than a police uniform would be. He had been called to the lofts at 9:30 on the night of the murders.

Paul Johnson began questioning him about the crime scene, and Fite admitted that patrolmen, PES, and ME were in the building.

"But no one entered the room until the evidentiary search warrant arrived," he said with authority.

Paul's eyes grew large.

"You didn't go inside that loft?" he asked in amazement.

"No."

"Did you give authority for the ME to take the bodies?"

He hesitated for a moment. "I talked to Mary Jean Pearle," he said. His mentioning the victims' mother placed him away from the crime scene, as Mary Jean had been downstairs. "No," he continued, "I don't recall telling the ME she could take the bodies."

"But you yourself didn't go into that crime scene?" Johnson asked for clarification.

"No. I just looked in from the door," Fite said.

Courtroom spectators exchanged questioning glances at the discrepancy with Ray's testimony.

Gigi Ray did not want to return to the witness stand, but now she was sitting there, dreading Johnson's next question. After he viewed the slides and asked the court to make photographs from them, he turned to Gigi.

"Okay," he said. "You heard what Detective Fite said. Was he telling the truth?"

Gigi was frozen, wishing she could magically disappear. She didn't want to paint a law enforcement peer in a bad light, but even more, she didn't want to perjure herself. She looked up at Judge Warder, feeling like a ten-year-old wanting her mother to tell her what to do. A sympathetic smile crossed the judge's face, then she gave Gigi a subtle nod that said, "You have to answer."

Gigi swallowed hard and said, "I guess he could have been mistaken." She looked down at her hands, and her face reddened with discomfort.

* * *

During the morning break, Paul Johnson and Gigi Ray just happened to reach the vestibule of the courtroom at the same time. Their eyes locked, and Paul stuck out his hand.

"I would like to applaud you on your honesty," he said, shaking her hand. "I'd have laid money that you would have covered for Fite."

When the evidentiary hearing continued after the break, Paul Johnson called James R. Vineyard to the stand. Vineyard had been a Dallas police officer for twenty-five years and worked as a detective with the crime scene response unit. When Paul Johnson questioned the experienced officer, he readily admitted to having been inside the loft without a search warrant.

"What did you do when you first got there?" Johnson asked.

"Shortly after I arrived, I helped the others mark evidence and then took photographs. I've investigated hundreds of crime scenes like this. I thought that in good faith we were doing the right thing."

His next statement lent credibility to Gigi Ray's testimony. Vineyard asserted that he and Fite were inside the loft discussing whether or not to get a search warrant. Around 10:30, they decided that one was necessary and left to find a judge.

Chief prosecutor Howard Blackmon was on his feet, defending the officer. "This was an emergency situation. They had to check on the children. Besides, anything in plain view doesn't need a warrant."

Standing taller and raising his voice louder, Paul

Johnson said, "The kids were obviously not in imminent danger. Besides, it was a chaotic scene. Nobody knew what they were doing. They were not maintaining the law. They had no right to collect evidence.

"I move to suppress all evidence collected at the scene," Johnson said. "This was an illegal search. All evidence would include the bodies, the guns, and the bullets."

The prosecution held its collective breath for Judge Warder's ruling.

She began thoughtfully, "I believe that the police had reason to act immediately. And all evidence in plain view is admissible—bodies, guns, everything. The evidence can be admitted under the emergency doctrine."

Paul stood, his face flushed, as he listened to the judge. She stated that, as there had been no itemization of seized evidence, Paul could not specify which bits of evidence had been moved or taken.

For the record, Paul objected that evidence was collected without a warrant and the judge nodded, noting his objection.

Johnson objected a second time. "The warrant wasn't specific as to what they were looking for. It was just a fishing expedition."

The judge noted the defense attorney's second objection.

"Your Honor," Johnson said, "my objections are for each piece of evidence that will be presented." Johnson appeared to be laying the groundwork for an appeal.

Officer James Vineyard was recalled to the stand. The crime scene investigator admitted to having searched Battaglia's truck around 2:20 A.M.

"Did you have a search warrant to do that?" Johnson asked.

"I didn't think a warrant was necessary. We were looking for weapons that were tied to the crime."

The three prosecutors looked at one another. They had not completely resolved the issue of the search warrant for the loft—and now they had the truck to worry about. The prosecutors busily flipped through reference books, then found the precedent they were looking for.

After listening to Blackmon, Judge Warder agreed with the prosecution's assertion that there was a motor vehicle exemption. "Evidence may be moved because it could become lost due to the movability of the truck," she said.

Johnson also objected to that finding. His objections were stacking up for the appellate court.

When the prosecution had its turn, it moved to admit John Battaglia's previous violations into evidence, including beating Mary Jean on Christmas Day and violating his protective order on April 17, 2001. Blackmon stated that Battaglia's motive for the murders was his impending arrest.

Paul Johnson had an advantage when he stood. Everyone had to look up to him. He objected to the admissions because the victim (Mary Jean) in those cases was a different person than the victims in this trial. In addition, he stated that this information on Battaglia's background might prejudice the jury.

Judge Warder disagreed. "I think these actions are highly relevant because they show a relationship."

Howard Blackmon stood in front of John Battaglia to read his indictment and begin the trial. Battaglia was told to stand.

"John David Battaglia, on or about the second day of May, 2001, did unlawfully, intentionally, and knowingly cause the death of Mary Faith Battaglia by shooting [her] with a firearm, a deadly weapon, and during the same criminal transaction said defendant did intentionally and knowingly cause the death of Liberty Battaglia. . . ."

Battaglia listened to the indictment and appeared about to yawn. When asked, he entered a plea of "not guilty."

The jury of seven men and five women entered the courtroom. The serious, unsmiling group ranged in age from their late twenties to their early sixties.

Chief prosecutor Howard Blackmon stood before them to give his opening statement.

He began by relating that Mary Jean's relationship with the defendant was marred by abuse culminating in the ultimate act of revenge.

He recounted the telephone call during which Mary Jean had been forced to listen to her girls being murdered. Blackmon mentioned the message that Mary Jean had heard the next morning. "John Battaglia told his girls how very brave they were, and how evil their mother was."

Blackmon led jurors along the path Battaglia had taken that night. He graphically itemized the shots that killed the children, then described John's night on the town: the girl, the drinks, the tattoos.

He concluded by saying, "Officer Dane Thornton was the first officer to stop. He was the first to see the horror of that scene. Now you will see what he saw."

The defense offered no opening statement.

* * *

The big, solid frame of Officer Dane P. Thornton entered the courtroom through double doors at the far end opposite the judge's bench. His head tan and shaved, he stood erect and walked with purpose. The veteran officer frowned throughout his entire testimony. There was just no way to appear pleasant and tell what he had witnessed. It had cost him three nights' sleep when it happened, and now he had to relive it. He described Mary Jean flagging him down, the arrival of Officers Murray and Rojas, their decision to kick down the door, and then their grisly discovery. He also detailed the massive manhunt for Battaglia that had lasted almost six hours.

Three days previously, on the Friday before trial started, an evidentiary hearing had been held. At that time, Paul Johnson had kept Officer Thornton on the stand for over an hour, pelting him with questions about that night. He had criticized him for initiating an illegal search and seizure merely on the word of Mary Jean, a hysterical mother. But during the hearing, Thornton had stood up to Johnson and had apparently won his respect—for after Thornton's trial testimony today, Johnson had no questions for the officer.

The prosecution called its next witness, Mary Jean Pearle.

FORTY-THREE

Mary Jean Pearle hadn't slept a wink the night before the trial. Even with all the incriminating evidence against John Battaglia, she felt a consuming dread that something would go wrong and he wouldn't be found guilty. Even if he were found guilty, he might not get the death penalty. She had promised her girls justice. Everything was resting on her testimony today.

Dressed in a conservative black-and-white-print dress covered with a black jacket, Mary Jean looked tired when she entered the courtroom.

Responding to Howard Blackmon's questioning, she described her early life in Dallas, her many years of working in her mother's antique shop, and her more recent management of her rental properties.

Mary Jean talked about her marriage to John Battaglia, and the arrival of the children. As Exhibit 12, the prosecution offered a colorful 18-by-24-inch photo of the girls at their elementary school carnival. It showed them hugging and grinning, crinkling their flower-painted faces.

The prosecution ventured into emotional territory as they began to question Mary Jean about her children.

"Liberty was in her third year of ballet," Mary

Jean said. "She danced like a swan compared to all the other children. She wanted to be a prima ballerina." As she struggled to say "prima," the first tears of her testimony began filling her eyes. "She had the best personality of anyone in the family and that's saying something for this family." She stopped to inhale and steady her breathing. "She had lots and lots of little friends . . ." More tears rolled down her cheeks.

Mary Jean mentioned that she had been Faith's first-grade room mother and had promised Liberty to be her first-grade room mother also. "But Liberty didn't make it to first grade," she said, squeezing her eyes shut. She had to stop talking for a moment.

Discussing her involvement with her children, she said, "Monday was ballet, Tuesday was violin, Wednesday was at the Y . . ." Everyone could see that the girls were her entire life. She didn't date because she didn't want to give John anything to blow up over.

She described how verbally abusive John had been during their entire nine-year marriage. "He got even meaner after he lost the RTC case. He screamed at me all the time after that, and that's when we separated."

Mary Jean was afraid that their relationship was turning toward physical violence, so she sought a protective order.

Her hunch proved correct. Mary Jean described her Christmas beating. As she sat at the witness stand, she pantomimed her physical motions during the fight—leaning down, ducking her head, and trying to fend off Battaglia's blows. The jury stayed with her every word.

"He pushed me to the floor," she said, ducking almost under the witness stand. "He started kicking me with his heavy shoe. Over and over again. And I only had on pajamas!"

After the attack, she said it got quiet. Mary Jean looked up from the stand as if she were looking for John. "He left Laurie with us and just took off."

She described her black-and-blue face, the hair she lost because John pulled it out, and all her other bruises. She complained that when she filed a criminal complaint against John, he only received probation. A few women on the jury shook their heads. She recalled that he was still on probation the night he killed the children.

Fifty minutes into her testimony, Blackmon guided her to the most emotional part: the call to the loft. Mary Jean described hearing Faith's voice, and that when she heard her scream, "No, Daddy, no, don't do it, please," she knew something terrible was happening because Faith had never said "no" to her daddy in her entire life. Mary Jean exploded into tears and pounded the witness stand with every "no, Daddy" she repeated. Then she beat out the sound of each gunshot by slapping the stand over and over again.

She described her dash to the loft. She told that she found the street empty and wondered where the police and ambulance were. Her frustration soared anew in the courtroom as she itemized every tragic revelation of the night.

Mary Jean described what it was like to return home the next morning and listen to Faith's recorded voice. That tape was played for the jury. Then she related how she had entered the children's room and listened to Battaglia's last message telling the girls how brave they were. The prosecution played that tape also. While it ran, every member of the jury glared at John. His chilling words made it obvious that all the pain John had inflicted that night was directed at Mary Jean. The girls were only tragic pawns in his scheme.

Wisely, Paul Johnson had no questions for Mary Jean.

Jennifer Esparza, the Highland Park 911 operator, was probably uncomfortable being called to testify. She had spent several weeks of the previous year trying to defend her handling of the 911 call.

The prosecution wanted to play the complete taped call for the jury. Paul Johnson objected, saying it would only be a second chance for Mary Jean to influence the jury.

The judge decided to run the tape outside the jury's presence; then the defense could object to various sections.

Esparza was heard saying that they [911] had had several disturbances with Battaglia. Her words made the call seem routine as she downplayed the emergency. On the tape, the full impact of Mary Jean's anguish could be heard in her sobs, her screams, and her cries.

When Mary Jean's taped voice screamed, "Oh, no, they're dead!" many of her friends in the courtroom bowed their heads, hair hanging over their faces as they cried.

After the airing, Johnson objected to several parts, calling it hearsay. He wanted the tape revised rather than simply muted during those sections because otherwise the jury would know that information was being kept from them.

The first day of the trial drew to a close. Paul Johnson still appeared vigorous. He never seemed to tire

of jumping to his feet, objecting, and nitpicking anything that could hurt his client.

During the trial, Mary Jean, her mother, and
Michelle Ghetti were cloistered in the witness waiting room. Mary Jean had to remain outside the
courtroom in case she was called again. Friends attended the proceedings, then reported to Mary Jean
what evidence was being presented at the trial.

Before the second day of trial, Paul Brauchle, the assistant defense attorney, went to the front of the
courtroom where Exhibit 12, the photograph of the
smiling girls at the carnival, was on display. He picked
up the picture and placed it facedown on the desk
next to the court reporter's station, out of the jury's
view.

Both dressed in black, John Battaglia's father and
stepmother entered the courtroom with John's
youngest brother, Trevor. They were soon joined by
the writer the Battaglias had hired to chronicle their
perspective of the story.

No bailiff had to bring the courtroom to its feet as
Judge Janice Warder entered. She was already at her
bench, busy working on legal papers and jotting
down notes.

The court reporter came in and noticed the girls'
photo. She picked it up and promptly returned it to
its proper place in front of the jury.

At the beginning of that day's session, the judge
warned that the testimony and evidence would be

graphic. She cautioned the spectators that if they felt
they could not handle the presentation, they should
leave now. She wanted no outbursts.

Jennifer Esparza, the Highland Park 911 operator,
was recalled to the stand. The argument over the tape
hadn't been resolved. It had not been re-recorded as
Paul Johnson had requested, so he was trying to have
the entire tape disallowed. As a compromise, the
judge allowed the first part of the tape to be played,
omitting the part where Mary Jean expressed concern
that John might kill her mother. After the tape was
aired, Jennifer Esparza was excused.

Melissa Lowder, the first of Mary Jean's friends to
arrive at the lofts, was the next witness. She was
smartly casual in a green sweater and gray pants.
Calmly, she portrayed the part she played in calling
911, going into the loft, and identifying the children.

Howard Blackmon questioned Melissa about her
knowledge of John Battaglia.

"I've known him since our oldest children were in
kindergarten. We socialized quite a bit as couples."

"Did Mary Jean ever describe John as bipolar?"
Blackmon asked, trying to preempt the defense on
the issue.

"We never discussed it," Melissa said.

Under further questioning, Melissa described
John as a great dad when their children were in
kindergarten, but how, toward the end of Battaglia's
marriage, she had heard about the very heated dis-
cussions that he had with Mary Jean.

Melissa said she was afraid to walk anywhere with
Mary Jean for fear that John Battaglia would come
by and take potshots at them. She also mentioned

John leaving phone messages calling Mary Jean a "fucking pig."

When Paul Johnson cross-examined, he said, "There were hundreds of phone calls from John asking Mary Jean to give him visitation with the girls. A hundred phone calls and only one with "fucking pig." You're only aware of the calls that John made that were rude?"

"I'm only aware that John called and made obscene remarks," Melissa told him.

When Melissa was excused, John Battaglia's probation officer, Debra Gibbs, was sworn in. She was a no-nonsense looking woman with short dark hair. Under Blackmon's questioning, she described her meeting with John Battaglia on April 30, two days before the murders. She had told the defendant that his file had been requested by the court, and had warned him that it probably meant his probation would be revoked.

"What was his reaction to that news?" Blackmon asked.

"He became very angry. Said his ex-wife was always trying to get him in trouble."

"How angry?" Blackmon asked, prodding her on.

"Intensely angry. Raised his voice. He had anger in his eyes."

Blackmon turned the witness over to the defense.

Paul Johnson continued his habit of standing next to the witnesses when he asked questions.

Johnson handed Gibbs the report she had written after her meeting with Battaglia on April 30. "Is this your report about the probationer?"

She squinted to read it, then nodded.

"You didn't mention any reaction by Battaglia in your report. Did he make any threats?"

She had to agree that none were listed in her report.

"When you were talking today," Johnson said, "you made him sound much more angry."

With Johnson inferring she was saying things she really hadn't experienced, she looked relieved to be excused.

Detective James Vineyard from the crime scene response unit again took his place in the witness chair. With his experience, he appeared relaxed in a courtroom setting. He was very precise, giving the exact location of the loft. "At the intersection of the I-45 overpass and Interstate 75."

He had the facts down cold. He talked about going to the loft that night. He had drawn a large floor plan of the loft, and he pointed to where the girls were found, where guns were located, and anything that would give the jury a better idea of the layout. Then he had the lights dimmed and began showing slides taken of the crime scene. Using a laser, he guided the jury through the assortment of shotguns and revolvers, bullet casings, and clutter strewn around the loft.

The most chilling point of the trial came next. He showed pictures of the girls. First there was Liberty. He flashed a slide on the screen showing her lying face down in a pool of blood, her toes turned in. In the next slide, Liberty's body filled the entire screen, adding to the impact of the image. An officer from PES had picked her up in her frozen position. Blood covered her features and obscured them.

Many people in the gallery gasped. They had not been expecting anything so graphic, even though the judge had warned them. One sobbing woman stood and left the courtroom.

Vineyard then showed the jury slides of Faith. Facedown. Blood. A young life wasted before it ever really began.

The Battaglias sat somber-faced, making no attempt to shield their eyes from the grisly photos. John Battaglia looked on with interest, as if they were someone else's children, someone else's murders. Members of the jury stared at him, most with frowns. When Liberty's bloody face had first appeared on the screen, a young male juror in the front row grabbed the rail of the jury box, looking ready to leap over and attack Battaglia.

Blackmon presented the revolvers, casings, hair and tissue samples, and all the slides into evidence. The dozen long guns and four pistols taken from Battaglia's loft were stacked around the base of the judge's bench. The courtroom looked like an arsenal.

With regularity, Paul Johnson objected to every bit of evidence that was photographed before the warrant arrived, saying it violated the Fourth Amendment on search and seizure. With equal regularity, the judge overruled his objections.

Vineyard's testimony was followed by a parade of experts. One was the trace evidence analyst, James Adams. He was young and dignified-looking in his dark suit, and he spoke with an extensive vocabulary. An expert in biology and chemistry, he had taken courses with the FBI and the CIA in forensics. It was his job to test and compare the hairs of the girls

taken from the two guns used in their murders. One
telling part of his testimony was that both girls' hair
appeared on the same gun, the Glock. It became obvious that their killer had simply gone from one girl
to the other inflicting the final execution shot.

Paul Johnson excused him without cross-examin-
ing, but, for the record, he objected to the evidence
Adams had presented on the now-familiar grounds
that it had been obtained without a search warrant.

FORTY-FOUR

The jury stayed focused through all the scientific testimony. The more than two months spent assembling this jury appeared well worth the effort. They were never late and, once in court, they listened intensely to everything that was presented.

Matthew Trent, one of the many people John Battaglia had spoken with on May 2, was called to the stand. The distinguished jeweler, with his dark suit and gold wire-rimmed glasses, looked like a witness anyone would want on his side. He recounted how John had come to his business and told him that he was concerned that his probation might be revoked and he might be arrested. He had asked Trent to get his wife to "talk some sense into Mary Jean."

Blackmon asked him about John Battaglia's demeanor.

"He seemed distracted, frustrated," Trent said.

Paul Johnson asked if he knew about John's frustration with Mary Jean, and Trent admitted he did.

Blackmon came back on re-direct. "John Battaglia didn't care very much for Mary Jean. Right?"

Trent had to admit that was the case.

* * *

If there was a distinctive feature of the trial, it was its brevity. Except for Mary Jean Pearle and Detective Vineyard, witnesses sat only briefly on the stand. Frequently, Paul Johnson did not take the opportunity to cross-examine. He didn't need to give the prosecutor's witnesses any more chance to damage his case.

Johnson took a brief opportunity to question Detective Katherine Justice when she was sworn to testify. Justice repeated the conversation she had had with Battaglia only four hours before the murders, in which she guaranteed him that she would not arrest him that evening in front of his children.

The defense attorney raised the unfairness of Mary Jean having the Highland Park Police Department in her hip pocket. He also wanted the jury to know that most of Battaglia's offenses were only phone calls.

Court spectators sat up taller to get a better look at the next witness, Missy Campbell, the woman with whom John Battaglia had spent the evening after he murdered his children. Her deep tan was striking against her white suit, and her long blond hair was tousled.

Missy sat down at the witness stand, glanced over at John Battaglia, and immediately burst out crying. Still sniffling, she recalled the events of that night. She itemized their visits to bars and the tattoo parlor, but she didn't mention the drugs they had inhaled.

* * *

Senior Corporal Lowell Bryant described spotting Battaglia's truck after he had driven around the city for four hours looking for it. Bryant told of trying to get Battaglia out of the truck and having to use a neck restraint so they could cuff him.

On cross examination, Paul Johnson reflected back to how John Battaglia had looked when Paul first met him. "Who did you observe kicking the defendant in the face?" Johnson asked. "Did you beat him about the face or was it someone from another office?"

"Police applied the force that was necessary," Bryant responded, holding his ground. "We kept yelling 'show us your hands.' He was on his stomach and he still wouldn't show us his hands. He just kept them at his sides."

Madeline Eltran was someone Mary Jean's Park Cities friends would be unlikely to encounter. The tattoo artist who had applied John Battaglia's roses had coal-black hair and wore a clingy, hot-pink satin blouse. Blackmon asked her about Battaglia's demeanor that night.

"He was having a good time. Talking, cracking jokes, just a standard good time." She described him as a willing talker. She said he had paid around $180 to $250 for the tattoos; she couldn't remember for sure.

The next witness, Dr. Joni McClain, had performed the autopsy on Faith. She entered the courtroom in a stylish business suit, her reddish brown hair cut fashionably short. In her ten years since graduating from the University of Oklahoma

School of Medicine, she had performed 3,000 autopsies. She and all the other medical examiners at the Dallas County ME office were highly qualified board certified forensic pathologists.

The jury watched Dr. McClain place an outline drawing of a person on the courtroom wall so she could demonstrate the places where bullets had entered. The soft-spoken doctor gave a more sterile presentation than Officer Vineyard (who had showed the jury the actual photos of the dead children), but Dr. McClain showed the jury what damage the bullets had done.

In describing the shot to Faith's shoulder, Dr. McClain said that the bullet entered the front of her body nine inches from the top of her head, traveled in a downward trajectory, and exited four and a half inches lower out her back.

The path of the next bullet indicated that Faith was on her stomach. That bullet destroyed her spinal column and perforated her heart and pancreas. The third shot to the back of her head caused additional damage around the bullet hole. The revolver had been shoved so tightly against her scalp that it made a muzzle stamp abrasion. The bullet had fractured her skull.

During the trial, John Battaglia's demeanor remained the same. He never looked away from the evidence being presented by the experts, in fact, he appeared absorbed in their findings.

Dr. Janice Townsend-Parchment, the medical examiner who had performed the autopsy on Liberty, also had 3,000 autopsies to her credit. An honors graduate from Princeton, she appeared professional, with a long, dark brown braid down the middle of her back. She wore a serious expression and no makeup.

She spoke with authority, using her hands when she made her presentation. She stated that Liberty had been shot five times from the back, and she detailed the damage caused by each shot. One bullet had lodged in Liberty's body; the doctor had extracted it from the muscles by her right chest.

Hearing the damage described had an effect on the jury. Many sat with crossed arms and frequently glared at Battaglia. He paid them no attention, nor did he show any remorse as the wounds were described.

After the witness concluded her testimony, the prosecution rested its case.

Now came Paul Johnson's difficult task of defending his client. Paul stood and asked that the jury be dismissed. After the last juror left the courtroom, he walked in front of the desk where John Battaglia sat with Paul Brauchle, and asked both men to stand.

Facing John, Paul said, "You have options available to you. You can bring in witnesses and present their testimony before the jury, or you can let the jury determine your guilt or innocence at this time."

Battaglia wasted no time in agreeing to turn the trial over to the jury.

Since the prosecution has the burden of proof, they always have two opportunities to address the jury in the closing arguments. The first closing argument was given by Assistant District Attorney Pat Kirlin. He straightened his jacket as he approached the jury. The young, thin attorney had a slightly receding hairline and a thick, dark mustache.

At first, he reviewed the evidence they had presented. He gestured with his hands as he described how the girls were found. He also stirred emotions by detailing Liberty running for her life as her father chased after her with a gun. "Obviously, he did not love his girls . . ."

Suddenly, a deep voice erupted from the direction of the defense table. John Battaglia blurted, "I did too love them!" he said. It was like hearing words from a stone, for that is what he had been during the entire trial. It was jarring.

After staring at John, everyone turned back to Kirlin. "Ladies and gentlemen, we have proven our case beyond a reasonable doubt." He turned and pointed his finger at Battaglia. "Find this man guilty of capital murder. You will not be telling him anything that he doesn't already know."

The defense's only chance to close was sandwiched in between the prosecution's closings. The job was given to Johnson's assistant, Paul Brauchle. The gray-haired man spoke softly as he stood in front of the jury. Jurors had to lean forward, straining to hear. Brauchle reminded them of their promise during voir dire that they would keep an open mind throughout the trial. He spoke of the credibility of the evidence—evidence that was admitted against the rules of the court. He pointed out that there was no proof that John had shot the children.

"There were no witnesses. The police entered the loft with no search warrant. They confiscated and photographed the evidence illegally." He concluded by declaring that the only fair verdict would be to find John Battaglia "not guilty."

* * *

Howard Blackmon always wore dark suits that complemented his dark brown hair and mustache. The chief prosecutor with eighteen years' experience walked to the railing of the jury box to begin his final argument.

He retraced the facts of the case so that they would be the last words the jury took with them to deliberate. "Just remember those photographs of the murdered children. And remember that phone call to Mary Jean. That was a savage effort by John Battaglia to emotionally destroy Mary Jean Pearle.

"John Battaglia killed his daughters for one reason and one reason only: revenge. This murder was a revengeful act against Mary Jean Pearle for filing charges and trying to have him arrested. He was afraid he'd be sent to jail. He was afraid he would lose his business. If he couldn't have his daughters, he didn't want Mary Jean to have them either. John Battaglia must be found guilty of capital murder."

As he strolled back to the defense table, Judge Warder turned to the jury. She reminded them that since John Battaglia was accused of killing *two* people, he could be found guilty of capital murder, punishable by either life in prison or by death. Then she gave them their instructions and released them to determine John Battaglia's guilt or innocence.

It had been a lopsided trial. John Battaglia's team had not called one witness. His own father had told *The Dallas Morning News* that his son had probably pulled the trigger.

Spectators stood at their seats, not venturing far

and not expecting to wait long. However, everyone was surprised that in only nineteen minutes the red light began to flash, indicating that the jury either had a question or had reached a decision. Word quickly spread that the jury had arrived at its verdict.

The spectators hurried to their seats and sat quietly waiting for the judge's announcement. She glanced over the document from the jury foreman and told John Battaglia to stand. His lawyers stood with him.

Reading from the jury's decision, Judge Warder said, "John Battaglia, the jury has found you guilty of capital murder."

The punishment phase would begin the following day.

FORTY-FIVE

Professor Michelle Ghetti walked quickly to the stand, looking poised and accustomed to being in front of a group of people. Her chin-length blond hair complemented her yellow linen dress and she looked much younger than her forty-eight years. When she spoke today, her words would be more emotional than when she addressed her law students at Southern University. She gave her impressive credentials, mentioning that she had drafted several abuse laws.

The pretty woman described her turbulent life with John Battaglia. She highlighted John's explosions—throwing Billy against the wall, hitting her with his cast-covered fist as she held Laurie—as well as all the trauma he'd inflicted after she divorced him.

With great detail, she described her six-year ordeal with John Battaglia.

Paul Johnson objected, and the jury was excused.

"Michelle is giving a narrative that is beyond what the state said they would ask," Johnson said.

Blackmon fired back. "What is this? All of a sudden you're surprised? You've known this information for months."

Judge Warder told Blackmon to ask questions and

let the witness respond without letting her give a monologue.

The jury was brought back, and Michelle continued to tell about the stalking, the threats, the beatings, and the frequent surveillance. She explained that she was constantly scared. Her stomach was always in knots.

She described the final beating in which he'd broken her nose and dislocated her jaw. Jury members either grimaced or shook their heads at the details. A photograph of her beaten and swollen face was entered into evidence. She testified that the only way she could save her life was to flee to Baton Rouge.

Paul Johnson stood to cross-examine. "You were pregnant when you married John Battaglia. Isn't that right?"

"I was," Michelle replied, embarrassed.

"Were you wondering whether or not to marry John?"

"Yes. My mother thought I should marry him."

"A marriage of convenience?" Johnson asked.

"We were married when I was two months pregnant."

"Before your marriage, you saw no physical violence?" Johnson asked.

"No, but I knew John was high-strung. A fast talker. I never saw him depressed. Even when he apologized for abusing me, he was high-strung. He was paranoid. Thought people were after him. He thought police were after him." Then, as a second thought, she added, "And they were."

Although her testimony was serious, laughter rippled through the courtroom.

"What changes did you see in his personality?"

"I could see anger in his face. His temperament would change."

Michelle told the defense attorney about John's hostility and how he panicked. He would fight, then flee.

"You're describing a person who changes personalities," Johnson said.

Michelle refused to agree with him, and the jury was excused for a second time.

"The witness is biased and is trying to step back from earlier statements," Johnson complained to the judge. "At one time she quoted John as saying, 'When I get like that, I don't know what I'm doing.'

"She knows what the defense approach will be and she's skewing her testimony to fit the state's position," Johnson said.

The jury returned.

Michelle said, "I don't know anyone else who does terrible things and then doesn't remember. I don't know if he can't remember or he says that to get out of trouble."

After the prosecution concluded itemizing the numerous ways John had violated his protective order, Johnson was still trying to get Michelle to admit that John had suffered from depression.

"I remember that he had never missed a day of work." Michelle said. "He had no trouble sleeping. I can't say that I ever saw him depressed."

The state rested in the punishment phase, and the court adjourned.

On Thursday, the defense began to make up for their lack of witnesses during the trial phase. Paul Johnson called James Jones to the stand. He owned a framing shop near Battaglia's accounting business. He thought that John was a fabulous dad, taking his kids back and forth from ice-skating and soccer. He told the jury he'd be hard-pressed to find a man as devoted as John was to his kids. Many times John had brought the children into his store to see the parrots he had there, and Jones had ample time to view how considerate and caring John was with his girls.

He first saw John depressed around the time of his divorce. John had dropped by the frame shop on the afternoon of the murders and claimed that Mary Jean was going to have him put in jail. He had never seen John so emotionally drained or more depressed.

Vida Hughes, a bookkeeper, also worked in the same building as John Battaglia. Hughes told the defense attorney about frequently chatting with Battaglia and seeing him with his daughters. She thought he was a wonderful, loving, and caring father. His children were his life. Her office was next to John's, and she would frequently hear his loud conversations with Mary Jean. She assumed he was having a difficult time trying to see his daughters. She said that these calls always depressed him.

At some risk, Paul Johnson recalled a hostile witness, Mary Jean Pearle, to the stand. Her tan suit and animal-print blouse were less severe than the dark outfit she had worn for her earlier testimony.

Johnson accused Mary Jean of doing everything she could to see that John got the death penalty.

"I don't feel that it is up to me. I'm leaving his fate to the hands of God and the jury."

"Isn't it true that your father was accused of murder?"

Mary Jean looked startled and said, "No. That's not correct!"

Johnson, holding notes as he stood, read, "Gene Pearle was accused of killing a man at 3601 Dickason on August second, 1982," Johnson said.

"He was no-billed for killing a burglar at that address," Mary Jean replied.

Judge Warder sent the jury from the room so she could discuss the charge. She let the police report stand as part of the record, but she disallowed the question because it was irrelevant and prejudicial to the jury.

Blackmon turned to Johnson and said that the question was improper. Johnson replied that it happened to be true. They began raising their voices, talking over one another. Suddenly, the judge rapped her gavel, and in her loudest voice of the trial cried, "Counsel!"

The court reporter could not take notes with three voices on top of each other and yelled, "Shut up!"

It was like a gun had blasted in the room. The following silence was deafening.

After the court had settled down, the jury returned.

Paul Johnson asked Mary Jean about her depression after the death of her father. Mary Jean told about being bedridden for four weeks and going into counseling. She had been on Zoloft ever since.

"So you agree that some mental illnesses can be treated with medication?"

With some hesitation, she acknowledged that it was possible.

John Battaglia listened nervously, chomping his gum and chewing faster and faster as his attorney hammered away at Mary Jean. It was the most emotion he had shown during the entire trial.

Mary Jean refused to say that John suffered from depression, stating that she had never seen him in any condition that was similar to hers when she had been depressed.

Psychiatrist Dr. Jay Crowder, director of forensic psychiatry at the University of Virginia, was the first expert witness called by the defense.

He had interviewed John Battaglia three times for a total of six hours and forty minutes. He had determined that John had an immature personality and was a substance abuser, which heightened his bipolar mood disorder. He classified the bipolar as "type one," which is a severe mental illness.

"John is sensitive to rejection by women ever since his mother's suicide," the doctor said. "Coupled with that, the prospect of going to jail made him feel persecuted."

The doctor felt that Battaglia wouldn't have killed his daughters if he had been medically treated.

"Are you telling this jury that John Battaglia had no choice in this murder?" Blackmon asked on cross-examination.

"I am saying that his bipolar disorder facilitated his murdering his children."

Paul Johnson asked if John would be a future danger.

"Improbable," the doctor replied. "His year in jail

produced no bad acts. We took him off of medication in October just to see what would happen. After he was drug-free, we did some psychological tests. Mr. Battaglia was mostly depressed, but he did have some periods of euphoria."

The prosecution wanted to depict the doctor as biased, so Blackmon asked, "Isn't it rare for you to consult on behalf of the prosecution?"

"I have never testified for the State on a capital murder case," he replied.

The next witness for the defense raised her hand to be sworn in. Dr. Judi Stonedale was a pretty woman with thick red hair who didn't look like she had spent five years as a prison psychiatrist. She was young, and this was only the second trial in which she testified as an expert witness.

She had spent a total of eight hours testing and talking with John Battaglia over three sessions. Occasionally glancing over at John, she testified that from the tests and interviews she had determined that he had a long-standing bipolar disorder characterized by hyperactivity followed by depression. She pronounced his condition as "one of the clearest cases I've ever seen." The first time she had talked with John, he was so manic that he was "bouncing off the walls." But once he was medicated, he could focus.

"He knew what he was doing when he killed his children," she said, "but he was acting under a delusion that he was protecting them from reliving his problems."

On cross-examination, Howard Blackmon asked, "Could John have an antisocial personality or be a sociopath as opposed to suffering from mental illness?"

"His history didn't indicate that he lacked a conscience."

"Could the defendant just be a plain mean, vindictive-type person and that's why he killed his children?" Blackmon asked.

"Of course he could," the doctor replied, "but that isn't my belief."

Blackmon asked Dr. Stonedale about John calling his ex-wife Michelle Ghetti and leaving a message that Mary Jean should lose her children.

"There's no proof that he ever called Michelle," the doctor said.

"Is it possible you could be mistaken in your diagnosis?" Blackmon asked.

Dr. Stonedale teared up and became defensive. "Of course, I'm not God," she whined. "I could make a mistake." But she reasserted her belief that Battaglia should be given a life sentence and not be sent to his death.

Judge Warder had hired Dr. Edward Gripon, a forensic psychiatrist from Beaumont, Texas, at the request of the prosecution to examine John Battaglia. On Friday, the older gray-haired man strode into the courtroom with confidence. He looked comfortable in court, having interviewed 8,000 people to determine their competency to stand trial.

After giving his distinguished credentials, he recounted his three-hour interview with John Battaglia. He spoke in a confident, relaxed manner and frequently made eye contact with the jury when he explained various points. He stated that John had described his mood swings of ecstasy and despondency. Upon further examination Dr. Gripon had determined that Mr. Battaglia had a long history of mood swings consistent with a bipolar disorder. With proper medication, the doctor felt Battaglia would be at a very low risk of committing criminal acts of violence in prison.

It was a crushing blow for the prosecution, as they had first asked for the highly respected doctor. Now he was testifying for the defense. The man was convincing; he spoke rapidly—facts on the tip of his tongue—and never had to grope for a word.

The doctor admitted that Battaglia was legally sane when he killed his children, but agreed with Dr. Stonedale that his was a classic case of bipolar disorder, possibly inherited from his mother. Dr. Gripon also leaned away from the antisocial personality aspect, saying that the Marine Corps is anathema to a person with that type of personality.

Dr. Gripon said, "My examinations suggest that Mr. Battaglia's violence almost always sprang from dysfunctional relationships with his wives . . . so with the removal of the victim pool, the [crime] would not likely occur again."

He said that it would be "simplistic" to suggest that Battaglia had murdered his daughters to get back at Ms. Pearle. He thought it was far more complicated than revenge, for John too lost his daughters.

Howard Blackmon asked, "Did you know that John Battaglia threatened his brother with a gun in 1975, and later pulled a gun on a car full of kids in Louisiana?"

"No," the doctor said. "I didn't know any of that."

Paul Johnson emphasized that the doctor had first been court appointed, which gave him the prosecution's original stamp of approval even though he lacked some of Battaglia's background information.

Howard Blackmon reminded the doctor that he had been called to evaluate the competency and sanity of Battaglia to stand trial, and had not been asked to investigate any bipolar aspect.

"It was the defendant who asked about the bipolar condition," the doctor admitted. "Truth is the truth regardless of who's paying for it. I didn't begin to investigate the bipolar aspect until after I had made my report to the judge."

The doctor smiled reassuredly and said, "I don't have a dog in this fight. I testified last Saturday at another trial, and I said then that that man was at risk and would be a danger. I'm giving you my opinion.

"Mr. Battaglia was not insane," the doctor allowed. "He had a choice of murdering his children. But his lack of sleep, distress, extra work, and taking drugs impacted his bipolar disorder."

On Monday morning, a week after the trial had started, John Battaglia's parents entered the courtroom with his youngest brother and Kelly, the blond girlfriend who had called Mary Jane the night of the murders to see if John could still keep his date with the girls. The faces of all four were sad and anxious.

The defense had presented a number of distinguished doctors. Now the prosecution had to rebut the testimony of those expert witnesses. They called Dr. Richard Coons to the stand.

Expensively dressed, the white-haired, bespectacled man seemed at home in the courtroom, as he had made 9,000 evaluations in the Houston area. He was both a psychiatrist and an attorney, and also had been a major in the Army Medical Corps, working as a forensic psychiatrist. Adding to his credentials, he had helped draft the Texas penal code on insanity, making it such a difficult defense to prove that it sent chills up defense attorneys' backs.

The doctor had been thorough, giving John Battaglia psychological tests in addition to interviewing him and poring over his divorce files and taped phone calls.

Most telling was the interview he had conducted with John. The defendant had not been consistent with his answers to the psychiatrists. He told Stonedale and Gripon that he had killed the girls to keep them from living his life—from having his problems.

But Battaglia told Dr. Coons he'd become upset when he found out the camping trip had been canceled. The doctor began reading from his report, giving John's account of the murders and it was quite a departure from what he had told the other psychiatrists. John told the doctor that some guns had been sitting out in his loft because he was going to get rid of them. That night in his loft, he heard a voice telling him to "do the right thing." Faith was looking at him saying, "No, Daddy, no." He told her that he loved her, and she said, "I know, Daddy." He put the gun behind the back of her ear. Then he did the same to Liberty. He said he'd believed they needed to go together.

The doctor turned fully to the jury. "He knew he was killing his children and he did so out of anger and retribution. He had the mother on the phone to punish her. He was extremely frustrated that things weren't going the right way. He felt that Mary Jean had her foot on his neck."

Dr. Coons had serious concerns about how John Battaglia would act in prison, saying that "In the pen, it's an in-your-face environment. John Battaglia had a significant violent history where neither protective orders nor probations were a deterrent to him."

Collectively, the jury was leaning forward, turned in their chairs to face the witness, their eyes concentrating on him as he spoke.

Under questioning by Paul Johnson, Dr. Coons admitted that there was a hereditary passage of bipolar disorder from mother to son. He also recognized that John was bipolar, but had a milder form that wouldn't prevent him from knowing he was killing his daughters.

Dr. Coons was the last witness. He stacked up his papers, stood up, and exited through the double doors of the courtroom.

Both sides rested.

FORTY-SIX

On Tuesday, the last day of trial, Judge Warder opened court by addressing the jury. She told them that since they had found the defendant guilty of capital murder, it was their duty to determine his punishment.

"You will be given two questions. First, you must determine if John Battaglia will be a continuing threat to society. If your answer to that question is 'yes,' then you will be required to answer a second question. Were there mitigating circumstances in the defendant's favor?

"But before you get to that, we'll have the closing statements." She nodded in the direction of the assistant district attorneys.

All three dark-haired prosecution attorneys wore dark suits, making them look like a handsome matched set. From that group, Pat Kirlin stood. He again had the task of leading the prosecution's closing argument. First, he reminded the jury of the state's position since voir dire—they were seeking the death penalty for what he phrased, "the ultimate act of revenge." He refreshed the jury's memory of the psychiatrists' testimony, recalling that Dr. Crowder had presented a laundry list of excuses for John Battaglia's actions.

"Would John present future endangerment? How about when he pointed a gun at his brother, Marc? It was not only his wives he assaulted. Now that assault has escalated to murder.

"He is capable of future violent acts against society. No one can force John to take his medication. There is no way to control what John will do in the future.

"John said that he shot his girls because he heard a voice telling him to 'do the right thing.' I ask you, ladies and gentlemen, when you are back in the jury room, do the right thing."

With fourteen years experience as a defense attorney, Paul Johnson strode confidently to the jury box. Normally he wore a brown or tan suit to blend with his sandy hair, but today he wore a more dramatic dark navy suit, blue shirt, and red tie.

He picked up on Kirlin's last line saying, "You are here because you told us you would do what was right. We wanted strong jurors, strong enough to give a life sentence.

"The defense never inferred that there was a question of guilt. The guilt is clear-cut. But can you not see that his mental illness plays a part? Did we not bring you medical credibility? It was the doctors' opinion that if it weren't for John's bipolar disorder, this crime would not have occurred. For you to send a mentally ill man to be killed shows no more compassion than John Battaglia gave to his children."

Johnson spoke unhurriedly, looking each juror in the eye. He kept his left hand casually in the pocket of his coat, while his raised right hand punctuated the air, giving emphasis to his words.

Recounting his impressive string of psychiatrists,

he mentioned Dr. Edward Gripon whom the judge had appointed. "Let's talk about credentials, folks. Both sides got his report the same day. That's when the prosecution backed off using him.

"Bipolar is like pouring gas on a lit match. What we had the day of the murders was an explosion. But with John under medication, this last year has been a good predictor of future behavior.

"Whatever you do, John will never set foot in the free world again. Don't put a man to death who acted out of illness. There are too many underlying causes for this to have been an act of revenge."

The jury had listened attentively to the defense attorney, and now watched the chief prosecutor approach them.

Howard Blackmon had spoken softly during the trial. However, for his closing statement, he raised his voice, speaking more forcefully as he addressed the jury.

"The defense would like nothing better than to turn this into a debate between psychiatrists. But lets look at the facts." He recapped the evidence that had been presented at the trial.

To show that this was no spur-of-the-moment, insane act, Blackmon reminded the jury that Battaglia had Faith call Mary Jean, and then waited until she could return the call and hear the slaughter of her children. Gesturing toward the defense, he said, "Their experts told you that bipolar made him do this. This was an act of meanness. This man has an unquenched thirst for vengeance.

"There is a confrontational environment in the

pen. I pity the poor inmate that angers him. I pity the guard.

"Based on what you have heard this week and last week, I ask you to find that there are no mitigating circumstances in this case. Answer 'no' to that second question."

At 11:22 A.M., the case went to the jury. By 2:44 P.M., the red button had flashed five times. Each time, the anxious attorneys stood waiting for the bailiff to answer the jury's call. Each time, he came back with a written question for the judge.

Spectators had rushed to the cafeteria on the first floor for a dry hamburger or a wilted salad. They didn't dare venture too far in search of better food. During the wait, John Battaglia's parents sat red-eyed, holding hands on one of the wooden benches in the corridor, not too far from the entrance to the courtroom.

Nervous assistant district attorneys paced between their offices and the courtroom. Everyone had an opinion about what the long wait indicated.

Finally, at 5:55 P.M., the light flashed again. The jury had reached its verdict.

Once the call went out, everyone came running. Suddenly, the courtroom pews were filled with excited people. The defendant huddled with his attorneys. Conversation grew louder as the gallery waited for the judge and the jury.

Judge Warder took her place at 6:15 P.M. and asked spectators to leave if they couldn't remain silent during the reading of the verdict.

The bailiff opened the door for the jurors, and twelve somber people trudged in. They looked physically exhausted—wrinkled clothes, tousled hair—and many had red eyes from crying. They made eye contact with no one.

John Battaglia and his attorneys again stood for the reading of the verdict.

Holding the form containing the jury's decisions, Judge Warder read the questions again. "Question One. Would the defendant commit acts of violence and be a continuing threat to society. Answer: Yes."

Question Two. Were there mitigating circumstances? Answer: No."

Judge Warder thanked and excused the jury, then turned to John Battaglia. She began, "You will be taken by the sheriff . . . on a designated date after six P.M. where [they] will carry out your sentence of death."

Battaglia's parents sat clinging to each other, their faces red and wet. As John stood he turned to them, and with a little smile he mouthed, "It's okay."

Mary Jean Pearle had waited for this moment one day short of a year. Somber faced, and looking drained and tired, she stood up and unfolded a wrinkled piece of paper as she walked to the front of the courtroom. In her mind, she had given the victim's statement for months, but she had spent most of last evening putting the finishing touches on it. Having avoided John's eyes during all of her testimony, she now stared directly at him as she began to read:

"On May 2, 2001, you chose to shatter my world forever by brutally terrorizing and executing the two sweetest, innocent, and kind babies in the world.

"The only two people in the world that cared for you and trusted you, their father, with their lives . . .

"You are one of the most heinous murderers of modern times. Hitler did not kill his own children. Dahmer didn't kill his own children.

"Faith used to tell me, 'I've got the worst father in the world.' I'd say, 'Oh, Faith, no you don't.' She'd say, 'Okay, the second-worst next to the daddy in University Park that killed the mommy in front of the kids.'

"Well, Faith, you were right! He was the worst father in the world. Liberty hid under the bed, not wanting to go to dinner with you that Wednesday night. But I said, 'Oh, it will be okay!' I trusted you with their lives.

"Your cowardly, evil, and selfish nature also took a father from Laurie. Much less the life she could have shared with her sisters that adored her . . .

"I am what's left of the goodness in them. They died with my love in their hearts and thought I might be able to save them. But to no avail. At least I know that I will be reunited with them in heaven forever.

"Until then, I will try to work to help others escape the domestic violence living hell you've put [us] through.

"Enjoy the new peers and lifestyle you have chosen. Don't ever give me a second thought. I would like to say the next time you see me is when they put the needle in your arm. But I'm not going to waste the time to be there.

"For what you have done, my family, friends, and myself hope you burn in hell forever."

Dorrace Pearle took the arm of her oldest son, Bobby Clark, as he escorted her through the crowd of friends congratulating them for winning the case.

Once they were out of the courtroom, Dorrace said, "Win? Win? What's all this 'win' business? All we've done is lose. Oh, we've lost so much."

Professor Michelle Ghetti teaches her family law students that domestic violence is always about power and control. John proved her point.

Since the murders, Mary Jean has remarried, but John's final act will haunt her the rest of her life.

John David Battaglia's power and control will finally end when he pays the ultimate price.

MORE MUST-READ TRUE CRIME
FROM PINNACLE

HORRIFYING TRUE CRIME
FROM PINNACLE BOOKS

Body Count
by Burl Barer   0-7860-1405-9   **$6.50**US/**$8.50**CAN

The Babyface Killer
by Jon Bellini   0-7860-1202-1   **$6.50**US/**$8.50**CAN

Love Me to Death
by Steve Jackson   0-7860-1458-X   **$6.50**US/**$8.50**CAN

The Boston Stranglers
by Susan Kelly   0-7860-1466-0   **$6.50**US/**$8.50**CAN

Body Double
by Don Lasseter   0-7860-1474-1   **$6.50**US/**$8.50**CAN

The Killers Next Door
by Joel Norris   0-7860-1502-0   **$6.50**US/**$8.50**CAN

Available Wherever Books Are Sold!

Visit our website at **www.kensingtonbooks.com**.

More Books From Your Favorite Thriller Authors